OBJECT
DEVELOPMENT
METHODS

ADVANCES IN OBJECT TECHNOLOGY

Dr. Richard S. Wiener
Series Editor

Editor
Journal of Object-Oriented Programming
and
Report on Object Analysis and Design
SIGS Publications, Inc.
New York, New York

and

Department of Computer Science
University of Colorado
Colorado Springs, Colorado

Additional Volumes in Preparation

OBJECT DEVELOPMENT METHODS

Edited by
Andy Carmichael
Object UK Ltd.
Southampton, UK

SIGS
BOOKS

New York

PUBLISHED BY
SIGS Books, Inc.
588 Broadway, Suite 604
New York, New York 10012

This book has been published in association with
UNICOM Seminars Ltd.
Brunel Science Park, Cleveland Road
Uxbridge, Middlesex UB8 3PH
United Kingdom
(p) +44-895-256484 (f) +44-895-813095
Compuserve 100142,1176
UNICOM offers seminars and training relating to Information Technology.
For further information, please contact UNICOM at the address listed above.

Library of Congress Catalog Card Number: 93-087695

SIGS Books ISBN 0-9627477-9-3
Prentice Hall ISBN 0-13-131591-9

This book is printed on acid-free paper.

Printed in United States of America
10 9 8 7 6 5 4 3 2 1
First printing May 1994

About the Editor

Andy Carmichael, Ph.D, MBCS, C. Eng., is a leading methods consultant specializing in object-oriented methods. As Director of Object UK Limited, Southampton, UK, he is responsible for training and consulting in object-oriented analysis and design. His current research interests lie in the unification of the semantics of multiple object-oriented methods. A leading advocate of the use of object-oriented methods, he has been involved with the use, specification, and provision of object-oriented CASE support and with the methods themselves for over 10 years. An active member of the British Computer Society, and an associate of IEEE, the editor is a regular speaker at international seminars and conferences and has published articles on topics such as object technology, CASE, and Software Development Environments among others. Andy Carmichael received the Ph.D. from University of Southampton, UK (1983), for work on computer methods of stress analysis. He also received the Bachelor of Science from University of Southampton, UK (1974), graduating with honors.

Series Introduction

The Advances in Object-Oriented Technology series seeks to present readers with books that provide incisive and timely information relating to object-oriented programming and programming languages, object-oriented requirements, object-oriented domain analysis, and object-oriented design. In addition, testing, metrics, formal methods and applications of object technology to areas including object-oriented databases, real-time systems, emergent computation, neural networks, and object-oriented distributed systems will be featured. The books are aimed at practicing software development professionals, programmers, educators, and students in computer-related disciplines.

I am delighted to introduce *Object Development Methods,* edited by Andy Carmichael. This book brings together the work of many important authors. The international roster of contributors includes Andy Carmichael, Ralph Hodgson, Gordon Blair, Steve Cook, Bruce Anderson, Martin Fowler, Colin Carter, Chris Raistrick, Grady Booch, Martin Rösch, Putnam Texel, Stuart Frost, Ian Graham, Ed Colbert, Ivar Jacobson, Magnus Christerson, Larry Constantine, Guido Dedene, Mike Goodland, and Richard Daley. The book provides insight into and comparisons of several important analysis and design methods. These methods include Shlaer/Mellor, Booch, Coad/Yourdon, Texel, OMT, SOMA, OOSD, OOSE, MERODE, and SSADM. In addition, environments for creating and maintaining object-oriented systems are described and compared. Part 1 of the book presents a general introduction to object orientation, dealing with the entire process from procurement to incremental enhancement; Part 2 includes four chapters that provide more detail of the concepts associated with the object model of computation; Part 3 focuses on a comparison of methods; Part 4 provides more detail about specific methods written, in some cases, by the originator of the method, and Part 5 discusses the evolution of object-oriented development environments. I believe that you will find this important book rich in content and rewarding in detail.

Richard S. Wiener
Series Editor

Preface

There is little doubt that object technology is the latest in a long line of pretenders to the role of "Silver Bullet"[1] — that mythical formula for slaying those fearsome and uncontrollable monsters: software development and maintenance. While we would be wise to heed F.P. Brooks' warning that there is indeed no such magic formula, the advances in the understanding of software development, and in particular object orientation, at both theoretical/mathematical and pragmatic/engineering levels, do promise to provide very significant benefits. Furthermore these advances do address both what Brooks calls the "accidents" in software production (of which experienced practitioners know there are many!), and the problems of "essence," such as complexity, changeability, and invisibility.

This book brings together the work of a number of authors who in different ways believe that the object paradigm can systematically improve what are arguably the most important aspects of system development, analysis, and design. Few if any subscribe to the view that object orientation, in and of itself, will transform the economics of software development. But we agree that it is an essential element of software engineering and it will contribute to the major improvement in analysis, design, and implementation that industry, and indeed society, requires.

As the title suggests, the focus of this book is object development, and in particular what has traditionally been called analysis and design. Analysis is primarily concerned with understanding and specifying the problem to be solved. Design, on the other hand, is concerned with the choices available in a problem's solution, choices of "buy versus build," and of modification and configuration, as well as the process of invention *ex*

---

[1] F.P. Brooks, Jr. (1987) No Silver Bullet: Essence and Accidents of Software Engineering. *Computer,* 20(4), pp. 10–19.

nihilo. Most object development models recognize that these activities do not necessarily operate in chronological order, followed by a distinct implementation or coding phase. The activities are inevitably intertwined with each other and with the three-way negotiation — explicit or hidden — between the user or beneficiary of the system (who wants the perfect system yesterday!), the manager of resources (money, people, and time, who wants to spend nothing at all and spread the expenditure over at least a decade!), and the technical or engineering manager who (being entirely objective and unbiased) can advise on the technical feasibility and cost of the various options.

In spite of this complex interweaving of phases, analysis and design are activities worthy of study and definition. To improve the process — any process — we must first define it and then apply it in a repeatable fashion. Software development is certainly no exception to this rule, and for this reason there is an emphasis in the book on methodology.

Methodology is variously defined. First, it is the study of methods (as biology is the study of life). There is much material here for those primarily interested in knowing about many methods, techniques, and notations. Second, methodology may be defined as a unified approach and process incorporating multiple techniques, notations, and tools — in short, a "method." (More usually this must be said in the marketing and promotional literature of software tools developers.) In the latter case, the book collects a number of papers that provide insight into the process and experience of some of the very many different object development methods that have been defined. I hope, therefore, that practitioners and academics alike will find material here to inform, inspire, encourage, warn, and guide in the improvement and maturation of the software development process.

BOOK OUTLINE — A GUIDE FOR READERS

The book is divided into five parts:

Part 1   Introduction
Part 2   Understanding and Adopting Object Technology
Part 3   Methods Comparison
Part 4   Perspectives on Specific Object-Oriented Methods
Part 5   The Evolving Development Environment.

Within each part the individual chapters contribute to the overall theme from different perspectives, as outlined below.

Part 1 is a general introduction to object orientation — or "object-think" — as an agent for change, not just in system development but in the whole process from procurement to incremental enhancement. Different methods are introduced, not so much to contrast their approaches, but to recognize the underlying commonality of the models produced and the change of structure introduced by object-orientation.

The four chapters in Part 2, entitled "Understanding and Adopting Object Technology," provide more detail concerning the concepts, techniques, and life cycles involved in an object-oriented approach. Chapter 2, by Ralph Hodgson, provides personal insight and guidance into the motivations for, and process of, "Adopting Object-Oriented Software Engineering." Beside discussing the problems, priorities, and cultural issues of technology adoption, elements of object-oriented techniques are introduced by example.

Chapter 3 builds on these examples to provide a more systematic model of object-oriented computing. Much of the criticism and trivialization of the object-oriented paradigm arises from a shallow definition of its scope. In this chapter, Gordon Blair introduces four dimensions of object orientation — encapsulation, classification, polymorphism, and interpretation — and shows that these have a wider and deeper significance than their implementation in any one method or language. This framework can therefore be used as a guide for assessing and improving the application of object technology. Chapter 3 also contains 20 questions and answers that provide straightforward definitions of many terms and a resolution of many frequently asked queries.

Steve Cook and John Daniels provide in Chapter 4 an outline of "Essential Techniques for Object-Oriented Design." The importance of the "insides and outsides" of objects, reusability achieved through classification and polymorphism, and the importance of modeling the world and the software — its structure and its behavior — are carefully explained. The chapter also introduces the concept of partial models and shows why such models are essential and how they can be managed and integrated.

In Chapter 5, Bruce Anderson addresses issues arising from "Evolution, Life Cycles, and Reuse." Object orientation should greatly improve the evolution of systems and productivity or production through reuse. However, the very real problems inherent in this goal are often overlooked. In this chapter key steps that software producers should take to capitalize on the potential within their organizations are outlined. In particular the software environment, manufacturing process, large- and small-scale architecture, skills, and tools are highlighted.

Part 3 focuses on methods comparison, but its two chapters provide different though complementary views of this complex subject. "Describing and Comparing Object-Oriented Analysis and Design Methods" is Martin Fowler's aim in Chapter 6. He first provides a framework for comparing the structureand techniques within methods, from three axes: Behavioural or Dynamic, Static or Structural, and Architectural. The paper then compares and contrasts six methods: Booch, Coad/Yourdon, Martin/Odell, Rumbaugh, Shlaer/Mellor, Wirfs-Brock, and Jacobson.

Ralph Hodgson's approach in Chapter 7 is broader in scope and lighter in touch. "Contemplating the Universe of Methods" provides a Hawking-like vision of methodological galaxies, black holes, and comets. The serious message of this chapter is that while we must live with a constantly evolving and changing universe of methods — including the blending of techniques and processes to form new methods — software development is a constant interaction between software liabilities (requirements for new systems) and software assets (previously developed components), as described by the "X-model." Comparison and transformations of methods is essential to preserve value in the existing software assets from previous iterations.

Part 4 provides, from the viewpoint of methodologists and practitioners of the various methods, "Perspectives on Specific Object-Oriented Methods." The aim is not to provide in-depth synopses of each method. Some of the chapters do provide an outline of a method, but each primarily seeks to provide insight into one particular aspect of the application or selection of that method. The methods discussed are:

Chapter 8   The Shlaer/Mellor Method
Chapter 9   The Booch Method
Chapter 10   The Coad/Yourdon Method
Chapter 11   The Texel Method
Chapter 12   The Rumbaugh Method (OMT)
Chapter 13   The SOMA Method
Chapter 14   The OOSD Method
Chapter 15   The OOSE Method
Chapter 16   The MERODE Method
Chapter 17   The SSADM Method

In Chapter 8, Colin Carter and Chris Raistrick discuss how object-oriented analysis and recursive development provide "A Formalism for Understanding Software Architectures." Recursive design is effectively a mechanism for parameterizing the development process — transforming analysis models into completed systems through a systematic, if not automated, process. This strategy is discussed in some depth in the context of the Shlaer/Mellor method.

Grady Booch discusses the "Process and Pragmatics" of object development in Chapter 9. This provides additional and complementary material to that in his books on his method, with insight into its application, particularly in the areas of the macro and micro development processes and practical advice for managers of projects using object-oriented methods.

Chapter 10 is concerned with the Coad/Yourdon Method; Martin Rösch expounds "Simplicity, Brevity, and Clarity — Keys to Successful Analysis and Design." Along with an overview of the Coad/Yourdon approach and notation and some of the principles that are applied in building models with the method, the chapter draws on Rösch's consulting experience in Germany to indicate which elements of the method have proven most beneficial in modeling business systems.

The Texel Method is perhaps less well known than those with published texts. However, in Chapter 11 Putnam P. Texel indicates that it is "A Pragmatic and Field-Proven Approach," drawing as it does on the best of methods such as Shlaer/Mellor, Rumbaugh, and Jacobson augmented by well-defined process definition, training, and tool support.

The discussion of the Rumbaugh Method (OMT) in Chapter 12 by Stuart Frost focuses on "The Selection of an Object-Oriented Analysis Method" for use in the development of a CASE tool — a selection that also applies to the method to be supported by that same tool. It provides an interesting perspective on the practical and other considerations that shaped his choice of methodology.

Ian Graham is the author of the SOMA Method and in Chapter 13 he discusses one of its key features, namely "Adding Rules to Classes." As well as outlining the SOMA notation, the chapter puts forward the case for describing object behavior with rules in the form of semiformal assertions. In this way business policies as well as system behavior can be captured and analyzed.

"Requirements Analysis with the Object-Oriented Software Development Method" is the aspect of the OOSD Method addressed by Ed Colbert in Chapter 14. This method makes particular use of object decomposition as a technique for discovering classes and class hierarchies. The chapter shows the use of OOSD in some detail as an example system for temperature monitoring in buildings, and discusses how the method can be used to verify and validate user requirements.

Ivar Jacobson, Magnus Christerson, and Larry Constantine outline the OOSE Method (Object-Oriented Software Engineering), which is "A Use-Case-Driven Approach," in Chapter 15. The organization of the method is based on understanding how the system under development will be used — the use cases. On this foundation, requirements analysis, robustness analysis, construction, and testing can be carried out according to a comprehensive process definition.

Chapter 16 by Guido Dedene, author of MERODE, looks at the method's use for "The Practical Realization of Object-Oriented Business Models." This chapter gives a most interesting insight into object orientation because the modeling technique used differs considerably from the others discussed in this book. For example, the use of "events," which are globally declared in the model and to which different objects respond polymorphically, has similarities but also significant differences from State Transition modeling, which occurs in many of the other methods. The author shows how, by using the event response analysis, class hierarchies and formal models of behavior can be derived.

SSADM is not considered by many to be an object-oriented method, prompting Mike Goodland's question in Chapter 17 — "An Object-Oriented Approach?" The SSADM notation is compared with some of the OO notations discussed in previous chapters, and the degree to which these involve minor changes or extension are considered. Such changes could effectively provide the benefits of the OO paradigm in a context and notation already familiar to the many users of this structured approach.

The book concludes with Part 5, which looks at a number of aspects of "The Evolving Development Environment." In Chapter 18 Richard Daley considers present requirements and future trends of "Object-Development Environments." In the final chapter the editor tackles just one of the requirements for the development environment, where multiple development methods coexist and there is a commitment to reuse as a basic strategy. In this scenario, one method (or tool supporting a method) must be able to interpret models developed with another method/tool and transform notational and presentational differences. Thus, "Toward a Common Object-Oriented Meta-Model for Object Development" — a mechanism for achieving transparent model transformations between methods — is a "forward-looking" (and some will feel optimistic) note on which to conclude.

The problem of bringing together the works of many authors and constructing from them a single and unified volume is not unlike the problem of software reuse and integration! In particular, the presentation of the chapters, classified by the five parts into which I have chosen to divide the volume, exhibits a problem familiar to all those who have used object-oriented analysis and design, or indeed any classification system. There are any number of valid classification schemes, and individual objects (in this case chapters) could be grouped very differently according to the different schemes. Needless to say, multiple inheritance complicates the picture yet further. As a result, gems sought under one category might well be hiding in another. The book therefore has comprehensive Subject and Author indices that allow not only the subjects presented by the authors to be studied in order, but common themes such as polymorphism and life cyle models to be explored across all the chapters. A more radical solution may yet be proposed by future editors skilled in the insights this volume provides. Their book — itself fully object-oriented — will accept a message from its users: "Book — read yourself".

Contents

PART 1 Introduction

PART 2 Understanding and Adopting Object Technology

PART 3   Methods Comparison

PART 4   Perspectives on Specific Object-Oriented Methods

PART 5 The Evolving Development Environment

Contributors

Bruce Anderson   *University of Essex, and Wizard Systems, Colchester, UK*

Gordon S. Blair   *University of Lancaster, Lancaster, UK*

Grady Booch   *Rational, Lakewood, Colorado, USA*

Andy Carmichael   *Object UK Ltd., Southampton, UK*

Colin B. Carter   *Kennedy Carter, London, UK*

Magnus Christerson   *Objective Systems SF AB, Stockholm, Sweden*

Edward Colbert   *Absolute Software Co., Los Angeles, California, USA*

Larry L. Constantine   *Constantine & Lockwood Ltd., Acton, Massachusetts, USA*

Steve Cook   *Object Designers Ltd., Bishop's Stortford, Hertfordshire, UK*

Richard Daley   *Richard Daley Associates, Bishop's Stortford, Hertfordshire, UK*

John Daniels   *Object Designers Ltd., Bishop's Stortford, Hertfordshire, UK*

Guido Dedene   *Katholieke Universiteit Leuven, Leuven, Belgium*

Martin Fowler   *Independent Consultant, Boston, Massachusetts, USA*

Stuart Frost   *Select Software Tools Ltd., Cheltenham, UK*

Ian Graham   *Swiss Bank Corp., London, UK*

Mike Goodland   *Kingston University, Kingston-upon-Thames, Surrey, UK*

Ralph Hodgson   *IDE Europe, Versailles, France**

Ivar Jacobson   *Objective Systems SF AB, Stockholm, Sweden*

Christopher H. Raistrick   *Kennedy Carter, London, UK*

Martin Rösch   *Rösch Consulting GmbH, Kaarst, Germany*

Putnam P. Texel   *p.p. Texel and Company, Inc., Eatontown, New Jersey, USA*

---

*Present Affiliation: IBM Consulting Group, Southbury, Connecticut, USA

part **1**

INTRODUCTION

chapter 1

Objects: Changing Software Production and Procurement

ANDY CARMICHAEL   *OBJECT UK LTD.*

Object orientation, a concept originally developed within programming languages, has a far wider-reaching impact on the overall process of procurement and development of systems than simply the coding of the software. Recently, a number of authors (e.g., Coad/Yourdon, Booch, Shlaer/Mellor, Colbert, and Rumbaugh) have published methods for the analysis and design of systems based on the object-oriented paradigm to gain the benefits in the early stage of the life cycle that object orientation has already brought to programming languages: benefits such as greater reuse, improved understandability and accessibility, and an incremental or evolutionary development process. In terms of how they differ, the resulting "object-oriented methodologies" are often compared from a competitive viewpoint. Of greater significance — the focus of this introductory chapter — are the concepts and principles they share and the change to "object-think" that they all demand from analysts and developers who have been brought up on more traditional approaches.

METHODS AND METHODOLOGISTS

It is an interesting (if unsurprising) fact that the methods that have been used to analyze and design automated systems have generally followed the concepts and principles embedded in the programming languages used to implement them. As it was with subroutine-based and data-oriented languages, so it is now with the new wave of computing languages that support object orientation. With programming languages such as FORTRAN and COBOL, which provided subroutines to programmers for localizing and reusing algorithms, the principal methods used in the design of large systems were based on functional decomposition, which is also a means of localizing, implementing, and reusing functionality. Along with the widespread use of relational database technology and the introduction of nonprocedural languages such as SQL for data definition, it was realized that the data structure of systems provided a more stable basis for the evolution of systems than their functionality. Methods based on the definition of the data model and subsequent and separate definition of the processing of the data were developed applying this principle (e.g., Structured Analysis/Structured Design and SSADM). More recently, however, a number of authors have proposed methods for analysis and design based on the concepts and principles of object-oriented programming; concepts such as the encapsulation of data and process within "class" definitions, inheritance and polymorphism,[1] and development by extension. These methods are now receiving wide attention in the market as they provide the potential to unlock the power of object-oriented development through systematic and controlled processes. The alternative to methods — using object-oriented languages without a systematic approach to the analysis of a system's requirements and the design of its implementation — has already, predictably, proved disastrous in some projects (Page-Jones 1989). This chapter draws examples from five methods:

- Coad/Yourdon (Coad 1991)
- Shlaer/Mellor (Shlaer 1988, 1992)
- Booch (Booch 1991)
- Colbert (Colbert 1989)
- Rumbaugh (Rumbaugh 1991)

These examples illustrate how analysis and design methods apply common concepts and principles of object orientation even though the notations and some of the prescribed processes of the methods differ.

---

[1]*Polymorphism*: This is a delicious buzzword to rival *paradigm* and *gestalt round-trip* from the current object-oriented crop! It is in fact a term borrowed from type theory and refers to languages where symbols (e.g., variable names in a program) can refer to objects of more than one type or class. Its importance to OO languages is that operations on objects can be specified without knowing the exact code that will be invoked to carry out the operations until, in the running system, the class of a particular object is known. Thus, in a statement such as *DRAW X* the operation called may be different every time the statement is executed if the variable *X* refers to objects of different classes (say "polygon," "circle," "bezier," etc). Classes can therefore be added, modified, and extended without modifying the programs that use them. Polymorphism is discussed in greater detail in chapter 3.

Concepts and Principles of Object Orientation

The change from traditional development methods to object orientation is not simply in the key buzzwords and notations of the languages, but requires a change of thinking in a number of areas.

The first and most obvious change is in the units of modularity, the building blocks of the system models. Whereas traditional methods' modules typically contain the specification of a process or function, in object-oriented thinking the *key* units of modularity become objects in the running system, and classes in the definition and design of the system.

Objects are units of encapsulated data — generally elements of the system's model of the real world. For example the object **Customer_A** may be a data structure storing details of a particular customer's name, address, and account details. However, the definition of the set of all similar objects, referred to as the *class*, contains not only the definition of the data structures (e.g., the attributes and their physical representation), but the operations or functions that operate on these data structures as well. In the case of the class **Customer**, such operations might include **validate_credit_rating**, **send_statement**, **invoice**, **mail**, and so on. The class is therefore the key element of modularity in the specification and design of the system. This is an important change (*the* important change) in thinking between traditional methods, which have very deliberately separated the definition of data and function (and have generally implemented them in different languages), and object-oriented methods, which require the data structures and the programs operating on the data structures to be defined together.

The second important change of thinking in object-oriented development is that systems are built to evolve and that the methods and languages are designed to support evolution by *extension* rather than by reimplementation. Boehm (1988) pointed out that the system development life cycle should be driven by an assessment of risk benefit and should therefore be incremental (many low-risk deliveries) rather than monolithic (one exceedingly high-risk delivery). Whereas this is widely recognized, and most projects follow this pattern at least to some degree, development methods often embed the traditional "waterfall" life cycle into their prescribed approach. Furthermore, it is only by using features of object-oriented languages such as inheritance (or generalization-specialization) that such incremental development becomes manageable.

Inheritance and polymorphism, for example, enable new features of classes to be defined by specifying new subclasses. Subclasses inherit all the existing features of the parent class, modified where necessary, without changing the original class definition itself or even the programs that will use the new subclass (provided they use it in the same way they would use the parent class). This maximizes the reuse of design and implementation information, while minimizing the parts of the system that do have to be changed when extensions are made. Inheritance can be used in the analysis and specification of systems, just as it is in the implementation stages, to reuse existing parts of a specification for new features. This is a most attractive feature of object-oriented approaches, and it follows a natural way for humans to organize information. Specifying general features of a class, and then defining subclasses where only the differences or extensions need be defined, saves much time and effort for both the reader and the producer of specifications. (Classification theory, of course, a mainstay of the organization of scientific knowledge, predates object-oriented languages and even computers by some considerable margin — a comforting thought for those concerned about the burgeoning of new and "untried" concepts.)

The use of inheritance in the analysis model has two purposes: the organization of specifications for clarity and compactness (reusing the specification of general classes in more specific subclasses), and, what is clearly a secondary goal in the analysis model, efficient and reusable class structure for implementation. Although it is likely that the designer will wish to use the same generalization-specializations in the implementation model as the analyst did in the specification, this need not be the case; in fact, it may not be desirable in some situations (e.g., where there are different limitations on inheritance in the implementation languages, or a different structure in the existing code is being reused). In these cases, consistency between class specification in the analysis and implementation models may still be enforced, but without necessarily preserving the inheritance structure from the analysis to the implementation models.

The third important change in thinking in terms of object orientation involves this continuity of models from analysis through implementation. Although a goal of most development methods, it becomes feasible when allied to object oriented features. This is because the same vocabulary, modularity, and abstractions can be used from the analysis model right through to the implementation. This is not to say that no additional terms or modules (classes) are introduced during the stages of detailed design and implementation — there will be many. But anything defined in the analysis and specification phases can be seen to map directly on to classes in the implementation stages. The use of the class as a universal unit of modularity means that analysis models are directly comparable to implementation models (even where the class hierarchy is not identical). In this way object orientation allows the "domain-experts," representing the procurers or users of the system, together with the designers and implementors of the system, to define a common vocabulary and ensure that vocabulary has a physical representation in the classes and objects of the final system. As the system evolves, the data structures and algorithms may change totally, but the analysis of the problem domain should remain relatively stable through the whole process.

These elements of object-think — modularity based on classes, development by extension, and continuity of design models — are present to some degree in all object-oriented development methods. In the next part of this chapter we consider how different methods support and represent four essential characteristics of an object-oriented approach to analysis and design:

- Classes and objects
- Scale
- Software architecture
- Evolutionary life cycles

CLASSES AND OBJECTS

As discussed earlier, *objects* are the units of modularity in the running system, they encapsulate a data structure representing a real-world "thing" or concept, and their structure and behavior are defined — along with the set of all similar objects, by their *class*. Each method provides notation for representing classes and objects (in this section, examples of their iconography and a brief discussion of the purpose of the diagrams on which they occur is presented). The principal concern in an object-oriented analysis or design is identifying and specifying the classes. Specifying the class will involve:

ITS GENERALIZATIONS AND SPECIALIZATIONS: what structure and behavior does it share with or inherit from more general classes, and what properties does it endow on descendants or specialized classes?

ITS ATTRIBUTES: including associations with other classes.

ITS SERVICES: an external view of the behavior of an object of the class.

ITS STATES AND TRANSITIONS: a means of specifying the dynamic behavior — how the internal state of an object changes through external stimulus or internal processing.

All these elements are represented in the five methods through different diagram types and textual specifications. The number of diagram types vary from just two (Coad/Yourdon) to at least seven (Shlaer/Mellor). More will no doubt be used in a specific project context, but the goal is common — the full specification and subsequent implementation of a comprehensive set of classes.

Examples of diagrams from the five methods are given in Figures 1.1 – 1.5, which show how the common elements of information can be displayed in varying levels of detail and emphasis. However, the diagrams do not show the full range of expressive power or types of diagrams that are available in the different methods.

The two diagram types of the Coad/Yourdon method are: the class diagram and state-transition diagram. Of these the principal focus is on the class diagram, shown in Figure 1.1.

The *Class_and _Object* icon shows the name of the class along with the names of the attributes (in the upper portion on the icon) and those of the services/operations (in the lower portion). Different layers of the information model can be suppressed or highlighted on the diagram to improve clarity when particular aspects are being analyzed or presented.

Rumbaugh uses a similar notation for classes, although the distinction between class and object is by icon shape (rounded corners for objects), and more optional information about the attributes and operations can be displayed on diagrams if required (e.g., data types for attributes and parameters for operations). An example of a Rumbaugh class diagram is shown in Figure 1.2. The method also uses object diagrams to specify the interaction between instances of the classes, state transition diagrams and, for specific classes or transactions, data flow diagrams.

Booch uses a "cloud" notation for objects and classes (dotted outline for classes) to convey through an "amorphous blob" the representation of a concept or thing. The details of attributes and services are documented through textual templates associated with each class. The method itself is focused more on the design and implementation phases than on analysis and therefore provides detailed notations for specifying the interaction between components. Other kinds of diagrams used in the Booch method include object, state transition, timing, and module diagrams.

Shlaer/Mellor (like Booch) hide the details of the services associated with classes, but show the attributes. This is closer to a more traditional entity-relationship model (the emphasis on identifying key attributes also contrasts with some OO methods that postpone these considerations to the detailed design stage, if relational databases are used). However, the Shlaer/Mellor method does follow the object-oriented principle of combining data and process definitions in the specification of the classes (generally and confusingly referred to in the method as *objects*; objects are referred to as *instances*). Again, a variety of diagram types are used, including state transition diagrams and data flow diagrams. This comprehensive methodology covers many stages of a project from initial concept to implementation.

Finally, Colbert uses a number of icons to represent different types of object (active,

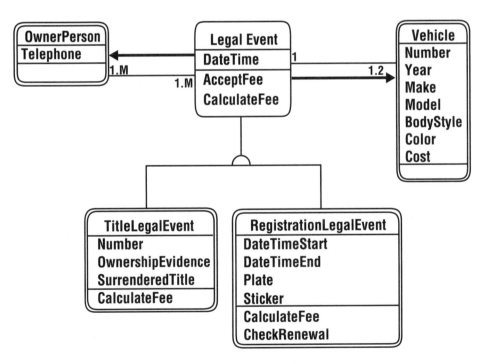

FIGURE 1.1. A class diagram in Coad/Yourdon notation.

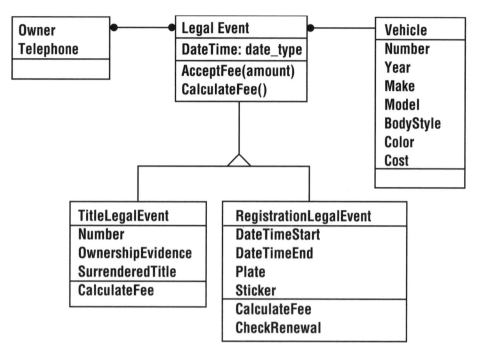

FIGURE 1.2. A class diagram in Rumbaugh's notation.

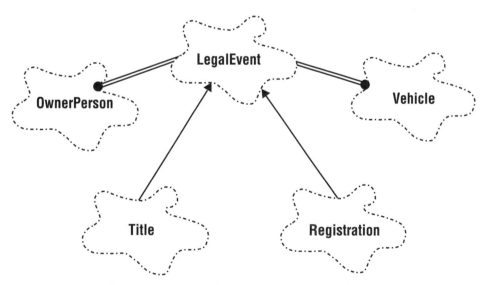

FIGURE 1.3. A class diagram in Booch's notation.

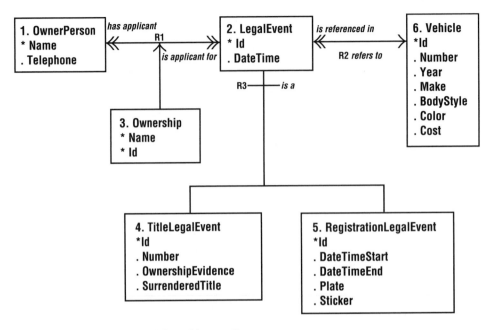

FIGURE 1.4. A data model in Shlaer/Mellor notation.

passive, and external) and the same shapes with dotted lines for corresponding classes. An interesting aspect of this method is that rather than starting the analysis from a consideration of the classes, a hierarchical object model is built from which classes can be identified. This is not an object hierarchy in the sense that some other methods use it,[2] but a set of object instances from which the generalizations into classes can be made. The class diagram shown in Figure 1.5 features only a small part of the notations that provide features for detailed specification of aspects of the requirements and design.

SCALE

Models with six to ten classes are common in training examples and text books, and are most helpful in grasping the concepts of methods. Unfortunately, in commercial systems

---

[2] *Object Hierarchy*: The object hierarchy in Colbert's method is quite different from that of HOOD although it uses a similar terminology. In HOOD (Carmichael 1992) the "objects" are in fact design components and in a "good" object-oriented design should correspond to classes, or collections of classes. In Colbert's object hierarchy, the objects are instances in the system at run-time. Thus, there may be many objects in the hierarchy of the same class. The classes are identified from this model and then implemented as classes in objected-oriented languages (e.g., C++) or abstract data types or packages in strongly typed languages (e.g., Ada).

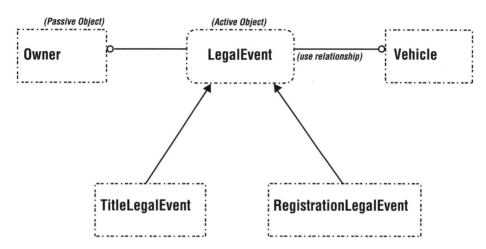

FIGURE 1.5. A class diagram in Colbert's notation.

there are likely to be many hundreds — even thousands — of classes. Naturally, as systems evolve, the number increases. For this reason, it is essential that methods help analysts deal with the scale of problems by partitioning them into manageable modules while preserving the integrity of the complete model.

Booch introduces a concept called the *class category* for precisely this purpose. It is a group of logically and closely coupled classes, probably sourced from the same team, subcontractor, or supplier, that may be versioned, controlled, and analyzed as a unit, independently from, or in conjunction with, other class categories. Class categories may contain other class categories, which results in a hierarchical structure [in this case, very similar to the hierarchy in HOOD (Carmichael 1992)]. The equivalent concept in Coad/Yourdon is *subject,* and in Rumbaugh and Colbert it is *module* — a grouping of related classes with their associations and generalizations. Shlaer/Mellor use high-level partitioning *domains*, which may not themselves be further partitioned, but which divide the overall problem into separate areas. *Bridges* in the Shlaer/Mellor method define the interfaces between domains and allow independent development of each domain.

The management of the scale of problems is not unique to object orientation, and therefore successful strategies from elsewhere can and should be applied. Grouping classes (the basic module in the analysis/design models) into larger modules means that configuration management tools and techniques can be used in the traditional manner. There is no doubt, however, that ensuring the integrity (completeness and consistency) of such very large models, which are by definition evolving independently over time, is no simple matter and still beyond the capabilities of current purely automated environments and tools.

SOFTWARE ARCHITECTURE

Software architecture is a term often used, but rarely defined. The analogy between the architecture of buildings and that of software has been developed by McDermid (1991). The chief architect's role in a new city development, for example, is to plan the major amenities, communications, and environmental constraints at the outset of the project. This structure, if not the detailed implementation, is likely to survive many changes in the use and scope of the development for decades to come. The chief architect may also decide the style and size of the buildings within certain parameters and how these components fit into the whole scheme. Certain critical elements of the design may be completed in full detail, but in other cases, provided the component buildings conform to the "architecture," new structures and changes to existing ones can be incorporated independently. The architectural design phase in software development is similar. Software architects can consider the requirements of the family of systems that will be built on their structures, or in the case of a single system, they can define the interfaces between the major components in such a way as to maximize reuse of existing components and minimize the cost of developing and subsequently replacing other components.

Shlaer/Mellor use a more specific definition of *software architecture* in their method, applying it to the mapping between concepts in an analysis model and those in the implementation languages being used to implement the system. For example, the rule that a class in the analysis model maps to an Ada package implementing an abstract data type in the implementation model would be just part of the definition of a specific software architecture. Clearly, formalizing the rules for transition from analysis to implementation not only assists designers and programmers in carrying this out, but allows for greater automation of the process with CASE tools. It is an approach that is equally applicable to other object-oriented methods.

EVOLUTIONARY LIFE CYCLES

It is an easy but unnecessary assumption that the logical ordering — analysis, design, implementation — is also the chronological one. A deep understanding of a problem domain is needed to specify the requirements for the enhancement of a system (even in the case of, say, a "green field" development). Usually, that understanding is gained only through building at least part of the system. Certainly, it is unreasonable to expect the highest risk activity — requirements specification — to be carried out reliably and completely at the time when the least is known about the application and its potential for automation. The fact that cancellations of very large procurements still occur after development but prior to systems entering service should convince us of this.

The object-oriented approach to development enables development to build on existing software and improve systems incrementally. This aspect of an evolutionary rather than monolithic life cycle is present in all the object-oriented methodologies. It is Booch who applied the term *gestalt round-trip* — a term borrowed from psychology — in this context. When psychologists failed to fully understand the human mind by partitioning it into separate compartments, they concluded that considering the whole form (gestalt) would improve their analysis. Software engineers may also gain from the insight that the activities of analysis (understanding the problem domain and the system requirements), design (inventing, selecting, and coordinating the elements of the solution), and implementation can occur simultaneously in their activities, although there is still a need to separately record and manage the resulting analysis models, design models, and code. As Parnas observed (Parnas 1979), the importance of a top-down model is in its logical presentation to the reader, rather than as a definition of the process to the writer.

Conclusion

Object-think involves three key elements: modularity based on classes, development by extension, and continuity of design models. It has not been our purpose here to carry out a full comparison of particular methods and notations (chapters 6 and 7, for example, go further). However, this chapter has focused on the common concepts and principles of methods for object-oriented analysis, design, and implementation (e.g., classes and objects, scale, software architecture, and evolutionary life cycles) and how the adoption of these principles requires a change of thinking on the part of the software professionals and system procurers involved. The aim of this change of thinking is not to replace one set of esoteric concepts and notations with another, but to address the problems of communication between the procurers of systems (and their associated application domain experts) and the developers of systems (with their associated experts in different aspects of the implementation systems). Object-oriented approaches can improve this process significantly and thereby provide an opportunity for the radical improvement of the quality, cost-effectiveness, and flexibility of automated systems.

References

Boehm, B.W. (1988) A spiral model of software development and enhancement. *Computer*, 21:61-72.

Booch, G. (1991) *Object-Oriented Design with Applications*, Benjamin Cummings, Redwood City, CA.

Carmichael, A.R. (1992) Defining software architectures using the Hierarchical Object-Oriented Design method (HOOD). *Proc. Tri-ADA '92 Conference*. ACM SIGAda, New York.

Coad, P., and E. Yourdon (1991) *Object-Oriented Analysis*. 2nd Edition, Yourdon Press, Prentice-Hall, Englewood Cliffs, NJ.

Coad, P., and E. Yourdon (1991) *Object-Oriented Design*, Yourdon Press, Prentice-Hall, Englewood Cliffs, NJ.

Colbert, E. (1989) Object-oriented software development: a practical approach to object-oriented development. *Proc. TRI-Ada '89*, ACM SIGAda, New York.

McDermid, J. (1991) In praise of architects, *Information and Software Technology*, 33:8.

Page-Jones, M., and S. Weiss (1989) Synthesis: an object-oriented analysis and design method. *Hotline on Object-Oriented Technology*, **1**(12).

Parnas, D.L. (1979) Designing software for ease of extension and contraction, *IEEE Transactions on Software Engineering*, SE-5(2).

Rumbaugh, J., M. Blaha, W. Premerlani, F. Eddy, and W. Lorensen (1991) *Object-Oriented Modeling and Design*, Prentice-Hall, Englewood Cliffs, NJ.

Shlaer, S. and S.J. Mellor (1988) *Object-Oriented Systems Analysis: Modeling the World in Data*. Yourdon Press, Prentice-Hall, Englewood Cliffs, NJ.

Shlaer, S. and S.J. Mellor (1992) *Object Lifecycles: Modeling the World in States*. Yourdon Press, Prentice-Hall, Englewood Cliffs, NJ.

part 2

UNDERSTANDING AND ADOPTING OBJECT TECHNOLOGY

chapter **2**

Adopting Object-Oriented Software Engineering

RALPH HODGSON   *IDE EUROPE**

Many organizations are now confronting the question of whether to go object oriented. For most, object orientation has to be assimilated into a trusted development life cycle process. Existing non–object-oriented software in the form of C, FORTRAN, COBOL, or 4GL applications, critical projects and timescales mean that going object oriented is not something that can be taken lightly. In this chapter we consider the motivations and strategies for adoption, which should be approached through responsible stages that allow an organization time to develop and learn. As for any technology adoption, organizational development should be informed by business strategy, interpretations of methodology as ideological imperatives, and the dynamics of technology transfer and cultural change.

INTRODUCTION

Object orientation is causing a reappraisal of methods for analysis and design and a rethinking of the role of systems architecture—the very terms *analysis* and *design* are open to question.

*Present Affiliation: IBM Consulting Group, Southbury, Connecticut

Questions arise from the need to place architecture as a central idea for the structuring of solutions. How should requirements be expressed so that existing architectures and design patterns can be used? What is the role of object-oriented modeling? Is it only to clarify an understanding of a problem (or problem situation) or is the model to be implemented so that it can serve as the core of the solution?

In this chapter and in chapter 7, I hope to answer some of these questions. If I achieve my purposes, I will have emphasized the importance of being clear on the motivations for going object oriented. I will have placed architecture and design patterns as a central concern for methods. I will have persuaded you that object-oriented methods continue to evolve and that an organization should be aware of the thinking behind all of them. Rather than choosing "the" method it will use, an organization should establish a set of engineering principles and define a process that combines techniques into an overall process for doing object-oriented software engineering. The focus of this chapter is the adoption of object technology: its intrigue, what it is and how it is different, its motivations, and how organizations can approach the problems of adoption.

The Intrigue and Dilemma of Objects

Perhaps every hour some manager somewhere in the world is being asked to use object orientation on the next project. This poor manager worries because he or she cannot suddenly go object oriented. For one thing, there will be many lines of existing non–object-oriented software, a history of existing FORTRAN, COBOL, or 4GL applications, critical projects, and timescales to contend with. Going object oriented is not something this manager can take lightly.

In response to all the promotion of the technology, other managers are insisting that their organizations get into objects. Here, the poor developers are the victims of the desire for object orientation. How should developers prepare themselves for changes in practice and in their development environments? Many temptations will be offered to these developers.

Whether the drive is from managers or developers, going object oriented has many meanings. Consensus on what impacts there will be at an organizational level will be needed — on the reality of the technology and on the benefits and the risks involved (Wasserman 1991).

The adoption of any new technology or practices may be viewed as a progression from a stage of curiosity (and skepticism), through investigations and demonstrators to pilot projects, and then to an attained software engineering capability that becomes part of the organizational culture. At the highest level, the distinctions of software engineering maturity assessment are relevant. Figure 2.1 suggests, using a pyramid, how at any given time many organizations will be at the stage of curiosity, fewer will be investigating, fewer will

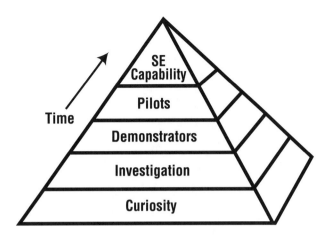

FIGURE 2.1. Maturity of technology adoption.

be building demonstrators or doing pilot projects, and even fewer organizations will be at a mature stage of adoption.

A managed process of technology introduction is a progression through stages with readiness checks (Figure 2.2). Readiness is reached through a dialogue guided by questionnaires and conducted among all interested parties, resulting in an expression of consensus that everyone can support.

Object orientation is not only a paradigm shift for how software systems are conceived and implemented, but for the organization, too. Is the organization going object oriented for greater productivity and a shortening of the time-to-market? Or, is it to be a solution to predictability of development times? Or for greater end-user satisfaction? Or as a long-term goal for asset-based development based on reuse? The answer will often be unclear. Moving from curiosity to investigation might be decided when there is consensus on:

- Motivations for going object oriented
- Expectations of the technology
- Objectives of the investigation
- The scope and method of the investigation
- Criteria for assessing the deliverables of the investigation

Readiness to move from investigation to demonstrations might include determining:

- Purposes of the demonstration
- Who owns the work and who the customer is (who needs convincing)
- Team structure and skills needed
- Review process and infrastructure

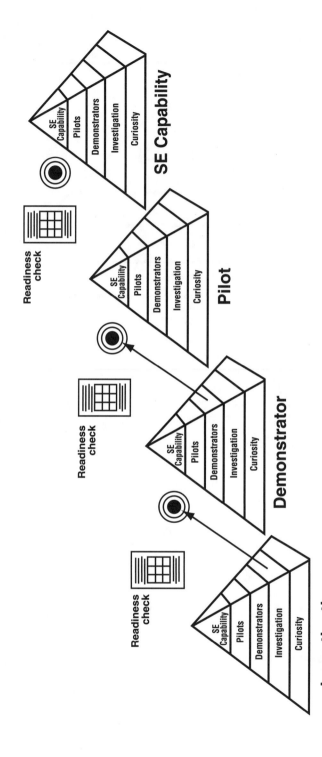

FIGURE 2.2. Technology adoption stages.

Deciding to do a pilot project is determined by:

- Clarity on the purposes of the pilot
- Degree of confidence on getting a successful result
- Ownership of the work and identification of the customer
- Team structure and skills required
- Risk assessment and management process

Assimilating new practices and technologies into the culture of an organization is difficult to understand as something that may be structured through "readiness" checks. Software maturity and capability assessment are relevant approaches. Some ways of undertaking such assessment are available in initiatives such as the SEI software maturity model, IMPROVEIT, BOOTSTRAP, and the ISO working group on software process standardization. Once an organization has new competence, skills and techniques become imbued in the organization. And readiness becomes implicit in the evolution of the organization's skills and norms. Some questions for clarifying readiness beyond pilots are:

- Is the organization willing to completely revise its ways of working?
- How will the assimilation of new ways of working fit with the existing organizational infrastructure and processes?
- How are the new ways of working congruent with business goals and strategies?

WHAT IS OBJECT ORIENTATION AND HOW IS IT DIFFERENT?

Object orientation is modeling — looking at some reality or domain that is of interest, and finding the key abstractions and the relationships between those key abstractions. For every entity in that domain, there is an object that represents that concept in the model.

An object encapsulates both function and data. Access and changes to the data can only be done by invoking an operation or sending a message to an object. Information hiding of this sort is not a new idea. It existed in the seventies with the work of Parnas. What is new for objects is the concept of object identity.

Objects can be treated as individuals. Their identity can be referenced by another object. When an object wants to invoke a message or operation on another one, it names that object uniquely. In Smalltalk, it is called a *message*, but in the Ada and C++ communities, the terms *operation* or *call* are preferred. Whatever expression we use, we simply mean that some action, which may or may not alter the state of an object as a result of the information or responsibilities that are being managed, is being requested.

Information hiding and object identity are only the starting point for understanding objects. There is also the concept of centralizing descriptions. The notion of a class may be understood as a specification for creating instances of objects. The idea of classification is the key to how descriptions are shared through the concept of inheritance.

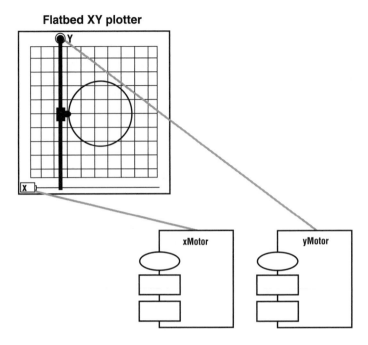

FIGURE 2.3. The concept of object identity, treating objects as individuals.

In the following examples, I will be using a notation called OOSD,[1] a design notation for object orientation (Wasserman 1990) that was influenced by the work of Booch, Constantine and Yourdon, and Hoare, and their ideas on monitors for concurrency.

An object in OOSD is indicated by a rectangle with operations as well as encapsulated data. I use the example of an **XY** plotter with an **Xmotor** and a **Ymotor** to illustrate the concept of object identity in Figure 2.3. The motors are referred to by their names. If I want to move either the **Xmotor** or the **Ymotor**, I invoke an operation called **move**. From the client's perspective, both motors behave according to a common interface or set of services. Object identity is important for describing scenarios of interaction. If I cannot distinguish the **X** and **Y** motors then I cannot describe specific patterns of execution.

If the motors are built differently and are of different classes, provided they can respond to the same operation name, the client's intentions are realized. Reference to objects of different classes using the same operation names is called *polymorphism*.

The concept of class can be understood in Figure 2.4. Two motors, of the same class, have their own private information for speed, direction, and running. Each may perform

---

[1]A different OOSD is discussed in chapter 14!—*Ed.*

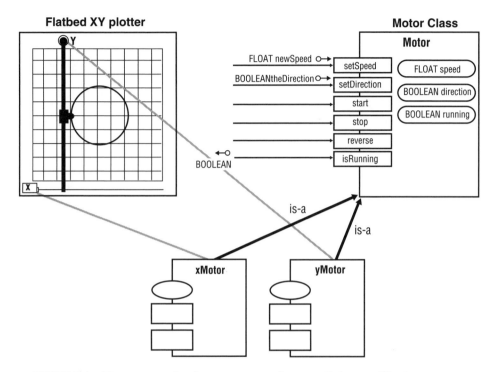

FIGURE 2.4. The concept of a class: a structure for centralizing specifications.

the operations of *setSpeed*, *setDirection*, *start*, *stop*, *reverse*, *isRunning*. A class allows us to centralize specifications or descriptions.

In object-oriented systems, classes may form relationships with each other through the concept of inheritance. Inheritance is a mechanism for sharing concepts and descriptions of behaviors. One class may inherit operations and properties from one or more other classes. It refers to these as its *ancestors* or *superclasses*.

Designing with inheritance requires decisions on where to locate operations. Inheritance is often used to stipulate an interface for conformance by subclasses. A popular example would be an inheritance tree of vehicles. The root of the tree would be the class *vehicle* abstracting common properties and behaviors of all types of vehicle, such as the registration number, number of seats, engine power, and capacity. Subclasses of *vehicle* would be *car*, *bus,* and *truck*. All vehicles can be started, stopped, parked, reversed, and accelerated. These operations would therefore characterize the generalized interface of the base class.

As a further illustration, I will use an example with which I have much experience — aircraft seat assignment. Figure 2.5 depicts an aircraft seat plan class that is specialized for different aircraft types: 737s, 747s, and 757s. Notice that there are two kinds of 747s: 136s and 236s.

Aircraft seat assignment can be given a standard interface by means of a generic interface that describes a protocol to which all aircraft seat assigners have to conform. If I go to a seat reservation clerk and say, "Find me a free seat," I will usually specify seat-class, non-smoking, aisle or window, left or right side, front or back, clear of the wing, or near another seat. These are the parameter arguments that characterize the interface of the generic root class. Irrespective of whether it is a Boeing 737 or 747, all aircraft have seat plans, and the interface on seat plans can be standardized as shown in Figure 2.6.

Generic interfaces need the concept of polymorphism, the idea that objects of different classes can be asked to perform a behavior known by the same name. A client object may reference server objects of different classes. The same operation name produces a

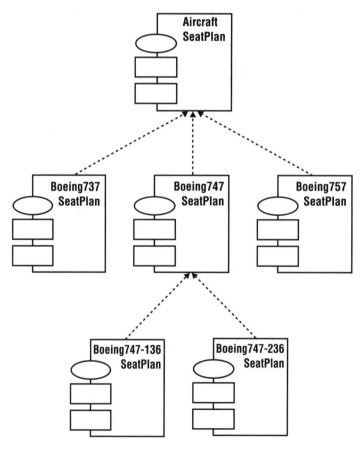

FIGURE 2.5. Designing with inheritance.

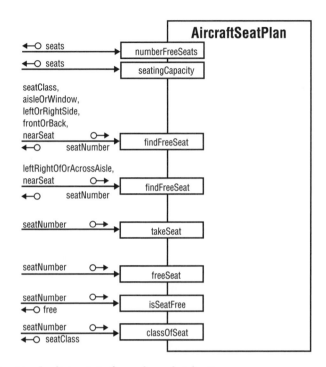

FIGURE 2.6. Standardizing interfaces through inheritance.

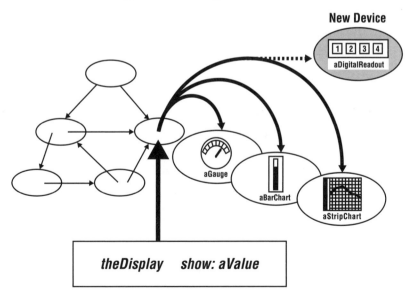

FIGURE 2.7. Polymorphism for display devices.

response in the server object, appropriate to what they represent and what they manage.

Figure 2.7 shows a client object invoking a ***show: a Value*** request on a display object. It does not matter whether that object is a gauge, a bar chart, or a strip chart; each behaves according to this protocol. The same request achieves a result appropriate to the particular responding object.

A new device of a different class can be added. All it has to do is comply with the protocol of use that has been specified. A key advantage of object orientation is that the client site does not have to change when new classes are introduced. In other words, components may evolve independently with no impact on clients. On this tenet rests the argument about the malleability of object-oriented systems.

WHAT ARE THE MOTIVATIONS FOR USING OBJECT TECHNOLOGY?

Most people, in my experience, are driven to go object oriented because of the promise of reusability. My own view is that it is not as realizable as malleability (changeability) and quality of design. These goals are more achievable. When the engineering implications of reusability are understood, organizations tend to retract that goal.

Malleability is the ability to refine and extend an existing set of classes in response to changing requirements or to operational needs such as adaptation to new computing environments. With object orientation, malleability depends on the quality of the abstractions expressed in the class hierarchies and, in particular, how interfaces are specified.

A notable example of good adaptability is given by CenterLine with their C++ development environment, ObjectCenter. Through good class design, the intricacies of platform dependencies were abstracted into more generic services for clients. CenterLine has been able to move to new platforms very quickly.

A requirement for methods is to recognize the importance of eliciting the ways in which changes might occur. Will it be more likely that new classes will be needed in the future,

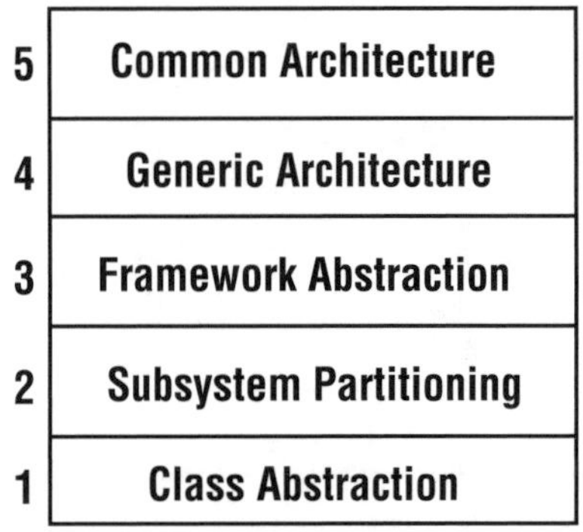

5	**Common Architecture**
4	**Generic Architecture**
3	**Framework Abstraction**
2	**Subsystem Partitioning**
1	**Class Abstraction**

FIGURE 2.8. Attainment levels of software reuse.

or new services to existing classes? In the latter case, it is advantageous to abstract the verbs of a specification as well as the objects. Class hierarchies that abstract services are called *algorithmic classes* (Hodgson 1992) or *strategy classes* (Anderson 1990).

Why is quality of design something that objects bring? Simply because the idea of modeling a world as objects fits very nicely with the way we communicate about the world. It is possible to focus on an application domain (or a computing domain) and model it very naturally with objects. Quality comes from a lack of distortion in the representations and transformations employed.

Reuse is possible and organizations that do see object technology as a means for both "design-for-reuse" and "design-with-reuse" will be positioned in the upper levels of the "reuse maturity" model of Figure 2.8. Large-scale reuse depends on architectural ideas that come from ways of organizing classes into structures of collaboration that express generalities about a domain (Eggenschwiler 1992, Johnson 1992). Such structures begin with discrete frameworks and lead to generic architectures that express the design patterns of a complete application. Figure 2.8 suggests that a common architecture that may be shared across different organizations would represent the highest level of reuse from an industry or user perspective.

Such a commitment to reuse must recognize that object orientation in a language such as C++ takes time to master. Reports from industry suggest the learning curve for mastering C++ shown in Figure 2.9.

OBJECT TECHNOLOGY ADOPTION

There is little doubt that object orientation is the most significant technology that will affect companies in the next three years. It has the potential to affect the very nature of the

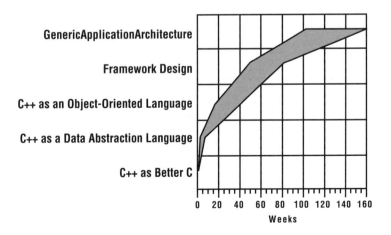

FIGURE 2.9. The learning curve for mastering C++.

business in which the enterprise is engaged. For example, with networked enterprises and telecommunications reaching every industry along connected value chains, we can anticipate interesting new opportunities. That businesses are undergoing reconfiguration as a result of information-technology–induced changes was well reported by the MIT90s project (Morton 1991).

Object orientation has the potential to affect all aspects of software development. For many the concerns are analysis and design. Traditional development is based on the transformation of a set of requirements into a design, whereas object-oriented development is a modeling process that produces systems with a domain-oriented architecture that supports an evolution of a system's functionality through iterative development. Architectures are structures that, through the partitioning of domains and component layers, offer the possibility of software reuse and an asset-based development philosophy.

Adopting any technology raises concerns in four major areas: technology supply, the external business environment, organizational infrastructure, and business strategy (Hodgson 1992). Figure 2.10 shows these areas as dynamic processes in a framework shaped like a four-leafed clover.

The framework starts with ideas from the Software Engineering Institute (SEI), Pittsburgh, PA. According to the SEI model, technology transfer is a progression from technology producers through advocates to receptors and end users (Fowler 1990). For the dynamics, I value Peter Senge's ideas of reinforcing and balancing processes within organizations (Senge 1991).

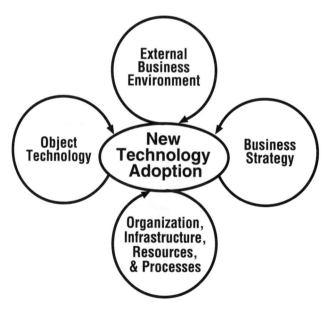

FIGURE 2.10. The "clover" model of technology adoption.

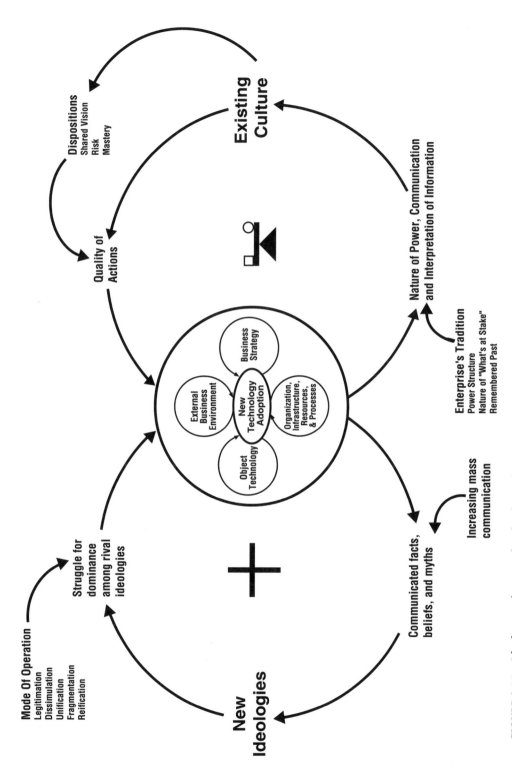

FIGURE 2.11. Ideology, culture, and technology adoption.

Thought must be given to the impact on the organization, the infrastructure, the processes of the organization, its resources, and how it sees the context of the business — what the business is and how competitors are behaving. Some of the barriers include the disposition of the organization to shared vision. Another barrier is the disposition to risk. Many companies have been oversold technology in the past, so there is a natural skepticism about so-called new advances. You have to be careful that you are not being oversold again.

There should be a relationship between the adoption of the technology and the business strategy. As an extreme example, a company might redefine its business by building class libraries and selling them to its competitors!

Ideology and culture also play a part in the organizational factors that surround technology adoption. Figure 2.11 suggests some of the forces at work. Ideological factors are evident in the rivalry between methods. Just as for political ideologies, there can be modes of operation in which methodologies appeal for attention, legitimation, and dissimulation (Thompson 1990).

Even if individuals in organizations make sense of the waves of ideology, cultural factors will ultimately determine the nature of organizational acceptance, which according to some recent surveys is cited as the greatest barrier to the acceptance of object technology. *Culture* is defined by Edgar Schein (1936) as:

> The pattern of basic assumptions that a given group has invented, discovered or developed in learning to cope with its problems of external adaptation and internal integration, and that have worked well enough to be considered valid, and, therefore, to be taught to new members as the correct way to perceive, think and feel in relation to those problems.

A software organization holds basic underlying assumptions that are the ultimate source of its values and justifications for its actions. This bedrock of axiomatic cultural knowledge — in all probability originally a result of sound rationale — becomes increasingly dislocated from the structures and processes that the organization adheres to as its operational logic. The challenge of objects is that they present a new axiom, and the very nature of organizational acceptance is to find a learning process to renew its deep cultural knowledge (Sackmann 1991).

Organizational change accompanies any new technology adoption. In Figure 2.12 I have tried to show the major processes. Through a perception of the possibilities of the technology, a shared vision must be agreed on. Then senior management's endorsement and motivation of the development team can be stimulated by the shared vision held in place through realistic technical and management expectations.

Once the work starts, endorsement and motivation must be reinforced by process and product visibility. Management must not become alienated, and developers must not become frustrated by misunderstood expectations. I emphasize process because it is important for everyone understand the nature of the work that is being done.

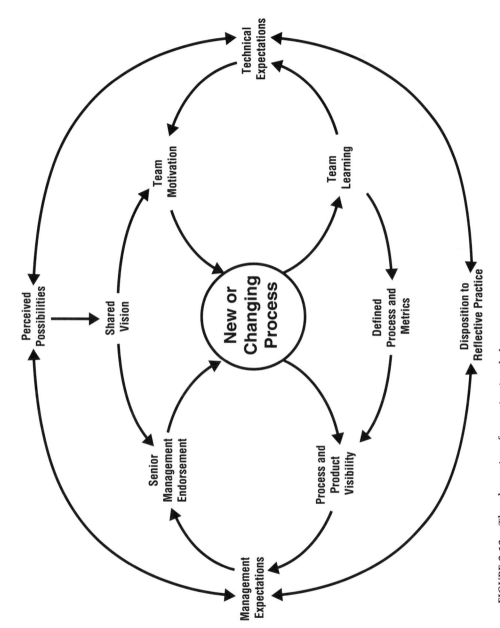

FIGURE 2.12. The dynamics of organizational change

The organization must also take the opportunity to learn. A learning process can reinforce or change expectations, and may also influence the definition of the process. The organization must be well-disposed to reflective practice, patterns of diagnosis that can imbue a sense of responsibility for organizational change (Reason 1988; Mohrman 1989).

CONCLUSION

As this technology matures, it is important to take an engineering approach. There is a growing adoption of the concepts, and many companies are using object technology in real projects now. A development process is vital, as are the tools, to ensure that radical improvement can take place across the object-oriented development life cycle.

REFERENCES

Anderson, D.B., and S. Gossain (1990) Software reusability using object-oriented programming, *UK IT 1990*, University of Southampton, UK.

Burke, W.W. (1987) *Organization Development: A Normative View*, Addison Wesley, Reading, MA.

Eggenschwiler, T. and E. Gamma (1992) ET++ swaps manager: using object technology in the financial engineering domain, *Proceedings of OOPSLA'92*, Vancouver, BC, Canada, 166–177, *ACM SIGPLAN Notices* 27(10).

Fowler, P.J. (1990) Technology transfer as collaboration: the receptor group. *12th International Conference on Software Engineering, Nice, France,* IEEE Computer Society Press, Piscataway, NJ, 332–333.

French, W.L. and C.H. Bell (1990) *Organization Development Behavioral Science Interventions for Organization Improvement*, Prentice-Hall, Englewood Cliffs, NJ.

Hax, A.C. and N.S. Majluf (1991) *The Strategy Concept and Process*, Prentice-Hall, Englewood Cliffs, NJ.

Hodgson, R. (1992) C++ in Europe. *C++ Report*, 4(3):56–64.

Hodgson, R. and B. Anderson (1993) *The Role of Architecture in Object-Oriented Software Engineering* (private communication).

Johnson, R.E. (1992) Documenting frameworks using patterns, *Proceedings of OOPSLA '92*, 63-76, *ACM SIGPLAN Notices* 27(10).

Mohrman, J.A.M., S.A. Mohrman, J.G.E. Ledford, T.G. Cummings, and E.E. Lawler III and Associates (1989) *Large-Scale Organizational Change*, Jossey-Bass Inc.

Morgan, G. (1986) *Images of Organization*, SAGE Publications, London, UK.

Morton, M.S.S., editor (1991) *The Corporation of the 1990s — Information Technology and Organizational Transformation*, Oxford University Press, UK.

Reason, P. (1988) *Human Inquiry in Action*, SAGE Publications, London, UK.

Sackmann, S.A. (1991) *Cultural Knowledge in Organizations*, SAGE Publications, London, UK.

Schein, E.H. (1992) *Organizational Culture and Leadership*, Jossey-Bass Publishers, San Francisco, CA.

Senge, P.M. (1991) *The Fifth Discipline — The Art and Practice of the Learning Organization*, Doubleday, New York.

Stroustrup, B. (1991) No good deed will remain unpunished, *Proceedings, ECUG Winter Conference*, Imperial College, London, pp. 40–51.

Thompson, J.B. (1990) *Ideology and Modern Culture*, Polity Press.

Wasserman, A.I., P.A. Pircher, and R.J. Muller (1990) The object-oriented structured design notation for software design representation, *IEEE Computer* 23(3): 50–63.

Wasserman, A.I. (1991) Object-oriented thinking, *Object Magazine* 1(3): 10–13.

chapter **3**

The Four Dimensions of Object-Oriented Methods and Languages

Gordon S. Blair   *University of Lancaster*

This chapter presents a view of object-oriented concepts based on four orthogonal dimensions: encapsulation, classification, polymorphism, and interpretation. A consideration of these concepts leads to an improved understanding and application of object-oriented systems, methods, and languages.

INTRODUCTION

There is now considerable interest in object-oriented computing from such diverse areas as language design, artificial intelligence, databases, parallel and distributed systems, software engineering, and operating systems. All are attracted by the general benefits of object-oriented computing in terms of data abstraction, behavior sharing, and support for evolution (Blair 1991). However, the requirements of each of these areas are often very different, for example, in terms of granularity of objects, performance, or semantic modeling capabilities. It is simply not possible for one set of techniques to solve all the problems in

This chapter is based on excerpts from Blair (1991). The material is reproduced here by kind permission of Pitman Publishers.

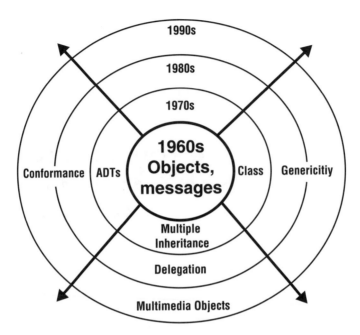

FIGURE 3.1. Variations in object-oriented computing.

each of these areas. Consequently, developers have experimented with various alternatives or variations of the basic object model in an attempt to tailor systems to their own needs. This situation is shown pictorially in Figure 3.1.

The range of techniques encompassed by the term *object oriented* is therefore vast. There is general agreement that all the aforementioned techniques are within the domain of object-oriented computing and yet, curiously, there is no accepted definition of object orientation. That is not necessarily a major problem. After all, a labeling exercise does not necessarily add to the understanding of a subject. However, a more serious problem is the lack of an agreed semantics of object-oriented computing. There is a real requirement for a model of object orientation that captures all the variations mentioned above and that allows reasoned debate about the relative merits of adopting one approach over another. Ideally, there should exist a design space for object-oriented computing that would allow designers to choose certain features to meet the requirements of their own specific areas.

This chapter presents such a model and is organized as follows. It begins with a presentation of the prevalent view of object-oriented computing. This view highlights the concepts of object, class, and inheritance as central to object-oriented computing. It is proposed that encapsulation, classification, polymorphism, and interpretation provide a set of orthogonal dimensions for object-oriented computing. The four dimensions are then examined in depth and alternative techniques for each dimension are explored. A number of key questions are analyzed using the model.

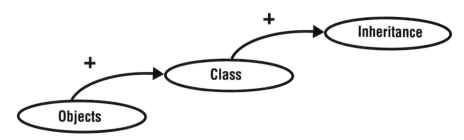

FIGURE 3.2. Traditional view of object orientation.

TRADITIONAL VIEW OF OBJECT-ORIENTED COMPUTING

Most work on object orientation has been carried out in the language domain. Consequently, it is not surprising that the most widely accepted interpretation of the term *object oriented* arose out of this field of study (Wegner 1987). In this view, object-orientation consists of a series of steps leading to full object-oriented systems (as illustrated in Figure 3.2).

This view of object-oriented computing is clear and precise, and provides a good framework for discussing most of the traditional work in object-oriented languages. However, limitations become apparent when the classification is applied to some recent developments. The main restriction of this classification is that it is based on a specific set of *mechanisms* that object-oriented languages should support. Languages that do not feature these mechanisms or those that adopt alternative mechanisms are therefore not considered to be object oriented. This is rather unsatisfactory, especially as new mechanisms for object-oriented computing are emerging all the time. In addition, the more interesting issues are concerned with what a particular system offers to the user rather than how it is implemented. This chapter presents the thesis that a more general view of object orientation is required. An alternative model is therefore proposed based on the more general *dimensions* of an object-oriented environment.

A MODEL OF OBJECT-ORIENTED COMPUTING

The model of object-orientation proposed in this chapter consists of the following four dimensions: encapsulation, classification, polymorphism, and interpretation. These are discussed in turn below.

Encapsulation Dimension

Encapsulation is the grouping together of various properties associated with an identifiable entity in the system in a lexical and logical unit, that is, the object. Access to the object should be restricted to a well-defined interface. All fields of object-oriented computing start with the basic concept that it is possible to describe the universe as a series of fairly autonomous, encapsulated objects that access each other through a protected interface. This notion is captured nicely below by Snyder (1986):

> Encapsulation is a technique for minimizing interdependencies among separately written modules by defining strict external interfaces. The external interface of a module serves as a contract between the module and its clients, and thus between the designer of the module and other designers. If clients depend only on the external interface, the module can be reimplemented without affecting any clients, so long as the new implementation supports the same (or upwardly compatible) external interface. Thus the effects of compatible changes can be confined.

The term *property* is used in the preceding definition of encapsulation in a general sense to convey any information pertaining to the object, including the internal data structures, the operations of the object, algorithms to implement the operations, attributes of the object, additional constraints, and triggers. Objects may also feature autonomous threads of control enabling them to act independently of the receipt of a message.

Different systems vary in the range of properties they support. It is therefore necessary in designing an object-oriented system to decide what properties should be associated with objects. This will inevitably vary from application to application. For example, it is common in object-oriented databases to limit the range of properties to attributes and constraints. However, in programming languages representation, operations, and algorithms will inevitably be encapsulated (although perhaps not attributes). Office information systems, on the other hand, place great emphasis on features such as triggers to provide support for various office procedures.

Once the properties of an object are defined, it is then necessary to decide on the visibility of the properties, that is, which properties are to be visible to the outside world and which are to represent internal state. It is at this stage that the interface to an object is defined. Normally, direct access to the actual representation of an object would be prevented; rather, the programmer would access the object through the operational interface. This property is usually referred to as *information hiding*. The visibility of other properties is not so clear cut. A discussion of the issues concerned with the visibility of attributes can be found in Snyder (1986). In the rest of this chapter, the visible interface of an object is referred to as the *(external) behavior* of that object.

Classification Dimension

In systems supporting encapsulation, the environment is represented by a finite set of objects in which each object exhibits certain behavior (i.e., external properties). It is very natural to extend this model to include classification. Classification is the ability to group associated objects according to common behavior. All objects within a particular grouping will share all the common properties for that grouping, but may have other differences. Classification is a very powerful tool and is absolutely central to most scientific and engineering disciplines.

In general, a classification is defined by a *predicate* over the environment of objects. For example, one valid classification would be all objects with an attribute color of red. All objects within this grouping are guaranteed to meet this predicate, but may have many other differences. A particular classification also has an *intent* and an *extent*. The intent of a classification is the description of the behavior of that classification. The intent denotes all the possible objects that exhibit a certain behavior and is, therefore, potentially infinite. By contrast, the extent of a classification is the finite set of objects in the current environment that feature such behavior. The intent of a classification is, therefore, specified by a particular predicate, whereas the extent is obtained by applying the predicate to a specific environment.

Both the intentional and extentional aspects of classification are important in object-oriented computing. This is particularly true in the object-oriented database community where it is vital to be able to represent both intentional and extentional concepts.

Various classifications can be formed representing different groupings in the system. The important question is which classifications should be represented in a particular system. The previous example is a general classification described in terms of attributes of objects. Another possibility is to specify classifications in terms of the operations provided by objects. For example, one useful classification would be the set of objects that support open, read, write, and close operations. The choice of how to model classifications in a particular object-oriented system is absolutely central to the design process. The most significant choices are discussed below.

- **Sets.** The most general way of representing classifications in a system is through sets. Sets are sufficiently powerful to model any possible classification required in a system. After all, the result of any predicate is a set of objects fulfilling that predicate. It is very uncommon to find sets in object-oriented languages. However, they are used more frequently in the area of object-oriented databases. For example, the semantic data model is based on simple set theory. The advantage of using sets is that there is an associated body of knowledge and a well-understood semantics from the field of mathematics. The intent of a set is given by a particular predicate or query. The extent is then given by all the objects answering that predicate or query. In the database community, it is quite common to denote the extent of a query by the term *class*. This illustrates the need for an agreed-upon terminology for object-oriented computing.

- **Abstract data types.** Types are also forms of classification. However, they are more specific classifications than sets in that they are purely concerned with the external interface to an object. A type is a set of objects that shares common behavior. Thus, all types are sets, but not all sets are types. An abstract data type is then the template that defines a particular classification. In effect, the predicate is given by the set of objects that meets the syntax and possibly semantics of the abstract data type. The intent of the classification is therefore the abstract data type description, whereas the extent is the set of all objects deemed to be of this abstract data type.

- **Classes (concrete data types).** The most restricted form of classification found in object-oriented computing is the class. Ironically, many people consider this to be the only classification compatible with object-oriented computing. A class is a template that fully defines the behavior of a group of objects in terms of the operations, representation, and algorithms (more generally, the complete internal and external behavior). A class can therefore be considered to be a concrete data type where the specification and implementation has been fully described. The intent of a class is given by the class template. In addition, the extent is the instances of a particular class.
- **Objects (prototypes).** To be complete, it is necessary to consider the individual object as a degenerate form of classification. This is needed to model the approaches based on prototypes (Lieberman 1986). The designers of such systems take the view that every object defines a new classification with only one element (i.e., a prototype).

Classification is, therefore, a sufficiently general concept to encompass sets, abstract data types, classes, and objects, that is, all the actual techniques found in object-oriented computing.

This also defines classifications in decreasing order of generality. This presents the designer of an object-oriented system with a spectrum of possibilities (ignoring the degenerate case):

Set > Abstract Data Type > Class

It is important to realize that the choice of one classification does not exclude the choice of a second classification. For example, several languages that allow abstract data types and classes to coexist have been developed (Black 1987; Meyer 1988). Similarly, there are several database models where set and class coexist. It is also possible to design a system or language that features all three concepts.

Polymorphism Dimension

INTRODUCING POLYMORPHISM

The concept of polymorphism has emerged from the field of type theory. In that context, polymorphism is defined to be an object's ability to have more than one type. Consequently, objects can be used in different contexts demanding different typed values. In this chapter, the term *polymorphism* is extended to take on a more general meaning. In terms of the model, polymorphism implies that an object can belong to more than one classification. This can be interpreted as meaning that objects can have more than one type. Equally, polymorphism can apply to other classifications; therefore, objects can belong to more than one set or class. Thus, polymorphism is an orthogonal concept to classification.

The power of polymorphism is that it supports a more flexible model of computing. In nonpolymorphic (i.e., monomorphic systems) objects can belong only to one classification. Hence, it is not possible for different classifications to share common behavior. Classifications therefore become protective walls that isolate objects into various disjoint categories. In polymorphic environments, however, classifications can overlap and intersect. Therefore, it is possible for two classifications to share some common behavior. Similarly, it is possible for one classification to have a subset of the behavior of a second classification.

Cardelli and Wegner, in a classic paper on polymorphism, distinguish between ad hoc polymorphism, which works on a finite number of types in an unprincipled manner, and universal polymorphism, which will work uniformly for a potentially infinite set of types in a principled manner (Cardelli 1985). Coercions and overloading were introduced as examples of ad hoc polymorphism. In addition, parametric and inclusion polymorphism were described as universal polymorphism techniques.

All styles of polymorphism are possible in an object-oriented language. However, it is *inclusion polymorphism* that really typifies this style of programming. Inclusion polymorphism supports a style of interaction in which one classification can be used in place of another because it exhibits all the behavior of the target classification. Classifications, therefore, do not exist in isolation. Rather, they are interrelated through a series of is-a relationships; that is, classification C_1 is-a C_2 if C_1 exhibits all the behavior of C_2. This form of polymorphism is normally associated with typing systems. However, it must be stressed that inclusion polymorphism is equally applicable to other classifications, in particular set and class. In typing, the is-a relationships are often referred to as *subtyping* relationships. Similarly, in set and class classifications, the is-a relationships are referred to as *subset* and *subclass*, respectively. In all cases, the is-a relationships provide a partial order over the environment and, hence, establish a lattice of classifications. This general interpretation of inclusion polymorphism is summarized in Table 3.1.

TABLE 3.1. **Inclusion polymorphism and classification.**[a]

Abstraction	Is-a Relationship	Resultant Lattice
sets	subset	set lattice
abstract data types	subtype	type lattice
classes	subclass	class lattice

[a]This interpretation of polymorphism is similar to the generalized view of inheritance described by Canning (1989).

IMPLICIT VS. EXPLICIT POLYMORPHISM

Object-oriented languages and systems are usually expected to feature inclusion polymorphism. However, one major question remains: how are the relationships between classifications established? There is a clear choice in object-oriented computing between the following options:

- **Implicit approach.** In this approach, the relationships between classifications is implicitly determined from the structure of classifications. Therefore, relationships exist between classifications because they share common behavior.
- **Explicit approach.** In this approach, the relationships between classifications is specified explicitly by the programmer. Therefore, classifications share common behavior because they are explicitly created this way.

In both cases, the net result is the same, that is, one classification can be used in place of another because they are related. There are advantages and disadvantages to both approaches. With the implicit style of polymorphism, the programmer makes a clear and full statement of the behavior of a classification and leaves the system to determine interrelationships. By contrast, in the explicit approach, the programmer makes a statement about the interrelationships and lets the system determine the full behavior. The implicit approach features a clear statement of how a classification should behave that is visible within the program. The explicit technique constructs classifications out of other classifications; hence, an element of reuse is achieved.

It must be remembered that the preceding discussion applies to all classifications (i.e., set, abstract data type, and class). It may well be that one technique might be used with abstract data types and a second technique with classes. For example, conformance rules illustrate the use of an implicit technique to determine relationships between abstract data types. By contrast, inheritance is an example of an explicit statement of relationships between classes.

ADDITIONAL FORMS OF POLYMORPHISM

It is also possible to introduce other styles of polymorphism in object-oriented languages and systems. This might be used to enhance inclusion polymorphism or it might be implemented as an alternative to inclusion polymorphism. The main alternatives are overloading and parametric polymorphism.

- **Overloading.** Using this technique, names can be overloaded to signify different properties (e.g., attributes or operations) in different contexts. Contextual information is then used to resolve the conflict. Overloading is an ad hoc technique, that is, it is introduced in an unprincipled way by the programmer. It can actually be shown that most inheritance systems support overloading in conjunction with inclusion polymorphism (Blair 1989).
- **Parametric polymorphism.** The form of parametric polymorphism most com-

monly found in object-oriented models is genericity. Briefly, genericity is the ability to parameterize a piece of software with one or more types. The parameterized types can then be used in the construction of the software element. Languages such as Ada and Clu support this form of polymorphism alone. Several other languages use genericity in conjunction with inclusion polymorphism. It should be stressed that genericity is not a replacement for inclusion polymorphism. Each provides different and complementary styles of polymorphism. Genericity provides a shorthand way of representing a number of different classifications that share a generic description. In effect, genericity saves the programmer from having to write the same descriptor for various uses of a common algorithm (e.g., to represent a stack of integers, a stack of characters, etc.). Inclusion polymorphism, by contrast, provides a more general mechanism for expressing relationships between classifications. It is therefore perfectly reasonable to employ both approaches in a particular design (Meyer 1988).

Interpretation Dimension

The final aspect of object-oriented computing to be discussed is the interpretation dimension. This dimension is responsible for the resolution of polymorphic behavior. In polymorphic environments, it is possible for an item of behavior to span many classifications. For example, a print operation is likely to have many interpretations within a system.

It is the task of this dimension to determine the precise interpretation of an operation in a specific context. It is therefore necessary to resolve the ambiguity that can exist in a polymorphic environment. On closer examination, this can involve two discrete steps:

1. Determine whether an operation is valid in the specific context.
2. Determine the precise implementation to be invoked.

The two steps correspond to type checking and binding, respectively. Type checking determines whether operations are supported by a particular object, and binding locates the correct implementation of the operation.

In both cases, the issue of when this interpretation procedure is carried out remains. There are two possibilities: the polymorphic behavior can either be resolved at compile-time or run-time. This choice applies equally to type checking and binding, giving rise to the following decisions:

- Static type checking vs. dynamic type checking
- Static binding vs. dynamic binding

Various combinations of static and dynamic type checking and binding are possible as shown in Table 3.2. The decisions made at this level can have a significant impact on the characteristics of a system in terms of flexibility and correctness.

TABLE 3.2. Combinations of type checking and binding policies.

Type of Binding	Static Type Checking	Dynamic Type Checking
Static Binding	Guarantee of correctness Inflexible interpretation	Invalid combination
Dynamic Binding	Guarantee of correctness Flexible interpretation	No guarantee of correctness Flexible interpretation

TWENTY QUESTIONS

A major test of the definition of object orientation described in this chapter is whether it supports constructive statements about some of the difficult semantic problems faced in object-oriented computing. It should be stressed at this point that definitive statements on some of these problems are still beyond the state of the art and will await more complete semantics for object orientation. However, the definition does provide a framework to clarify most confusing issues. This is demonstrated in an informal way by considering 20 questions commonly asked about object-oriented computing.

1. *What is object-oriented computing?* This chapter proposes that object-oriented computing is best understood as an aggregation of techniques that fit within the design space outlined above. Furthermore, the temptation to place a more rigid interpretation on object orientation ought to be resisted.
2. *What are the benefits of object-oriented computing?* The benefits commonly claimed for object-oriented computing all tend to be manifestations of the benefits of encapsulation, classification, polymorphism, and interpretation.
3. *Is object-oriented computing a certain frame of mind?* The question is often raised of whether object-oriented computing is a completely new model of programming. It is probably more accurate to say that object-oriented programming is a recogntion of the benefits of encapsulation, classification, polymorphism, and interpretation.
4. *What is an object?* An object is any identifiable encapsulation in the system that probably represents a concept in the world being modeled. The task of identifying objects in a particular application of object-oriented computing is fraught with difficulties and comes under the banner of object-oriented design (Blair 1991).
5. *Is message passing fundamental to object-oriented languages?* No. Message passing is one possible technique for implementing object-oriented systems. It is equally possible to adopt other solutions. However, message passing is conceptually a very good way of viewing object-oriented programs.
6. *Is dynamic binding essential?* Dynamic binding (or the dynamic interpretation of polymorphism) is not essential to object-oriented environments. However, the

benefits to be gained from dynamic binding should not be underestimated.

7. *Is inheritance fundamental to object-oriented computing?* Again, inheritance is not essential within the proposed definition. Other methods of obtaining polymorphism may be used. However, inheritance has proven to be a very useful technique in many environments and should not be overlooked lightly.

8. *What is the relationship between class and type?* Class and type are alternative techniques for modeling classification in object-oriented systems. The distinction is that type is solely concerned with the external behavior of objects, whereas class is also concerned with how this behavior is implemented. Both concepts can coexist in the same system.

9. *Is static type checking possible in object-oriented languages?* Yes. It has been demonstrated that it is possible to statically type check object-oriented languages. This can be most satisfactorily achieved by having a clean separation between the concepts of class and type.

10. *What does conformance provide?* Conformance provides an alternative technique for achieving polymorphism in languages. By contrast with inheritance, conformance is concerned only with the type of an object. Conformance uses this typing information to implicitly derive the subtyping relationships between types.

11. *What about genericity?* Similarly, genericity provides a mechanism for implementing polymorphic types. Essentially, genericity allows generic algorithms that can operate across a range of types to be written only once. The same description can then be reused in several different situations.

12. *Is Ada object oriented?* This is one of the most common questions in the object-oriented community, partly because of the interest in using Ada in object-oriented design. In short, this is the wrong question to ask. For one thing, it can only have a yes or no answer, which is not particularly helpful. The more interesting questions are concerned with the properties Ada possesses in comparison with, say, Smalltalk or Eiffel. Ada certainly provides encapsulation and classification through the package mechanism. In addition, polymorphism is supported through genericity. Therefore, it is right that Ada should be compared with other languages within the object-oriented community. However, there are some limitations to Ada that ought to be pointed out. Firstly, genericity is not a replacement for inheritance or conformance; it is a specific style of polymorphism that helps with the construction of generic modules. Secondly, the resolution of this polymorphism is carried out at compile-time in Ada. This decision sacrifices many of the benefits associated with dynamic binding. An entertaining discussion of this issue can be found in Touati (1987).

13. *Is genericity compatible with inheritance?* Yes. As mentioned above, inheritance and genericity are different styles of polymorphism that perform different jobs. Inheritance establishes code and behavior sharing between classes, whereas genericity provides a shorthand way of specifying the same algorithm on different types. It would therefore be possible — and probably very sensible — to use both styles in the same language. Similar comments apply to the question of whether genericity is compatible with conformance.

14. *What does enhancement provide?* Enhancement is an example of a mixing of styles of polymorphism (Horn 1986). Enhancement combines aspects of inheritance, conformance, and genericity, thus combining the benefits from each technique.

15. *What is delegation?* In systems with delegation, objects are encapsulated entities as in any object-oriented model. However, objects do not belong to classifications, nor are they created from classifications. Instead, objects exist as freestanding entities and are created using other objects as prototypes (this corresponds to the degenerate form of classification mentioned earlier). The technique of delegation is used in such an environment to implement behavior sharing, but at the level of individual objects (Meyer 1986).

16. *How are languages such as Miranda and Hope related to object-oriented computing?* The answer to this question is that a whole range of polymorphic programming languages, such as Miranda and Hope, ought to be considered within the object-oriented community. Often the style of polymorphism is different. For example, Miranda and Hope support parametric polymorphism. However, a lot can be learned from studying such languages. It should also be mentioned that most of these languages also support classification.

17. *What is the relationship between class and set?* Class and set are alternative ways of modeling classification in an object-oriented system. As mentioned above, a class represents a set of objects that share common behavior and a common implementation. In contrast, a set is a collection of objects that share some common properties. Set is therefore a much more general concept than class. Sets are commonly used in the object-oriented database community where, confusingly, they are often referred to as classes.

18. *What is the semantic data model?* The semantic data model is a leading data model that has emerged from the object-oriented database community. It is based on sets as the unit of classification and exploits set operations such as intersection and union.

19. *Can object-oriented languages be used in a parallel or distributed environment?* There has been some doubt about whether some object-oriented techniques translate into a parallel or distributed environment. For example, Wegner has stated that inheritance is incompatible with distribution (Wegner 1987). However, taking a more general view of object-oriented computing allows other techniques that might be more suitable than traditional techniques such as class and inheritance to be explored.

20. *How generally applicable are object-oriented techniques?* In general, a wider view of object-oriented computing increases the suitability of the techniques for other fields of application. Particular techniques can be employed to meet the needs of a particular application area. The concepts underlying object-oriented computing are more important than specific mechanisms.

CONCLUSION

This chapter has presented a model of object-oriented computing that is intended to encompass all the techniques discussed in the first part of the book. The important feature of this model is that it is based on a design space for object-oriented systems rather than on specific implementation mechanisms. In particular, the model consists of four dimensions, namely encapsulation, classification, polymorphism, and interpretation. This more general interpretation widens the scope of object-orientation and includes alternative techniques such as delegation, conformance, and genericity. In addition, such a definition encourages debate on the relative merits of different techniques and allows system designers to select appropriate techniques for particular application domains. Such flexibility is crucial if object-oriented computing is to adapt to the many new fields of application.

Object-oriented computing is still a relatively immature and fast developing subject. There is, inevitably, still a lot of confusion about the merits of different techniques. This chapter has attempted to resolve some of the confusion by discussing some pertinent questions in light of our definition. In so doing, we hope that we have made some progress toward answering the sorts of questions often raised in the literature.

REFERENCES

Black, A., N. Hutchinson, E. Jul, H. Levy, and L. Carter (1987) Distribution and abstract types in emerald. *IEEE Transactions on Software Engineering*, SE-13 (1): 65–76.

Blair, G.S., J.J. Gallagher, and J. Malik (1989) Genericity vs inheritance vs. delegation vs. conformance vs. . . . (toward a unifying understanding of objects). *Journal of Object-Oriented Programming*, 2(3): 11–17.

Blair, G.S., J.J. Gallagher, D. Hutchison, and W.D. Shepherd (eds.) (1991) *Object-Oriented Languages, Systems and Applications*, Pitman Publishing, London.

Canning, P.S., W.R. Cook, W.L. Hill, and W.G. Olthoff (1989) Interfaces for strongly typed object-oriented programming. *Proceedings of the Conference on Object-Oriented Programming Systems, Languages and Applications (OOPSLA '89)*, 457–467.

Cardelli, L. and P. Wegner (1985) On understanding types, data abstraction, and polymorphism. *Computing Surveys*, 17(4): 471–522.

Horn, C. (1986) Conformance, genericity, inheritance and enhancement. *Technical Report*, Department of Computer Science, Trinity College, Dublin, Ireland.

Lieberman, H. (1986) Using prototypical objects to implement shared behavior in object-oriented systems. *Proceedings of the Conference on Object-Oriented Programming Systems, Languages and Applications (OOPSLA '86)*, SIGPLAN Notices, 21, 214–223.

Meyer, B. (1986) Genericity versus inheritance. *Proceedings of the Conference on Object-Oriented Programming Systems, Languages and Applications (OOPSLA '86)*, SIGPLAN Notices, 21, 391–405.

Meyer, B. (1988) *Object-Oriented Software Construction*, Prentice-Hall, Englewood Cliffs, NJ.

Snyder, A. (1986) Encapsulation and inheritance in object-oriented programming languages. *Proceedings of the Conference on Object-Oriented Programming Systems, Languages and Applications (OOPSLA '86)*, SIGPLAN Notices, 21, 38–45.

Touati, H. (1987) Is Ada an object-oriented programming language? *SIGPLAN Notices*, 22(5): 23–26.

Wegner, P. (1987) Dimensions of object-based language design. *Proceedings of the Conference on Object-Oriented Programming Systems*, Languages, and Applications *(OOPSLA '87)*, SIGPLAN Notices, 22, 168–182.

chapter 4

Essential Techniques for Object-Oriented Design

STEVE COOK AND JOHN DANIELS   *OBJECT DESIGNERS LTD.*

Object technology holds the promise of a breakthrough in software productivity. But this breakthrough will not be achieved by continuing to develop systems in the same old way using object-oriented languages instead of procedural ones. The breakthrough will be a consequence of building systems by assembling them from prefabricated parts, instead of repeatedly starting system development from scratch.

Many technological and organizational changes are needed to bring about this revolution. In this chapter we focus on the technical issues that enable robust systems to be built from prefabricated parts. We propose that there are two fundamental and essential notions in object technology:

1. Distinguishing between insides and outsides of objects
2. Building and composing models

We discuss specific techniques for object-oriented design with a critical eye on how they support these fundamental notions. These techniques form part of Syntropy, a software development approach currently under development within Object Designers Ltd.

Our objective is that Syntropy should be precisely specified and should offer a complete and rigorous design environment. By doing this, we are attempting to address the

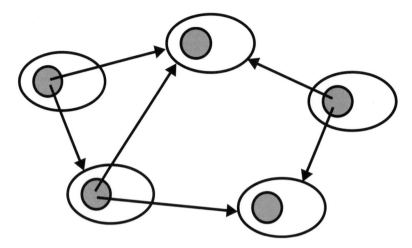

FIGURE 4.1.   The boiled egg model of objects.

difficulties faced by software developers, who in many cases must determine the precise semantics of published object-oriented methods for themselves.

INSIDES AND OUTSIDES

One of the fundamental principles of object technology is the distinction between the outside and the inside of an object. Objects encapsulate data together with the operations that act upon those data. Objects are accessed only via operations, which provide services to the object's clients. A single object can be thought of as a stimulus-response mechanism, where a stimulus is a message causing the invocation of one of the object's operations. From the perspective of the message sender, the response is a value returned from the operation. From a more global perspective, the response includes a set of messages sent by the object to others, each of which causes its own response.

The distinction between the insides and outsides of objects is captured by the "boiled egg" model (Figure 4.1). If an object is a boiled egg, then the yolk of the egg represents the object's data. Completely surrounding the yolk is the white, which represents the object's operations. On the very outside is the shell, representing the interface that the object offers the world. The only visible part of the egg is the shell. The white and yolk are inaccessible to the observer outside the egg unless the egg is broken open — this would be called a *violation of encapsulation* in object-oriented terms.

Reusability

Object technology is often said to encourage reuse. This ability is a direct consequence of pursuing the distinction between insides and outsides. The inside of one object contains assumptions about the outsides of the other objects it uses. Any object that offers an out-side conforming to these expectations is a valid partner in this relationship. Building software systems by assembling prefabricated components is made possible by software technology that allows many different actual outsides to conform to a single expected out-side (see Figure 4.2). This property is called *polymorphism*.

Bertrand Meyer has emphasized this idea using the phrase *design by contract* (Meyer 1988). Each relationship of usage between two objects has a server and client. The server offers the client a contract. In Meyer's language, Eiffel, such a contract is specified in terms of preconditions, which the client must satisfy before calling an operation, and postcon-ditions, which the server promises to satisfy afterward.

Distinguishing insides from outsides minimizes the knowledge that one component of a system needs to have about another. The essence of object technology is a set of tech-niques that permits the construction of software components that rely as little as possible on the details of the surrounding environment. As a result, software can be made sub-stantially more resilient to changing circumstances than it would be otherwise.

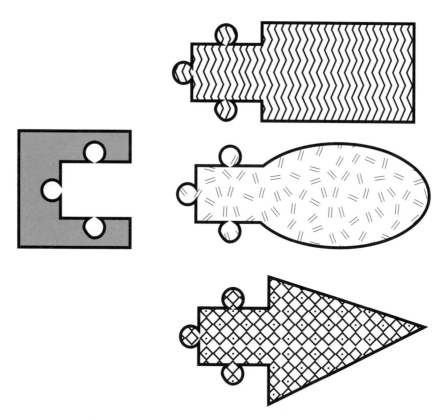

FIGURE 4.2. Polymorphism.

The reusability of a software component is inversely related to the amount it depends upon the rest of the world. The less dependent it is, the more situations it can be used in. Building reusable software requires the developer to identify the abstractions that reduce dependencies between software components as far as possible. This can be a highly skilled task, and the techniques used for object-oriented design should encourage it strongly.

The distinction between insides and outsides contrasts strongly with the more traditional distinction between data and processing, which is fundamental to the design of third-generation programming languages and forms the basis of many familiar design methods and, indeed, the architecture of most computer systems.

MODELING

The second fundamental principle of object technology is modeling. Of course, modeling is also fundamental in the tradition that splits data and processing; object modeling shares many of the ideas of data modeling. The main difference lies in the distinction between insides and outsides: Data modeling is concerned with creating data structures (insides), which represent the state of something, whereas object modeling is concerned with creating interfaces (outsides), which both represent the state of something and provide loosely coupled encapsulated software components.

The similarity between object modeling and data modeling has led to some confusion in the methods world. It is becoming unfashionable to speak of entity-relationship modeling; it must be *object modeling*. There is a real danger that the benefits of object technology, which primarily result from following the distinction between insides and outsides rigorously throughout the software design process, are lost or diluted as a consequence.

Reasons for Modeling

Any introductory article about object technology is likely to tell you that objects can model the real world. But the real world is an infinitely complex place, and there are many reasons why you might want software to model some part of it. As well as modeling the world, the software has to provide services to the world, and is often responsible for changing the world.

Simulation, where object technology has its roots, is the most direct reason for modeling. In simulation, the software models a system in its environment for the purpose of understanding the system itself. The model does not correspond in real time to any portion of the world; instead, it is used to ask what-if questions about the system being simulated.

Representation of current facts is another major reason for modeling. Traditionally, this purpose is fulfilled by a database system, which is kept up-to-date with a set of facts about a system and can be queried by people interested in discovering these facts.

Creating an artificial reality is a third major reason for modeling. These are systems that allow users to create and interact with information structures that correspond to concepts in their minds. Typical examples would be word processors, graphics editors, mathemaical processing systems, and music composition systems. The world modeled by the software is the language of the particular activity, whether words, pictures, mathematics, or music.

Controlling a process is another major reason. In processes such as chemical plants or aircraft, software responds to stimuli generated within the process and produces appropriate responses to control the future development of the process.

Some systems combine aspects of each of these. For example, software that supports trading activities on financial markets is currently one of the most demanding applications of object technology, and such systems often combine elements from all of these kinds of modeling.

THE ENVIRONMENT

Every software system exists within an external environment: some system or systems that the software is to represent and perhaps control. Typical environments contain human activity systems, such as:

- Banking systems containing various kinds of accounts, customers, transactions, etc.
- Library systems containing books, borrowers, loans, etc.
- Manufacturing systems containing manufacturing cells, schedules, plans, etc.

The environment might also contain designed systems, such as:

- A part of mathematics, such as differential calculus or some algebra
- The design of a particular building or physical structure
- A system of music notation
- Words, sentences, and paragraphs as used in a word-processing system

Computer systems are not always directly connected to their environment. Often they are operated by human intermediaries who observe and interpret the world, input information to the computer system, and interpret the results.

Figure 4.3 shows a general architecture of how a software system is connected to its environment. On the left is the world of things and occurrences that the software must represent and affect. This is the environment. It would exist whether the software were there or not, although the software may alter it.

At the top right is the concept model, a software representation of relevant aspects of the world. Every software system has a concept model, although in some cases, it may be enormously complex and in others, extremely simple.

Direct input devices are sensors that directly detect some aspect of the world and translate the signals or measurements into messages sent to the concept model.

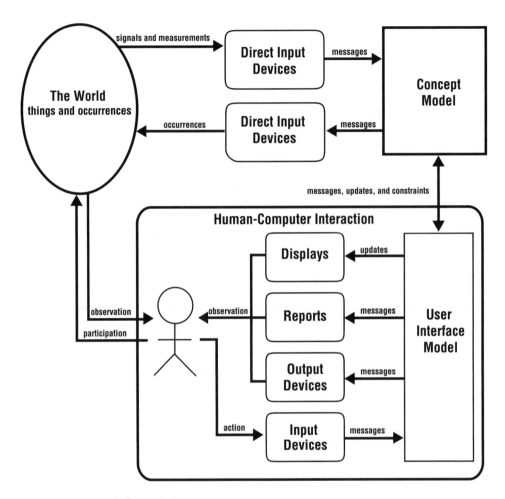

FIGURE 4.3. Software in its environment.

Direct output devices receive messages from the concept model and translate them directly into occurrences in the world.

Human-computer interaction (HCI) is itself a designed system consisting of people, devices, and software. The people observe and participate in the world, observe displays, reports, and other signals generated by the computer systems and act upon input devices.

The user interface model has a similar relationship to concepts in the user interface as the concept model does to concepts in the environment. Concepts in a typical GUI interface include windows, views, lists, buttons, scrollbars, and the like.

Displays provide continuously updated views of aspects of the concept model and the user interface model.

Reports are visual outputs from the system generated on demand, either on a display screen or on paper.

Figure 4.3 is intended to be very general. All software systems fit into it to some extent. It is quite hard to think of a system in which one or more of the parts of the diagram is completely absent: The control system for a guided missile in flight is probably the nearest thing to a system without any human-computer interaction component.

DOMAINS

A complete software system is subdivided into areas of concern, which we call *domains*. At the core of the system is a special domain called the *concept domain*, which corresponds to the concept model discussed earlier.

It is appropriate to deal with a domain as a separate, coherent whole. A domain can be identified both statically in the system model, where it consists of a set of associated types, and dynamically in the running system, where it consists of a set of objects of those types.

The concept domain implements a model of the state of an external system in the environment. A large system might have more than one concept domain, because the software deals with more than one distinct external system.

The concept domain consists of a set of objects of types corresponding to relevant concepts in the environment. The combined state of these objects represents the state of the environment. As well as the concept domain, interactive systems have a user-interface domain. This is usually divided into two subdomains: a generic subdomain, often consisting of preexisting software components such as a GUI class library, and an application-specific subdomain responsible for coordinating these components for the purposes of the application at hand.

Object persistence and sharing are central issues for most object systems. They are implemented in an object management domain responsible for storing, retrieving, and sharing object representations. Many of the concepts modeled in the object management domain are the concepts of object systems themselves. The interface between the object management domain and other domains may be different from the normal interface between domains, because the object management domain needs access to the implementation of objects rather than their external interface.

Networked systems probably have a communications domain, modeling the concepts of network communications such as protocols, datagrams, and connections. Systems with direct input and output devices have a domain of sensors and switches, modeling the interfaces to specific hardware components.

Figure 4.4 shows how a typical system is broken down into domains. Boundaries between the areas in the diagram indicate that there is an interface between adjoining domains. For most systems, a diagram like this is sufficiently expressive to show domains and their connectivity.

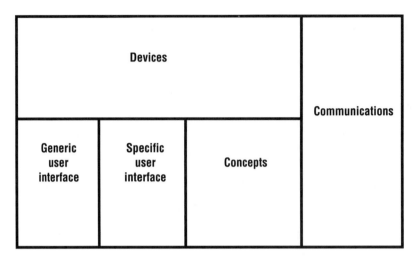

FIGURE 4.4. Domains.

Events

Environments change, both independently of the software and as a consequence of it. When the state of the environment changes, objects in the concept domain must eventually change correspondingly. We think about changes of state in terms of events: discrete occurrences associated with specific phenomena in the environment.

We are not interested in all events in the environment, only the essential events, which correspond to changes in state modeled by the objects in the concept domain. When an essential event occurs, there is a corresponding state change in the concept domain. The mechanism for communicating between the environment and the concept domain might be direct, using some kind of sensor, or indirect, using an operator interacting via a user interface. There are several kinds of essential event:

- Some occur regardless of whether the software system is there or not
- Some occur because the software system needs information
- Some are directly caused by the software system

For example, in a central heating control system:

- The events of external temperature rising and falling would happen whether the heating system were installed or not.
- The event of setting the desired temperature for a room provides necessary information for the software to operate.
- The event of igniting the boiler occurs because the software causes it to.

It is often helpful when thinking about events to identify the agents that participate in transforming an event in the environment into a stimulus applied to the software or transforming a response of the software into an event in the environment. An agent might be a person, a mechanism, or even a natural cause like the weather. We identify three kinds of agent:

> PHYSICAL AGENT: responsible for actually causing a stimulus to be transmitted between the environment and the software. This might be a sensor or a component of a user-interface. Physical agents are usually not modeled in the concept domain, but may be modeled in other domains.
>
> LOGICAL AGENT: responsible for collecting events into logically coherent groups. These are modeled in the concept domain.
>
> ORIGINATING AGENT: the primary source or destination of an event, and often not modeled within the software at all.

Events can be described at different levels of abstraction. The event "clicking the mouse button" at one level is the same event as "selecting the Add menu entry" at another level, which is the same as "adding a new book to the library system" at a third. We choose the appropriate level of description for the domain under consideration. If we are analyzing the concept domain for a library system, and are dealing with concepts such as books, borrowers, and loans, clearly the third level of abstraction is correct. If, on the other hand, we are designing a user-interface domain for the same system, one of the lower levels of abstraction is most appropriate. The connection between these levels is made at the interface between domains, where objects in one domain send messages to those in another.

Events at a certain level of abstraction may logically group together. For example, all of the events associated with a certain book (adding it to the system, borrowing it, returning it, deleting it, declaring it lost, etc.) logically belong together. Finding such groups is an important part of analysis because it helps us to build a coherent concept domain model. We call the concept around which the events are grouped the *logical agent*; the logical agent is modeled as an object in the concept domain and will be the source or destination of messages associated with stimuli corresponding to the grouped events. Essential events are described at the level of abstraction of the concept domain and are associated with the logical agent.

On the input side, essential events are communicated to the software either by means of direct input devices or indirectly by means of a human operator. On the output side, the software may affect the environment directly via output devices, or indirectly when a human operator responds to some displayed information. We normally include as essential events all of the input events, but only those output events that are directly communicated to the environment.

STATE AND BEHAVIOR

We can summarize the relationship between a software system and its environment as follows:

1. The concept domain models the state of the system in the environment, in terms of users' concepts about the environment.
2. Events occurring in the environment that correspond to changes in the state modeled by the concept domain are called *essential events*.
3. Agents act as intermediaries for events between the software and its environment.

The behavior of the software is the way it responds to stimuli. We might formalize behavior quite generally as follows:

> We assume that a software system responds to a set of stimuli with a set of responses. For simplicity, we assume that no response occurs without a corresponding stimulus, and that every stimulus produces a response. This would be a reasonable assumption for an infinitely fast processor. Then the behavior of the system is a functional relationship between sequences of stimuli and sequences of responses.

However this simple formalization of behavior is quite useless in practice. We never think about the behavior of systems in terms of indefinitely long histories of events. Instead, we think about a system as having at any time a state that determines its response to stimuli. We think of behavior as a function that takes a stimulus and a current state, and gives a response and a new state.

It follows that we cannot usefully describe the behavior of a system without talking about its state space. But we cannot talk about its state space until we decide how that state space is going to be modeled. Hence building a structure for modeling the state space of the concept domain is a vital early activity in the overall design of an object-oriented system. This activity is often called *object-oriented analysis*.

PARTIAL MODELS

If reuse is to be a serious aspect of our software process we must be able to construct and compose partial models. Starting from scratch every time is not a practical approach for complex software systems.

One approach to partial models is "copy and paste." When a new system is seen to resemble an existing one, models describing the old one are copied and modified to create the new one. This approach has the benefit of flexibility: without rules, anything goes.

But object technology, at least in the programming sense, has introduced a number of precise mechanisms (such as inheritance) for controlling reuse of partial system descriptions, and such mechanisms should exist throughout the entire software development process, not just programming.

We propose that an object-oriented modeling method should offer means by which models can be constructed from models: Models should be recursively composable. It should be possible to modify and/or extend existing models, and incorporate the consequences of these actions into a system without compromising its overall integrity.

The technical key to partial modeling is the idea of conformance between outsides, or design by contract. It is the ability of many different objects to act as suitable servers for a client that allows models to be composed in many different ways.

Partial models are the fundamental assets of a software development organization. It should be possible to share them between different larger models, and when they are refined and enhanced, the improvements should propagate through their extensions. Full support for partial models is a fundamental requirement for CASE tools, which will bring about the real benefits of object technology.

MODELING THE WORLD VS. MODELING THE SOFTWARE

Having discussed the relationship between the software system and its environment, we can think about techniques for describing these things. In the remainder of this chapter we discuss two diagrammatic modeling techniques: type diagrams and state diagrams. In particular, we focus on their ability to support the key ideas we have identified as essential:distinguishing between insides and outsides, and defining conformance or contract relationships.

Each of these techniques can be used for two distinct purposes: describing certain aspects of the environment and describing certain aspects of the software. It is important to be clear about which purpose a technique is being used for. Often this distinction gets blurred in descriptions of object-oriented modeling techniques. The real world does not consist of objects sending messages and executing methods, and it is not useful to pretend that it does. A technique used for modeling the world provides understanding, but does not attempt to be executable. In the world, we are concerned with phenomena and their properties, and build models in order to understand; in software, we are concerned with objects and their relationships, and build models in order to specify these accurately. We attempt to create a systematic relationship between the models of the world and the specification of the software, because this allows us to find the parts of the software that must be changed when the world changes. But it is much too simplistic to imagine that we simply build a model of the world and then submit it to a compiler.

Figure 4.5 shows the relationship between the world, the software, and models of both.

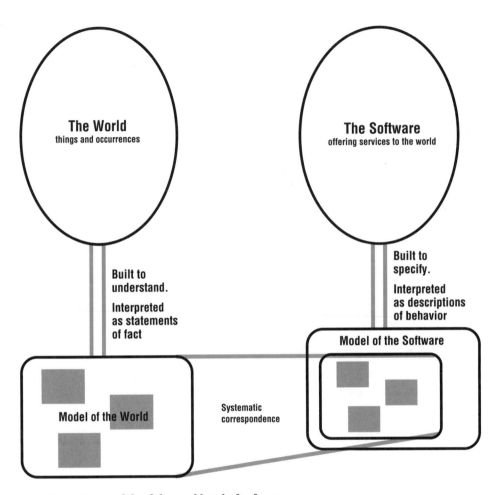

FIGURE 4.5. Models of the world and of software.

STRUCTURAL MODELING: THE TYPE DIAGRAM

Most published methods on object-oriented analysis and design include some kind of technique based on entity-relationship modeling. There is considerable consensus that these models are very useful when designing object systems. Where methods diverge is exactly what the elements of these models are, and how they are to be interpreted.

Consider Figure 4.6, which uses the OMT notation (Rumbaugh 1991). The figure has three boxes, labeled *Person*, *Employee*, and *Company*. Inside these boxes are additional

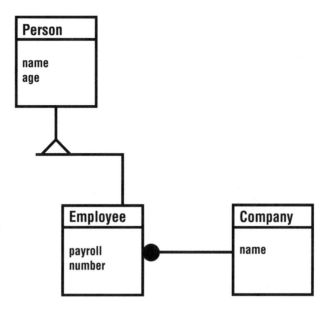

FIGURE 4.6.   A type diagram.

names, such as *name* in the **Person** box. Between the boxes are various connectors. There are at least three distinct interpretations of what this diagram means:

- The real world meaning
- The data modeling meaning
- The object-oriented meaning

The Real World Meaning

The real world meaning is an interpretation in terms of English statements. The diagram is equivalent to the following statements:

> A Person has a name and an age
> An Employee is a Person
> An Employee has a payroll number
> An Employee is associated with exactly one Company
> A Company has a name
> A Company is associated with zero or more Employees.

The diagram is understood to the extent that these statements are understood as statements of fact about the world being modeled. Building this model serves to define terms and to establish rules about how these terms are understood. For example, the model establishes that within the current area of concern, Employees are not associated with more than one Company.

With this interpretation, the diagram says nothing at all about software. If we want it to say something about software, we have to apply a different and more precise interpretation.

The Data Modeling Meaning

In the world of data modeling, the meaning of the diagram is quite precisely understood. The diagram indicates that there is a set of entities called Persons, each of which has attributes *name* and *age*. Some of these entities are, in addition, Employees, with an additional attribute *payroll number*. Every Employee entity is associated with a single Company entity, and every Company entity is associated with many Employee entities. In a database, the information described by this diagram could be held in two tables of records, one representing Persons with the columns *name*, *age*, *payroll number,* and *company id*, and the other representing Companies with the columns *company id* and *name*. Those Persons who are not Employees would have null entries in the payroll number and company id columns.

This interpretation says nothing about processing. A database constructed using this approach stores certain facts about the world, such as which employees are associated with a particular company. How these facts are established, updated, and otherwise processed is a separate matter.

The Object-Oriented Meaning

The object-oriented world gives different interpretations again for the symbols in the diagram. However in this world, there is no well-established agreement about what they mean, and we have to think about it rather carefully.

The reason for drawing this particular diagram is the fundamental notion that objects model the world; that if there are Employees and Companies in the environment, there should be Employees and Companies in the software, and the relationships between the software objects should in some way correspond to the relationships between the real phenomena.

We want the diagram to describe only the outsides of objects, to preserve the crucial distinction between outsides and insides. The primary purpose of the diagram is specification: describing software accurately and unambiguously.

The obvious candidate for the boxes are classes, and indeed most object-oriented methods call them that. It is tempting for CASE manufacturers to latch onto these diagrams and decide that C++ code can be generated from them by equating a class with each box. That kind of thing sells. But there are serious questions about whether it is the most appropriate interpretation for the diagrams.

So what is a class? All of the following definitions (among others) are valid in different circumstances:

1. A set of instances implemented from the same template
2. A set of instances offering the same set of operations in their interface
3. The programming language definition of a template for instantiating a set of similar instances
4. The definition of an interface consisting of a set of operations

The simple equation of boxes with classes in an object-oriented programming language, coupled with the interpretation of the subtype or extension symbol (like the one between Person and Employee) to mean inheritance, gives the boxes definition 3. Unfortunately, all well-known object-oriented programming languages differ in detail about the meaning of the class and inheritance constructs. Hence, the consequence of such a definition is that the meaning of these diagrams are defined by the semantics of a particular programming language.

Further problems arise with the meanings of attributes and associations in this context. Attributes are usually equated with instance variables (in Smalltalk terminology) or data members (in C++ terminology) of the class. The difficulty here is that instance variables are decidedly an aspect of the inside of a class. It is clearly wrong that such an implementation-dependent decision should be made in this model, and in any case this interpretation would destroy the distinction between insides and outsides that we insist on preserving.

A final problem is with the interpretation of associations. These are often interpreted in terms of implementation constructs, such as pointers or keys. Once again, these are *implementation-dependent* decisions that violate the most basic principle of object-oriented design, keeping the insides and outsides separate.

We prefer the boxes to have the interpretation of definition 4; that is, to define an interface. To emphasize this interpretation, we call the boxes in the diagram *types*. A type defines a set of operations, together with the conditions under which those operations can validly be invoked. Each object of the type is able to respond to the operations when properly invoked.

A type can be implemented using many strategies, of which a class in a programming language is one. The attributes of a type are simply accessor operations that return values and are valid in all states. The presence of an attribute does not imply the ability to update it, by contrast with the database interpretation.

Associations are abstract indications of the state of objects playing types. The association between Employee and Company in Figure 4.6 indicates that given an object playing the type Employee, a single associated object playing the type Company may be found. More precisely, there is an operation in the interface defined by Employee that will deliver the associated Company, and vice versa.

The subtyping or type extension connector is interpreted to mean conformance, or substitutability, in the following sense: if *B* extends *A*, then a client of *A* can be given a *B* without causing any errors to occur. Another way of putting this is that B behaves exactly like an *A* under the operations of *A*. For the example in Figure 4.4, this means that an object playing the type Employee (i.e., offering the interface defined by the type Employee) can successfully play the type Person within the software system.

From the modeling perspective, this seems to be exactly the right choice. In the real world, there is no doubt that employees can do whatever people can do. For the software model to be a good one, the same property should hold, regardless of the actual operations offered by Employee and Person objects. Inheritance, as defined in most object-oriented programming languages, does not necessarily result in conformance in the sense described here, although with discipline it may be used to implement conformance.

Implicit in the discussion so far is a distinction between objects and values. Objects can be distinguished by having a unique identity, quite apart from other aspects of their behavior. Values simply stand for themselves. We find this distinction useful because we think it is unintuitive to deal with a system where the number 3 can be represented by more than one distinct instance, as would be implied if it were an object. Numbers, points, dates, strings, and similar sets are usually best thought of as values when doing object-oriented modeling. We define value sets using algebraic, rather than diagrammatic, methods. However, when implementing a design, value sets may well be implemented by classes, especially in C++, which provides many constructs specifically for this purpose. This is another reason for decoupling boxes on type diagrams from the concept of class.

Partial Models with Viewpoint Diagrams

Looking again at Figure 4.6, we might notice that different levels of abstraction are depicted. The box labeled Person exists at a more general level of abstraction than the others. Other parts of the same system may refer to the box Person, but do not need to be concerned with Employees in any way. As we have said, we wish to create partial models and provide ways they can be composed into larger models. Without the ability to create partial models, reuse is fundamentally impossible.

We address this need by introducing viewpoint diagrams. These are type diagrams considered from the viewpoint of one or more types. Figure 4.7 shows the same example, redrawn as a viewpoint diagram from the perspective of the Employee type only.

In the diagram, a full description of Employee is given, but only vestigial descriptions of the types it is associated with are provided. A hire operation has been added to Employee to emphasize that a type defines operations. We call Employee the *subject type,* and the others *reference types*. The presence of the extension connector between Person and Employee tells us that Employee is an extension of a type Person, defined elsewhere; similarly the association with Company tells us that an employee is associated with exactly one Company, whose definition is elsewhere. It tells us that the type Employee defines an operation to find the company. However, the diagram says nothing about the Company type apart from the fact that it exists, hence the question mark on the near end of the association.

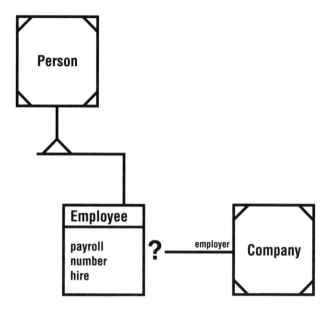

FIGURE 4.7. Employee viewpoint.

These diagrams can be composed using a fairly straightforward set of rules. The result of composing two diagrams with one target type each is a diagram with two target types. Figure 4.8 shows two diagrams that can be composed with the Employee viewpoint diagram to produce the original composite diagram.

Notice that the Person viewpoint does not show any knowledge of the Employee viewpoint. The Person role could participate quite separately in other models.

Viewpoint diagrams indicate association visibility. An association might be visible only in one direction because it could be shown in the viewpoint for the type at one of its ends but not the other. When viewpoint diagrams are composed, the resulting associations may be annotated with an arrow to indicate association visibility in one direction only.

As we have said, the ability to compose models from parts is absolutely vital for component-based software reuse. The simple viewpoint-based scheme proposed here goes one step toward that goal.

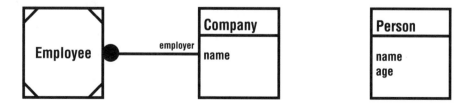

FIGURE 4.8. Viewpoints for Company and Person.

STATE MODELING: STATECHARTS

A second popular technique for object-oriented analysis and design is the state transition diagram. Figure 4.9 shows a state machine for a simple telephone, using the statechart notation originated by David Harel and popularized by Rumbaugh (Rumbaugh et al. 1991).

As with type diagrams, there are several distinct uses for state machines in software design, each with its own interpretation. They can be used as a technique for understanding the behavior of phenomena in the world, such as telephones, electronic calculators, and microwave ovens. For this purpose, the events that cause their transitions are named in terms of the world being described (e.g., *handset lifted*, *press clear*, or *open door*). Although this well-understood and useful technique has no particular connection with the concepts of object technology, if the mechanism being described is implemented using object-oriented software, there is likely to be a systematic (but not necessarily isomorphic) relationship between this kind of statechart and the statecharts used to describe objects.

An important use of statecharts in object-oriented systems is to describe the external behavior of software objects. Specifically, a statechart may be associated with each type to

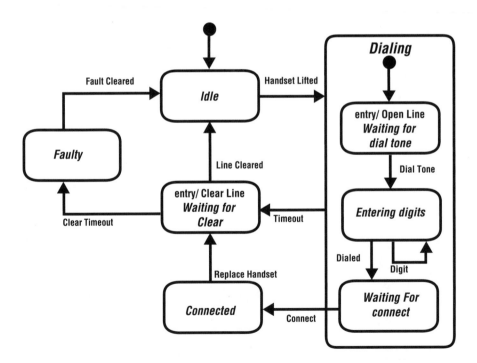

FIGURE 4.9. Telephone statechart.

describe valid sequences of operations for objects of that type. The constructs of the statechart can be given a precise meaning in terms of the external interface of the object:

- Transitions are triggered as a consequence of messages sent to the object.
- Transitions may be guarded by Boolean expressions constructed over the accessors of the object.
- The results of transitions may be stated in terms of Boolean expressions constructed from the before and after values for the accessors of the object.

A statechart that uses these ideas to describe a simple stack is shown in Figure 4.10.

This is not the place to go into the detailed semantics of these notations. The essential point to make here is that these diagrams are wholly concerned with the external behavior of objects, specifically the sequencing of their operations, and contain no reference to their implementations. Any expressions that describe message sending and updating of data variables are concerned with implementation and belong elsewhere.

Conformance

We have to define what it means for one statechart to conform to another. This is necessary to give a consistent meaning to the concept of type extension and, thus, to allow models to be composed. Whenever we draw a diagram of the form shown in Figure 4.11, we mean that type *B* extends, or conforms to, type *A*. What does that really mean? We have said it means that a *B* behaves exactly like an *A* under the operations of *A*. One thing we can be sure of is that an object of type *B* will have a defined response to every message for which an object of type *A* has a defined response. That is, the set of

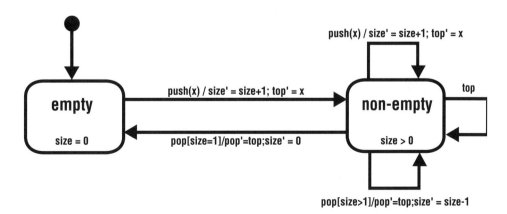

FIGURE 4.10. Statechart for a simple stack.

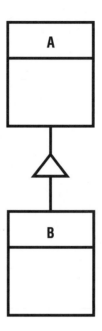

FIGURE 4.11.   Conformance.

messages that make up the interface to type *B* equals or is a superset of the set of messages that make up the interface to type *A*. In addition, objects expect messages to arrive in a defined order, and for *B* to conform to *A*, these orders must conform. Every valid message sequence for type *A* is also valid for type *B*.

The statechart in Figure 4.12, representing an extended stack, does conform to the stack in Figure 4.10, because it can be substituted for it in all working systems without affecting any clients of the original stack. In general, there are a number of detailed rules that can be applied to test if two statecharts conform in this sense. The following kinds of transformation are valid:

- Adding certain transitions
- Adding certain new states
- Subdividing existing states

In a sequential system we do not require *B* to conform to *A* in the sense that wherever a program using *A* will fail, one using *B* will fail, too. To require this would impose such strong restrictions on conformance as to render it useless.

Concurrency makes the situation much more complex. In a concurrent system we want to ensure that synchronization behavior is also preserved when conforming roles are substituted. If we were to interpret Figures 4.10 and 4.12 so that Figure 4.10 means that a

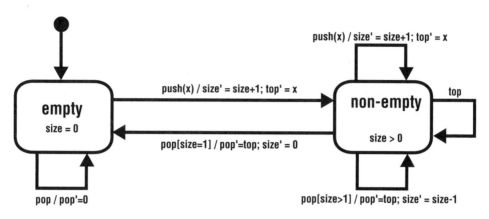

FIGURE 4.12. Statechart for extended stack.

pop message is blocked in the empty state, and Figure 4.12 means that a pop message is accepted in the empty state, these diagrams cease to conform in a useful way. However, it turns out that if synchronization behavior is expressed as a property of the *client* of an object, in terms of the states of the server, then conformance continues to have a useful meaning for concurrent object systems. This contrasts with typical approaches that attach synchronization behavior to the server only.

CONCLUSION

The pursuit of the distinction between data and process has led us into a world where software applications are purchased more on the basis of what hardware they run on and which data formats they can interpret than for the services they offer to their users. In consequence, the world of software is struggling to escape the clutches of proprietary instruction sets and primitive operating systems.

The answer is to lift our gaze from these matters and start looking for ways to compose software systems from prefabricated parts, regardless of implementation technology. We claim that the key is to distinguish strongly between insides and outsides, rather than between data and processing, and to build precise and reusable models using techniques that maintain this distinction.

In this chapter we have discussed the principles behind designing software systems with a focus on these essential ideas. We have shown how software relates to its environment, and described some specific techniques that can be used to model software in its environment. We believe that object-oriented analysis and design methods must take these imperatives on board if the vision of a breakthrough in software productivity is to be realized in practice.

REFERENCES

Meyer, B. (1988) *Object-Oriented Software Construction*, Prentice-Hall, Englewood Cliffs, NJ.

Rumbaugh, J., M. Blaha, W. Premerlani, F. Eddy, and W. Lorensen (1991) *Object-Oriented Modeling and Design*, Prentice-Hall, Eaglewood Cliffs, NJ.

chapter 5

Evolution, Life Cycles, and Reuse

BRUCE ANDERSON   UNIVERSITY OF ESSEX AND WIZARD SYSTEMS

In this chapter our thoughts concerning experiences with object technology are synthesized into a framework for both working in and looking at the task of producing software using object technology. We do not say *object-oriented programming* because programming is the least part of the task; that is, we hope to structure the task to facilitate programming. The ideas are based on research, including the development of a series of applications (Gossain and Anderson 1990; Anderson and Gossain 1990), on consulting experience, and on discussions with practitioners.

SOME OF THE PROBLEMS

One of the main difficulties facing users and potential users of object-oriented technology is that they are searching for methods and processes for software production while they are actually producing software products. Allocating adequate resources for this requires bold decisionmaking, especially from management that is already successful with conventional methods.

There is no doubt that current commercial methods are not helpful enough. First, they are often based on specific application areas (mainly information systems and real time) with well-known problem decompositions that do not carry over to others. Second, they are based mainly in older methodologies that ignore the notion of application domain and the central role of the class hierarchy:

Reuse: reusing the current hierarchy to solve the new problem
Design for reuse: augmenting the hierarchy for current and future use
Hierarchy as theory of domain: providing a way to look at problems
Process abstraction: creating procedural subhierarchies
Class hierarchies: provide a structured expression of insight into application
  domains and solution strategies.

There are many kinds of application, and no initial reason to expect commonalities of class or method among them:

- Supervisory control and data acquisition
- Direct control systems
- Command and control systems
- Scheduling systems
- Resource management systems
- Decision support systems
- Interactive design tools and environments
- Information systems
- Noninteractive tools

The framework should be bigger than the problem. An aircraft manufacturing company has a definite style and range of products. For example, Boeing does not produce jet fighters. Why not? Because their processes — their expertise, their range of parts, their construction facilities — are geared toward a range of airliners. As software shifts toward being a manufactured product with a large investment in procedures, tools, and reusable code, the same kind of specialization will take place. The size issue is also important. Boeing could not continue to exist (i.e., could not afford this investment) without continuing to produce a series of products and, thus, the value of the company is much greater than the value of an airplane.

In object-oriented software engineering, we are currently developing our own methods and processes whether we like it or not. We are bound to be better off if we realize this; we can allow for it, but it is far better to capitalize on it; that is, to make specific plans to develop (or acquire) method and process as we proceed (Gilb 1989).

BOUNDING THE PROBLEM

Just as Boeing does not see the "problem" of designing an airliner in a vacuum, but within its own framework, what might the framework be for a software group? I suggest the following components: software environment; manufacturing process, large-scale architecture, small-scale architecture, skills, and tools. These components must be present in some way, but perhaps not expressed or defined or regulated. Although they may be difficult to construct, they help by bounding the problem of creating some software. Our focus here on artifacts as well as processes is unfashionable, but it is intended to aid the search for process by delimiting it.

THE COMPONENTS OF THE FRAMEWORK

Software Environment

The class hierarchy provides at any point more than just a repository for potentially useful components; it is a theory of the domain at hand, and a powerful guide to problem-solving in that domain. As an example, a child asked to build a house from Lego will take a different approach than when asked to use Meccano — the idea that the child would make a design and then implement it freely in either is ludicrous. Of course, this implies a large investment both in creating a hierarchy and in learning to use it. A well-known electronics company spent over a year designing — and redesigning — a class *WaveForm*. They thought this effort well worthwhile.

KINDS OF CLASSES

We have found it productive to categorize our classes as follows. The categories have been very useful to bear in mind while looking at new problems (Gossain and Anderson 1990):

Domain classes: have counterparts in the real world and, as such, attempt to map real-world entities into the software. Using inheritance, the hierarchy aims to depict the natural taxonomy of the problem space.

Factor classes: model the processes of the solution domain and manipulate the entities of the domain. They are so named because they factor out code into reusable functions.

Application classes: characterize the common abstractions between all solutions in the domain, so that each application is made up of a set of objects, each an instance of a subclass of an application class.

Bridging classes: provide the link from basic math or computer science classes (such as *List* and *Map*) to the other classes.

These categories are useful not just for describing architecture, but in the design process, where we create them at different stages and in different ways. Such categorization is recognized by other practitioners (Whiting 1991) and is becoming incorporated into commercial analysis and design methods.

We reject the notion of "finding" classes, stressing the fact that analyzing and designing are creative acts, even if done in a structured and organized way. For each kind of class, the first step is to create candidate classes (such as the following) that can then be further evaluated and abstracted (Gossain and Anderson 1989).

- **Domain classes.** Here, it is relatively straightforward to use a domain analysis, or data-modeling, method (Prieto-Diaz 1987, Shlaer and Mellor 1989) that identifies objects and relationships, then generates a list of candidate classes.
- **Factor classes.** This is inherently more difficult, depending on the designer's own view of the problem domain and understanding of the solution domain. There are no given concrete entities to model. It is necessary to design the domain classes first, look at the functions on them, and list solution processes. Then each operation can be evaluated with a view to objectifying it (Beck 1988) by asking these questions:
  - Is it reusable over a number of contexts? A useful class can be seen to take part in several scenarios.
  - Is it a meaningful abstraction? Good classes have definite operations and responsibility.
  - Does it depend on the type of its arguments? An operation should not be too bound to a particular representation or a single client.
  - Can it be generalized or specialized? This question can be answered only on the basis of a growing picture of the solution space.
  - Is it a locus of change? We can answer this by thinking about the implications of the kind of changes we foresee in later versions of the system.
- **Application classes:** These cannot be designed until several applications exist so that we can see the classes that they will coordinate. Making them requires intuition and experience.

These designing ideas are just the kind of skills that ought to become easier to acquire as the field of object-oriented software engineering grows, but clearly the design "methods" available, while providing useful frameworks and checklists, do not themselves help in the learning process. The best deliverable outcome of design research is problematic.

DEVELOPING THE HIERARCHY

The hierarchy is likely to be under continuous development. In our project on writing a series of applications for PCB/VLSI routing (Anderson and Gossain 1990) we found, to our surprise, that the hierarchy/environment did not converge, but that there was a process of continuous refinement and addition and growth.

Why didn't we expect this? Although we took what we considered to be a sophisticated view of the software life cycle, namely that applications are never finished and that evolutionary methods are essential, we unconsciously adopted a waterfall model for the life cycle of the component kit. Of course, we must have known that the domain would develop, requiring the kit to expand, but we didn't see that new solution strategies would introduce new concepts. This has to be true, otherwise there would be no progress in engineering, no papers would be published, and there would be no surprises.

The growth of the class hierarchy was not uniform, and in the initial stages we did not experience the changes needed later. Different domains, different requirements in terms of change and improvement, and longer sequences of applications all affect the pattern of change and growth. So will the commitment to refactoring, to constantly improving the hierarchy, and to working for reuse rather than just adding to it.

In particular, in a more data-intensive system we might expect an initial analysis of the data to be more long-lasting; witness the various systematic procedures for database design. However, much of the variation in database systems is in the application code, and much of the interest in object-oriented databases is due to the possibility of putting this code "in the database." It seems likely that if this is done, the same kit-expansion phenomenon will occur. For example, in banking an important tactic is to be able to create new financial instruments (e.g., kinds of loans with varying risks and payback profiles). As such concepts move from the application to the database there will be much scope for their creation and classification in the manner of RApp's factor classes.

The kit remains a powerful tool in the software process, as it does encapsulate the current knowledge and understanding of the domain. But it cannot be built a priori, and it will be in a constant state of change. The shift that has to be made is in one's attitude to this fact — change must be our ally, not our enemy (Peters 1987).

One consolation is that we did not reconceptualize the domain in any major way during the project. This may be due to our lack of creativity or to our initial perspicacity, but looking at models of scientific progress in the large (Kuhn 1970), we might expect this to be a relatively rare occurrence. Even if it did happen, we would be able to decide whether to implement the new view in the usual way that engineering decisions are made.

Our work might also be criticized in a related way. Perhaps we are incompetent, and a better team would have made a more abstract and more complete initial domain analysis. This may well be true, but there is no doubt that we are "good enough," and so, for practical purposes, a way to keep control of change will be essential. The difference in farsightedness is one of degree, not kind.

PATTERNS OF EVOLUTION IN THE HIERARCHY

While of course classes are improved internally, there are patterns of change in the hierarchy as a whole. As classes are added we see simple growth both horizontally (i.e., new root classes or subclasses near to roots), as new concepts are introduced, and vertically (i.e., from more deeply derived classes), as current concepts are extended. However, reorganization of the hierarchy is an essential activity. One pervasive pattern of reorganization is that of splitting, where a class is split into a new class and subclass. There are two complementary processes here, of specialization and generalization, but usually one is the focus of the change.

In generalization, a class becomes more abstract, shifting upward in the hierarchy. In specialization, more responsibility and functionality is added to a class. Specialization and generalization differ only in the focus of the change; which of the new classes does the old name refer to? Both are examples of the promotion of structure, and the detailed examples illustrate how powerful abstractions are often developed bottom-up.

We also find horizontal reorganization when we decide to break objects into composable parts.

These changes provide us with a more useful hierarchy, a more powerful set of concepts. Implementing the reassignment of functionality is usually a long and tedious job, even though conceptually clear. This task, now dubbed "refactoring" (Opdyke and Johnson 1990) could be greatly eased by software tools, though implementing them for a language with such complex semantics as C++ would be extremely difficult.

Manufacturing Process

What life cycle models are involved? We need models at least for components, for the hierarchy itself, and for the applications that are produced; that is, for three interlocking life cycles.

THE COMPONENT LIFE CYCLE (ABOUT GOODNESS)

Here, we take the interface to be given. Changes involve work on the implementation of the component, perhaps to make it faster. Indeed, alternative versions might be provided with different properties such as the amount of checking or the total capacity. At this level, we may make internal measurements on components (e.g., cyclomatic complexity) and evaluate the interface (e.g., degree of encapsulation).

THE APPLICATION LIFE CYCLE (ABOUT USEFULNESS)

By *application life cycle* we refer to the sequence of software products, which may be versions of a single application or a series of applications. We may ask which components are useful, and which need modification. We can measure the amount of reuse in the application.

THE HIERARCHY LIFE CYCLE (ABOUT REUSEFULNESS)

The really new element in the model is that the collection of components is a rich structure central to the software process. New classes are added and the hierarchy is reorganized. We need to track this process and to gain experience in evaluating progress. There are many questions to ask. How much inheritance is there? How different are classes?

Large-Scale Architecture

One key aspect of an excellent design is that, at least to the discerning eye, it exhibits a purposeful architecture. Any aspect of a piece of software that is to be worked with must have visible structure that provides the overall philosophy and locates the individual parts. Object-oriented programming provides a very significant step forward in the technology of program building precisely because it provides for the expression in the software itself of architectural information. We know many architectures, such as:

- Big switch
- Model-view-controller
- Blackboard
- Pipeline
- Client-server
- Relational database
- Junkyard
- Software bus

We need to have these architectures available to us. One way to do this is to have a class that is the (application) architecture, and create applications as instances of it. These generic applications, such as MacApp, RApp, and ET++ (Weinand et al 1989), are currently the most powerful uses of object-oriented programming. However, their expressive power is limited, especially in expressing configurations of interconnected objects, so that we must go to new structuring methods beyond object-oriented programming in order to describe and reuse many architectures. This is currently a vital area of investigation (Helm et al. 1990).

Small-Scale Architecture

In contrast to the overall philosophy, we must have a style at the component level. For example, we may wish to use "pluggability"; that is, abstract classes that require their subclasses to implement certain methods. We may wish to use functional classes rather than alter methods, and we may wish to legislate on the use of private data.

As an example, consider an application to devise good routes for traffic in a city. A naive approach, and one also derived by some systematic methods, would locate such algorithms as methods of "streets" or "places," so that we might have

myRoute = startPlace->routeTo(finishPlace)

or

myRoute = (startPlace->streetOf())->routeTo(finishPlace->streetOf())

This sounds classically object oriented ("streets know how to explore their connections to find routes"), but is unlikely to be a good engineering choice, as such algorithms are a common locus for change, both for straightforward improvement (new search algorithms) and strategic improvement (e.g., varying the algorithm by time of day). A better solution is to incorporate such code directly into a hierarchy of function-like objects, perhaps better called *strategy objects*. We can then more easily contain changes in this hierarchy, rather than in the hopefully more stable **Street** or **Place** classes.

```
myRoutingTask = new RoutingTask(startPlace, finishPlace, otherInfo);
myRoutingMethod = new SomeRoutingMethod;
myRoute–myRoutingTask->apply(myRoutingMethod)
```

This immediately encourages us to ask what the other properties of such objects might be. For example, in a numerical domain, we might have a hierarchy of matrix inverters and ask them for effort bids before choosing which to use:

```
theFastestInverter = allInverters->chooseLeast(myMatrix, timeEstimate);
myMatrixInverse = myMatrix.apply(theFastestInverter)
```

Underlying Skills and Tools

All the high-level knowledge must, of course, connect to choices and competencies in skills and tools. In particular, there are many rules — some conventions and some rules of thumb — to be codified. For example, hints on the process include:

- Don't over-inherit; aggregation may be clearer and better
- Put functionality high up
- Use pluggability with generic methods
- Stick to is-a; maintain a strict hierarchy
- Some objects are process-like
- Spend time choosing and reviewing names
- Separate logic from control
- Encourage abstraction—can *(A B)* become *(AandB (OnlyA OnlyB))*?

Also, there are exemplary systems, such as ET++, to be digested. This is not the place to discuss languages and their features and support, but clearly it is not possible to take full advantage of the potential of object-oriented software engineering in a language that does not directly support object-oriented programming. Some languages are good enough, some are not. Ada has no inheritance, and so does not support the approach to software that we are discussing here. To complicate the picture further, the fact that a project or process is intellectually feasible does not make it commercially successful, and there is already a documented history of projects based on object-oriented methods that were cancelled (Leathers 1990).

NOTES ON THE COMPONENT CULTURE

We believe that current object-oriented technology does not support domain libraries as products. Libraries will be in a state of constant evolution, an evolution reflecting the current needs, views, and solutions of a software team. These factors are unlikely to overlap extensively with those of another team unless the teams cooperate. Despite talk of a market in libraries for several years, there are basically only three kinds of library in use: collections, mathematical algorithms, and graphic interfaces. The first implements the result of several thousand years of evolution, the second a well-agreed and simply-structured set of methods, and the last is the result of wide agreement. None of these criteria are true of users' problem domains. Additional problems include:

- **Specifying and testing.** It is not currently possible to test the code of a class in such a way as to guarantee that no errors will occur in it when it is subclassed (Perry and Kaiser 1990). Similarly, when plugability is used, it is usually very difficult to state just what the requirements are on the subclass in terms of the messages or member functions that it must implement. These difficulties mean that with current technology, it is necessary to supply source code to library users.
- **Need to subclass but also to split.** A class library is more valuable than a subroutine library because the classes can be augmented and altered using inheritance. However, we have seen that as a hierarchy evolves it is necessary to move functionality between classes in the splitting operations. This cannot be done without access to source code, and the changes will not be shared with other users of the library.
- **Hierarchy concepts too valuable to share.** In our work on routing we developed some interesting and powerful approaches to the problem — particularly the functional classes, such as *Expander*, and descriptions of the surface, such as *Grid*. The corresponding commercial advantage of this intellectual property would be better realized through exploitation in a product than in sale as a library. As a concrete example, the large electronics company that spent over a year designing and redesigning a class *WaveForm* for use in embedded instrument code thought this effort well worthwhile.
- **Configuring/architecture is not expressed.** At the level of architecture, we have many structures available to us, such as Blackboard, Model-View-Controller, and Client-Server. The expressive power of OOP is limited, especially in describing configurations of interconnected objects, so that we must go to new structuring methods beyond OOP in order to describe and reuse many architectures. The importance for libraries is that they must be augmented by considerable description, in text or program examples, in order to be useful; we cannot yet provide reusable structures at the architecture level. Our Meccano still needs a handbook.

INTUITION, VISION, AND CREATIVITY IN THE DESIGN PROCESS

Insight is in short supply, so our first move is to limit and structure the area where it is needed. The elements discussed above, which bound the problem, do just that. But some creative activity is still essential — this is the classic "problem" of design. In fact, design looks unproblematic only in domains that are well understood. Much of the demand for object-oriented "methods" comes from those who have seen the success of structured approaches in, for example, information systems, where database design and use has become a powerful technique. Two things need to be said here. One is that there are many similarities between the problems in question, and that the processing of the data is often less of a problem than representing it consistently. The other is that the methods do not extend to the procedures or code that manipulate the data; indeed, this is the focus of research and development in object-oriented databases. There is no reason to believe that such approaches will be available before much experience is gained, some of it painfully. The idea that there is a "method" that can be "applied" to yield "the solution," independent of the creativity of the person applying it, is feasible only in domains that have essentially been understood and "solved" at the meta-level.

In particular, the notion that object-oriented design (or analysis) is about "finding objects" is misleading. Of course, the initial foray into a domain will be helped by an entity-relationship analysis, but this is only part of the picture. Classes are not "found," but created. A look at the Smalltalk image, at ET++, or at RApp will reveal many insightful design steps from which we can learn. Even very recent texts are quite incomplete, if not misleading, in their discussion of software engineering in the object-oriented paradigm.

In particular, the creation of a class hierarchy, rather than just abstract data types, gives us a major opportunity to think deeply about the structure of the problem and to create very powerful solution structures.

As an example, I recently had to use a new PC-based system in the library at the University of Essex to find a book. My selection actions retrieved about 30 books, more data than would fit on the screen, and I was presented with a complex method of viewing this information in screen-sized chunks. It struck me that the invention of the scrolling, resizable, user-controlled window was a major creative act, not in any way to be "found."

All the problems at the application-design and class-design level are repeated at the architecture level, both in decisions about reuse and in the creation of new architectures.

REFLECTIVE PRACTICE AND THE WAY FORWARD

The key to progress, that is, to better understanding and more effective manufacture, for individuals, groups, and the profession, must lie in a more reflective practice. The working cycle is a learning cycle

decide; work; assess and reflect; decide; work

in which we can choose to work with awareness, to make as much as possible as explicit as possible in order to be able to benefit from our experience.

One focus for such expression is the creation of catalogs:

* Architectures
* Techniques/rules
* Ideas for finding classes
* Powerful examples

as illustrated above. Unfortunately, in the competitive commercial world, exemplary code and catalogs will be too valuable to share.

It is not easy to develop and introduce methods of reflective practice, and this is itself an area of research and development (Reason and Rowan 1981). However, it is clearly a component, sometimes covert, of successful work. Whatever is needed, it will not be produced as "principles" from separate "research." Software manufacture in the object-oriented paradigm is an exciting challenge at every level.

ACKNOWLEDGMENTS

I would particularly like to thank Sanjiv Gossain, Ralph Hodgson, Kim Harris, and Larry Constantine among the many who have helped me develop my ideas.

REFERENCES

Anderson, D.B. and S. Gossain (1990) Hierarchy evolution and the software lifecycle, *Proceedings of the Second International TOOLS Conference, Paris 1990*, Editions Angkor, Paris, 41–50.

Beck, K. (1988) Experiences with Reusability — Panel Session. "Proceedings of the Third ACM Conference on Object-Oriented Programming Systems, Languages and Applications (OOPSLA)." *SIGPLAN Notices* 23(11): 372–376.

Gilb, T. (1989) *Software Engineering Management*, Addison Wesley, London.

Gossain, S. and D.B. Anderson (1989) Designing a class hierarchy for domain representation and reusability, *Proceedings of the First International TOOLS Conference, Paris*, 201–210, Prentice-Hall, Englewood Cliffs, NJ.

Gossain, S. and D.B. Anderson (1990) An iterative-design model for reusable object-oriented software, *SIGPLAN Notices* 25(10): 12–27.

Helm, R., I.M. Holland, and D. Gangopadhyay (1990) Contracts: specifying behavioral compositions in object-oriented systems, *SIGPLAN Notices* 25(10): 169–180.

Kuhn, T. (1970) *The Structure of Scientific Revolutions*, University of Chicago Press, Chicago.

Leathers, B. (1990) Cognos and Eiffel: a cautionary tale, *Hotline on Object-Oriented Technology* 1(9): 1–8.

Opdyke, W.F. and R.E. Johnson (1990) Refactoring: an aid in designing application frameworks, *Proceedings of the Symposium on Object-Oriented Programming Emphasizing Practical Applications*, Poughkeepsie, NY, 145–160.

Perry, D.E. and G.E. Kaiser (1990) Adequate testing and object-oriented programming, *Journal of Object-Oriented Programming* 2(5): 13–19.

Peters, T. (1987) *Thriving on Chaos*, Knopf, New York.

Prieto-Diaz, R. (1987) Domain analysis for reusability, *Proceedings of IEEE COMPSAC'87*, IEEE, Piscataway, NJ, 23–29.

Reason, P. and J. Rowan (eds) (1981) *Human Enquiry: A Sourcebook for New Paradigm Research*, Wiley, Chichester.

Shlaer, S. and S.J. Mellor (1989) An object-oriented approach to domain analysis, *SIGSOFT Software Engineering Notes* 14(5): 66–77.

Weinand, A., E. Gamma, and R. Marty (1989) Design and implementation of ET++, a seamless object-oriented application framework, *Structured Programming*, 10(2): 63–87.

Whiting, M. (1991) Report on "finding the object" workshop, Addendum to OOPSLA/ECOOP'90, *SIGPLAN Notices Special Issue*, 99–107.

part **3**

METHODS COMPARISON

chapter **6**

Describing and Comparing Object-Oriented Analysis and Design Methods

MARTIN FOWLER   *INDEPENDENT CONSULTANT*

Many object-oriented analysis and design methods have been published. Upon close examination, their similarities may be greater than their differences. This chapter looks at the popular methods and provides a framework for understanding the techniques that make them up.

DESCRIBING METHODS

An analysis or design method is a coherent approach to describing a system. This system may be a computer system, or it may be the business process that a computer system is going to support. Such systems are very complex, and thus a common approach is to use a number of different techniques, each of which provides a distinct view of the system. Each technique emphasizes some aspect of the system and neglects others. For instance, the Entity-Relationship model looks at the data of a system and does not describe any processing. Typically, a method will use several such techniques to cover all aspects of a design. Techniques are not usually exclusive to one method, and the same technique may turn up in a wide range of different methods. Although the basic techniques are the same, each methodologist has a habit of altering them, introducing some new modeling concepts and a new notation. Thus Shlaer/Mellor (1988) and Rumbaugh (1991) are two methods using different dialects of the Entity-Relationship technique. They differ in some concepts (e.g., there is no concept of aggregation in Shlaer/Mellor), and in notation (e.g., cardinality notations are different).

Each modeling technique presents a particular view of a system. In general, we can consider three general views of systems: data, behavior, and architecture (Figure 6.1). The data view describes the static or structural parts of the system and neglects processing. In database systems, this is the database schema; in object orientation, it is the types, attributes, and the relationships between them. The Entity-Relationship technique is one example of a data view. The behavioral views describe how the system changes. Ideally it should be executable, in that a compiler can be written for it, and the description will run. The state-transition diagram is an example of a behavioral view. Between them, the data and behavioral view can provide a complete description of a system for the purposes of computerization, but this description can all too easily become too complex to comprehend. Thus, an architectural technique can break the system down into subsystems. The data-flow diagram is an example of the architectural view.

This three-way split is not the only option. It is very common to see a two-way classification of process and data, but I prefer to separate behavior and architecture, since I believe that there is a significant difference in emphasis. In my classification, behavior defines sequence and control flow, while architecture defines how a system is broken into modules.

There are two key aspects of a technique: its rigor and its comprehensibility. A rigorous technique does not permit any ambiguity in its interpretation. This is stressed to its utmost in formal methods, such as Z and VDM. Rigor is very important, since without it any ambiguities in a model will be resolved in implementation, in a way that may not be consistent with the rest of the model. Comprehensibility is often understressed (especially by the formal methods community), but is equally important. One reason for this is that a technique that is difficult to comprehend is difficult to teach and, thus, is more difficult for new people to understand. This is important in that it reduces the chances of users making an effective contribution to the analysis process and reduces the chances of models being reused — and reusing models is a key element to reusing software.

A second, less commonly stated but equally important reason for using comprehensible methods is that to produce a good model it is vital that the modeler has a good view of the system. If a model is difficult to comprehend, it makes life more difficult for the analyst and designer, and will result in a lower quality model. Although rigor and comprehensibility are often regarded as mutually exclusive interests, they can be resolved. Most data modelers find Entity-Relationship diagrams a very comprehensible view of data that can easily be defined in such a way as to make them completely formal.

Thus, a method consists of a number of different techniques that combine to form a coherent model of a system. As well as these modeling techniques, a set of heuristics is required to describe how to construct a model. I use the term *heuristics* because these are always somewhat loosely described, but they do give useful guidelines in where to go from the blank sheet of paper. Much of the process of analysis and design is impossible to

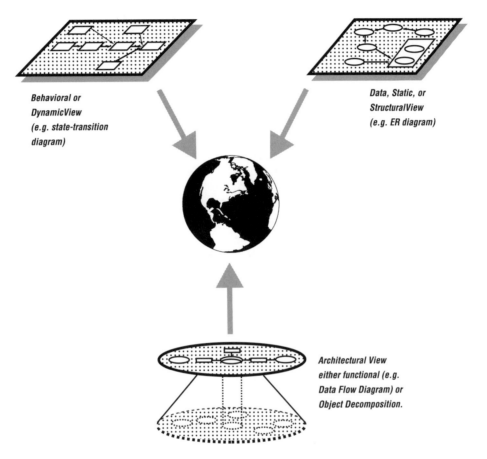

**Behavioral or
DynamicView
(e.g. state-transition
diagram)**

**Data, Static, or
StructuralView
(e.g. ER diagram)**

**Architectural View
either functional (e.g.
Data Flow Diagram) or
Object Decomposition.**

FIGURE 6.1. **Three views of a system.**

describe in a book. Analysis and design is at least as much art as it is science.

The attentive reader will have noticed that I have not attempted to strike a boundary between analysis and design. I follow Bailin's view that the distinction is "useful but infuriating." Each method gives its own interpretation of where the break exists (if there is one). It is worth pointing out that most would agree that analysis is the design of a conceptual (logical) model, and there is arguably more "design" in analysis than there is in design!

The rest of this chapter is divided into several sections. First I describe the various techniques used by different methods to define the three views of a system defined above. Then I give an overview of the different analysis and design heuristics, followed by a set of very brief overviews of the different methods. Finally, there is a section providing some advice in choosing a method. I cannot claim to have tried all these methods in detail, and I apologize to the authors concerned for any misrepresentations of their ideas I may have made.

Data View

Types and Classes

The data, or structural view of a system, concentrates on describing the types of objects in the system and various kinds of static relationships that exist between them. Three principal kinds of relationships are important: associations (e.g., a customer may rent a number of videos), subtypes (e.g., a nurse is a kind of person), and aggregation (e.g., an engine is part of an aircraft). The various object-oriented methods all use different (and often conflicting) terminology for these concepts. This is extremely frustrating but inevitable: object-oriented languages are just as inconsiderate. My choice of terms is entirely arbitrary — it's what I like. For those used to Entity-Relationship modeling, types correspond to entity types, associations to relationships, and subtyping is just the same.

The notion of types is, of course, common, and they are represented as a box on a diagram, although the shape of the box varies from method to method. Some other subtleties are worth pointing out. Martin/Odell (1992) distinguish between object types and classes by saying that object types are conceptual while classes are part of implementation and that (in the same way as the Object Management Group's distinction) one type might be implemented by a number of classes with different vendors, reliability, and speed characteristics. Coad/Yourdon (1992a) distinguish on diagrams between abstract classes (called *class*) and nonabstract classes (*class* and *object*), as does the Booch (1992) notation. Indeed, the Booch notation also adds distinctions for metaclasses and parameterized classes. Most methods make a distinction between classes and attributes, although the Martin/Odell method follows the binary modeling approach of not making such a distinction. This practice is also implied by Booch.

Jacobson (1992) classifies types as entity objects, interface objects, or control objects. Entity objects are used to hold stored information, interface objects are used to communicate with external actors (e.g., users), and control objects are used for processing.

TABLE 6.1. Terms Used in the Data View.

My Term	Booch	Coad/ Yourdon	Jacobson	Martin/ Odell	Shlaer/ Mellor	Rumbaugh
Type	Class	Class & Object	Object	Object Type	Object	Class
Association	Uses	Instance connection	Acquaintance association	Association	Relationship	Association
Subtype	Inherits	Gen-Spec	Inherits	Subtype	Subtype	Generalization
Aggregation	Containing	Part-Whole	None	Composition	None	Aggregation

Associations

Associations represent relationships between instances of types (e.g., a person works for a company, a company has a number of offices). These are similar to pointers in object-oriented languages, but with the important distinction that they are usually considered to be bidirectional and can be navigated in either direction. Jacobson (1992) is the notable exception here: a pity his counterexample to bidirectionality is erroneous..

One of the key aspects of associations is the cardinality of an association (sometimes called *multiplicity*). This specifies how many companies a person may work for, how many children a mother can have, etc. This corresponds to the notion of mandatory, optional, 1-to-many, many-to-many relationships in the Entity-Relationship approach. Each method uses a particular notation to indicate the cardinality; it is a sad fact that they are all completely different. In structured methods the crow's-foot style (Martin/Odell 1992) was beginning to become a standard, but the object-oriented community has wiped that standardization out in a stroke. For the purposes of comparison, it is best to consider cardinality as an expression of an upper and lower bound. The most common values for

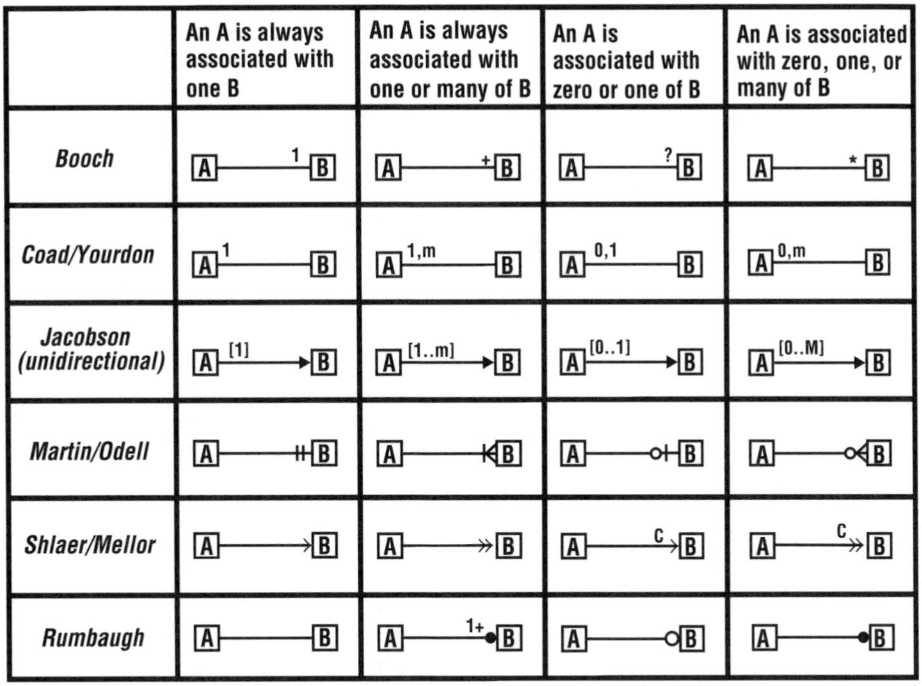

FIGURE 6.2. Different cardinality notations.

the lower bound are zero and one; for the upper, one and many. This results in the four combinations shown in Figure 6.2. It is important to stress that a particular association has a different cardinality in each direction. Other bounds can exist (such as a meeting having a lower bound of two) but are much rarer. None of the methods show symbols for this case. Instead, they prefer to show the numbers in a similar way to Coad/Yourdon (1991a). Rumbaugh (1991) also mentions the possibility of a discontinuous cardinality (e.g., a car having two or four doors), but these are even rarer.

Associations are full of additional subtleties to be picked out by different methods. One of the most important is that of derived or computed associations discussed by Rumbaugh and Martin/Odell, who describe how associations can be defined based on other base associations (thus, grandfather is an association defined by running the parent association followed by the father association). This concept can be further extended to bring in derived types, attributes, and subtypes. It can be used to define queries, views, and higher-level constraint rules.

Martin/Odell describe associations as either being a pair of unidirectional functions that are inverses of each other (e.g., employer and employee), or as a relation (employment) that is equivalent to the relation of relational databases. The distinction of functions is particularly valuable for computed functions where the bidirectional nature of associations is not always sensible. Rumbaugh has much the same concept of relations in defining association classes that allow associations to have attributes and operations. Both Martin/Odell and Rumbaugh allow associations to be subtyped just like types that define how subtypes can place further constraints on inherited associations.

Conventionally, it is assumed that multivalued associations are sets (e.g., the children of a person is a set of people). Rumbaugh provides notations for supporting other kinds of collection. Marking a line with *{ordered}* indicates a list rather than a set (the curly brace notation is also used to mark constraints). A qualified association allows the set to have a look-up key (such as *directory: file name*), which is a useful conceptual notion of what object-oriented languages support with dictionaries.

Figure 6.3 shows the basic set of constructs necessary for the data view. Cardinality is recorded by numbered upper and lower bounds. Aggregation is given a prominent role. Note also that the cardinality of the relationship is shown on the end closest to the class and object, in contrast to most other notations of this kind. Other notations for the data view are shown in Figures 6.4–6.8.

Subtyping, Aggregation, and Attributes

Subtyping is the most important addition to Entity-Relationship diagrams for use in object-orientation. Subtyping indicates that instances of the subtype class inherit all the attributes, operations, and associations of the supertype class. Subtyping is handled in different ways by different methods. The simplest approach, used by Booch and Jacobson, is to show one type as a subtype of another. The usual object-oriented programming rules apply, indicating that an object is of only one type and inherits from that type's supertypes. This is also the assumption implied in all the other methods, with the exception of Martin/Odell. Martin/Odell's view is that an object may belong to many types (multiple classification) and, indeed, may change types during its lifetime (dynamic classification). A partition notation is introduced to show how a type may be subtyped in different ways according to separate specializations. Although the use of partitions in this way is only described in Martin/Odell, a number of other notations can be used in this way (and recent articles describe some of them as being used in this way). The use of partitions is a notable break from object-oriented programming conventions and is not directly supported by most object-oriented languages.

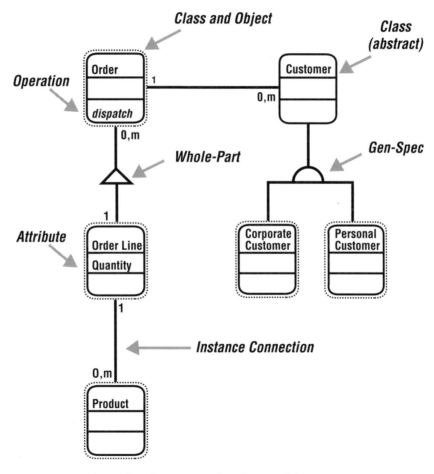

FIGURE 6.3. Coad/Yourdon object-oriented analysis model.

Aggregation relationships are introduced by most methods, although Coad/Yourdon makes the best use of them. These indicate part/whole relationships (e.g., a hammer is made up of a head and a haft). It is notoriously difficult to define the difference between an aggregation and an association, or to indicate whether the distinction is useful. The distinction is used most by the methods that use object decomposition in the architectural view (Figure 6.3), especially Coad/Yourdon, who use it nicely in their analysis approach.

Attributes and operations are generally handled in a similar way. Methods show attributes and associations within the type box, but wisely remark that this is only appropriate for small models. For larger models, it is best to note them on a separate text list. Rumbaugh indicates the importance of putting the attribute type for attributes, and operation return type and arguments on operation definitions. Booch adds a very wide range of possible indications, including concurrency and persistence. An example of a Booch diagram is shown in Figure 6.4, which also shows the slightly awkward notation. It is difficult to draw on a whiteboard or with a computer drawing package. UNIX ed symbols are used to indicate cardinality — try explaining those to users! Martin/Odell point out that attributes are essentially the same thing as associations (also implied by Booch); interestingly, they do not suggest listing operations with classes. Rather, they define this by a correspondence between types and event types on their event schema.

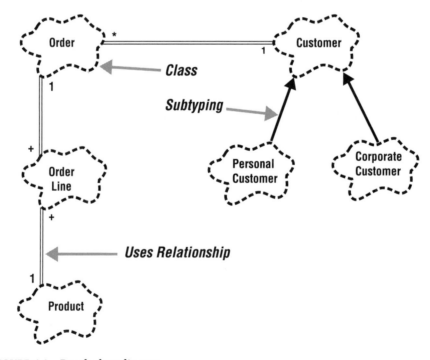

FIGURE 6.4. Booch class diagram.

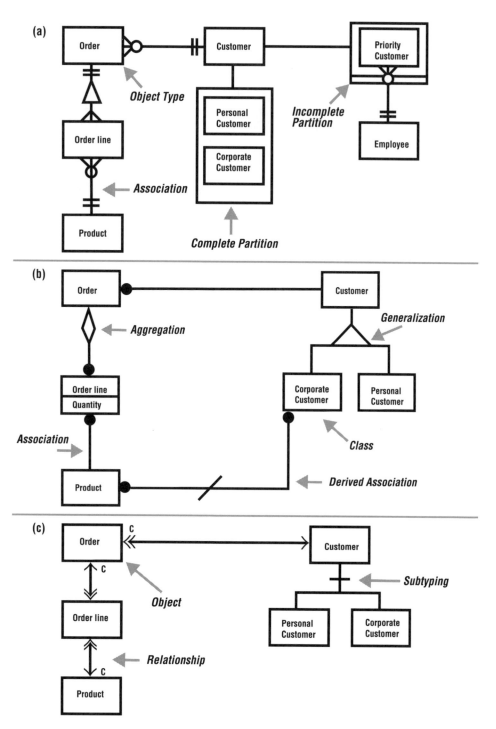

FIGURE 6.5. Three data views: (a) Martin/Odell; (b) Rumbaugh; (c) Shlaer/Mellor.

Against this large-scale usage of data models, it is important to note the dissenting voice of Wirfs-Brock (1990). This method provides only a simple representation of subtyping relationship. No attempt is made to provide modeling of the other concepts shown above. This is a reflection of their focus on a responsibility-driven approach, discussed under analysis and design heuristics.

The Jacobson approach (Figure 6.6) has a number of interesting features. In particular, note the classification of objects into entity objects, control objects, and interface objects. Jacobson's associations are unidirectional, which means that bidirectional relationships require a pair of lines.

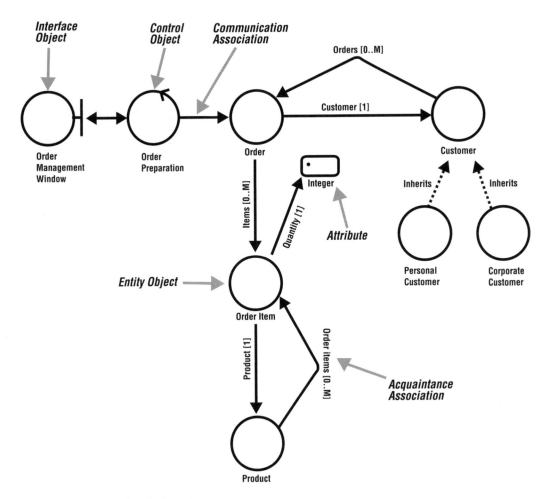

FIGURE 6.6. Jacobson's data view.

BEHAVIORAL VIEW

In structured methods the comparative unanimity of the Entity-Relationship technique for modeling data has never had an equivalent for representing behavior. Various approaches have been used, many of which combined the notions of behavioral and architectural modeling. The most common approach for behavioral modeling is still the flow chart — or its nondiagrammatic equivalent of pseudocode. The defects of any of these procedure-based techniques for large, complex behaviors has been well documented. However, both techniques are probably still unrivaled for the description of a single algorithm, providing it is not too long or wide ranging.

A technique that has received a great deal of attention — particularly in the real-time world — is the state-based state transition diagram. This has many advantages: it has a fairly well-worked-out formal basis and is executable. It takes the form of a diagram with boxes that are the states of the system being modeled connected by directed lines that represent transitions between these states. Each transition may be labeled with an event. When an event is received, the system reacts depending on which state it is in by undertaking the marked transition for the state and the event. Although this general framework applies to all state transition diagrams, they vary widely in detail. All state transition diagrams, however, share the disadvantage of requiring all the states of the system to be defined as nodes in the diagram. While this is all right for small systems, it soon breaks down in larger systems as there is an exponential growth in the number of states. This "state explosion" problem leads to state transition diagrams becoming far too complex for much practical use.

To combat this state explosion problem, object-oriented methods define separate state-transition diagrams for each class. This pretty much eliminates the explosion problem since each class is simple enough to have a comprehensible state transition diagram. It does, however, raise a problem in that it is difficult to visualize the behavior of the whole system from a number of diagrams of individual classes. This problem led to the development of mechanism and event-based modeling techniques that enable the modeler to describe how several classes cooperate in a real system. These techniques will be described later.

Varieties of State Transition

One of the principal differences between various kinds of state transition diagrams is where actions fit into the technique. The Mealy model approach is to link actions to transitions, so that when a transition occurs an action may be carried out. The system then waits in its various states. The Moore model, however, links actions to states: When a state is entered, an action is carried out. This is a subtle difference, but one that is very important in producing different diagrams for the same situation.

This difference is illustrated by comparing the state transition diagrams for Proposed Action, which consider states of actions. Actions pass from proposed to initiated to

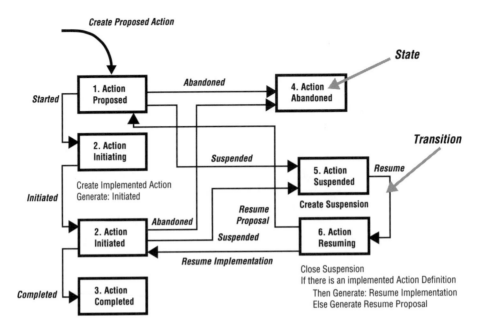

FIGURE 6.7. Shlaer/Mellor state transition diagram.

completed. Before they may be abandoned or suspended. Suspended actions may be resumed. A separate suspension object is created to record the suspension and a separate object is created to record the implemented action.

The two diagrams to consider initially are the Shlaer/Mellor and Booch versions, Figures 6.7 and 6.8 respectively. Booch uses a Mealy model while Shlaer/Mellor uses a Moore model. The immediate thing to notice is how the Shlaer/Mellor diagram introduces two extra states (Resuming and Initiating) to handle the actions associated with the resume and started transitions in Booch. The Booch model requires the notion of conditional transitions, in that the resume event can lead to two different transitions from the state suspended. Each transition thus needs some form of condition attached to it to indicate which one should be called — the logic for this is captured explicitly in the Shlaer/Mellor diagram.

Another level of sophistication for state transition diagrams was described by David Harel and was taken up and described by Rumbaugh (1991). (They are also used by Booch 1992.) The most noticeable extension is the notion of superstates and substates, which can be clearly seen in the Rumbaugh version of Proposed Action (Figure 6.9). This allows behavior that is common across states to be captured (e.g., the suspend and abandon events). The linking of actions to the diagram is also more sophisticated, in that processing may be linked to either states or transitions, thus combining the advantages of the Mealy and Moore approaches. This style distinguishes between actions that are considered

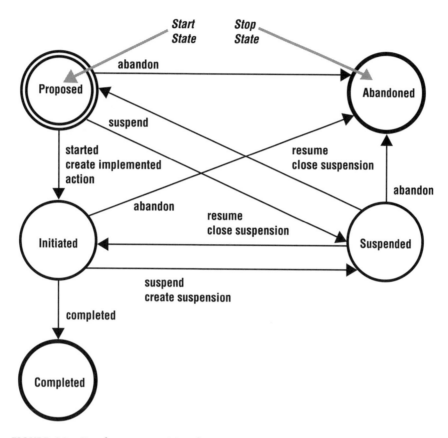

FIGURE 6.8. Booch state transition diagram.

to be instantaneous within the context of the model and activities that take significant time. Actions are linked to transitions and activities to states. Furthermore, actions may be linked to the entry of a state or the exit from a state. Thus the actions to create and close suspensions are very neatly handled in this approach.

Actions (and Rumbaugh's activities) are further specified by pseudocode in Rumbaugh and Booch, and by Action Data Flow diagrams in Schlaer/Mellor. Action Data Flow diagrams are based on the real time extensions to Data Flow Diagrams. A single, unlayered Action Data Flow Diagram is prepared for each action on the state transition diagram using data and control flows between processes. Conditional control flows exist to handle conditional processing.

The Coad/Yourdon approach (1991a) uses states in a much simpler way than the other approaches, developing a simple state transition diagram (without actions) simply to identify the different states an object may go through. This is used to help identify the services a class must provide. Each of these services is an algorithm described by a flow chart.

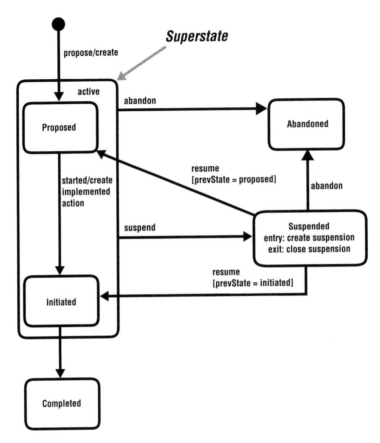

FIGURE 6.9. Rumbaugh state transition diagram.

Behavior Between Types

Limiting state transition diagrams to single classes succeeds in generally eliminating the state explosion problem, but does generate a different problem. Although the behavior of a single class is easy to visualize, it is still difficult to visualize the behavior of a system of many different classes working together. There are three basic approaches to this. One way is to not attempt to deal with this problem in behavioral modeling at all. This approach describes interclass behavior only in an architectural sense. In this approach, the messages and events that classes may send each other is described, but no attempt is made to describe the sequence of how these messages are sent. It is important to realize that this does not affect the rigor of the approach — state transition diagrams for each class fully describe the behavior of a complex system. The problem lies purely in visualization.

A second approach is the mechanism-based approach, which attempts to visualize the

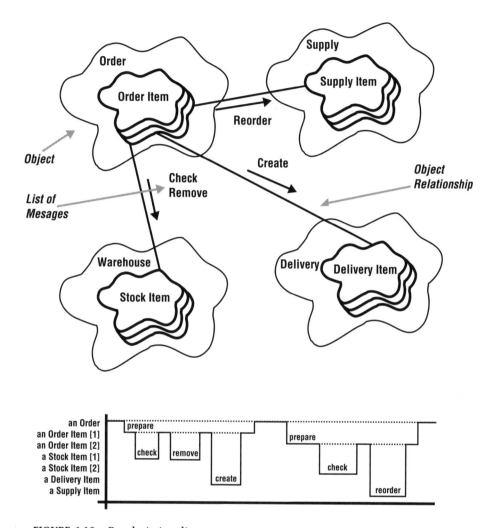

FIGURE 6.10. Booch timing diagram.

interclass behavior. The term *mechanism* was coined by Booch to describe "the means whereby objects collaborate to provide some higher level behavior." Descriptions of mechanisms are provided next to the object diagram (an architectural view describing which messages are sent from object to object). Booch gives three ways of describing mechanisms:

1. To number the messages in sequence
2. To provide pseudo-code
3. The timing diagram that provides a diagrammatic version of mechanism 1

The most visual of these is the timing diagram (Figure 6.10), but this has the disadvantage of not being very good at defining (as opposed to describing) behavior. In particular, there is no way of showing conditional behavior on the diagram. This mechanism approach (although not in those words) also appears in a number of other methods (i.e., Coad/Yourdon, *service layer*; Jacobson, *interaction diagram*; Rumbaugh, *event trace*). Only Jacobson uses pseudocode so that behavior can be defined rather than merely described. This is probably due to the fact that less emphasis is given to state-transition diagrams.

The mechanism concept does allow for inter-object behavior, but has disadvantages. The first problem is the lack of a diagrammatic construct rich enough to be computationally complete. The second problem lies in the fact that mechanisms are essentially algorithms and describe a single thread of control — there is no way of combining mechanisms to show a wider view of system behavior. At this point, we should talk about the method whose behavioral view has so far been conspicuous by its absence: the Martin/Odell method (1992).

Unlike all the other methods discussed here, the Martin/Odell method makes only a fleeting mention of state transition diagrams. Its behavioral view is based on another kind of diagram entirely: the event diagram. The event diagram begins from a very different basis to the state transition diagram; instead of treating states as the principal building blocks, it focuses on events (hence, it is an event-based approach). Events are produced by operations that are connected by trigger rules, a structure not entirely dissimilar to the Action Data Flow Diagram of Shlaer/Mellor. The event diagram, however, is not drawn for a particular state-based action, but is used to (potentially) describe the entire system behavior. Although an event diagram can be used to describe a state transition style action or a mechanism in much the same way as pseudocode, its great strength lies in being able to go further to describe behavior with many different interacting threads of control.

The contrast between state- and event-based descriptions is shown by the order example (Figures 6.11 and 6.12). Both the state and the event diagrams are equivalent descriptions of behavior with equivalent rigor: The event diagram (Figure 6.11) has the advantage of being more comprehensible since all the interactions between the different state diagrams are shown on the diagram. It also allows for triggering of methods on a set of objects, conditional behavior and looping. There are disadvantages, of course. The most noticeable is the lack of indication of which operations are bound to which classes, thus, there is no sense of objects collaborating in the sense of the Booch Timing Diagram. Whether that is due to the event diagram not being object oriented or due to a wider failing of the object paradigm is a matter for (often vigorous) debate. There is a wider issue: The presence of an event diagram suggests some behavior that is outside the class definition, while state diagrams imply that all the behavior is tied to the class definitions. This leads to wider questions about where system-level behavior should be defined.

Thus, there are four ways to tackle behavior modeling: procedure-, state-, mechanism-, and event-based. As always, the most important thing to remember is that there is no best modeling technique for all problems. In describing the states of actions, state transition

FIGURE 6.11. A comparison of diagrams for order processing: (a) event-based diagram (Martin/Odell); (b) state-transition diagrams.

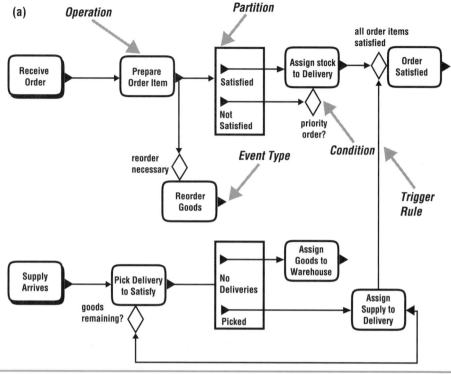

(a)

Operation — Prepare Order Item

Partition

Event Type — Reorder Goods

Condition

Trigger Rule

Receive Order → Prepare Order Item → [Satisfied / Not Satisfied] → Assign stock to Delivery → all order items satisfied → Order Satisfied

priority order?

reorder necessary → Reorder Goods

Supply Arrives → Pick Delivery to Satisfy → [No Deliveries → Assign Goods to Warehouse] / [Picked] → Assign Supply to Delivery

goods remaining?

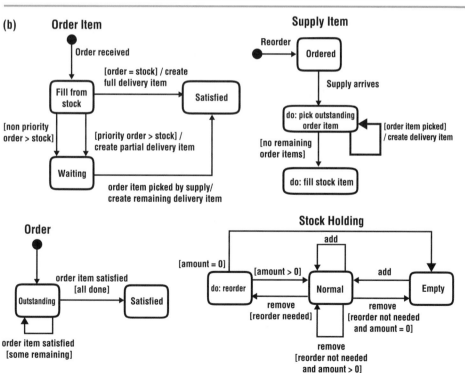

(b)

Order Item

Order received → Fill from stock

[order = stock] / create full delivery item → Satisfied

[non priority order > stock]

[priority order > stock] / create partial delivery item

Waiting

order item picked by supply / create remaining delivery item → Satisfied

Supply Item

Reorder → Ordered

Supply arrives

do: pick outstanding order item

[order item picked] / create delivery item

[no remaining order items]

do: fill stock item

Order

Outstanding

order item satisfied [all done] → Satisfied

order item satisfied [some remaining]

Stock Holding

add

[amount = 0]

do: reorder

[amount > 0]

Normal

add

add

Empty

remove [reorder needed]

remove [reorder not needed and amount = 0]

remove [reorder not needed and amount > 0]

diagrams provide a better picture than a rather disjointed event diagram. Event diagrams are superior when large-scale system behavior across many classes needs to be defined. The mechanism approaches are halfway houses that are insufficient on their own, but useful when combined with lower-level descriptions of a class's response to messages. All of these approaches are no better (and often inferior) to "old fashioned" flow charts and pseudocode in describing algorithms.

ARCHITECTURAL VIEW

The architectural view corresponds to breaking a large system up into components. Traditionally, this has been done functionally — a high-level function is broken into (inevitably 7 ± 2) subfunctions that are further broken down until a sufficiently low level is reached. Since it is difficult to do this without some form of guidance, the notion of data flow allows the designer to describe not only the modules, but the data that is passed between them. This allows the modeler to concentrate data flows in a particular model to reduce coupling. The arrival of object orientation heralds a different way to decompose systems — by object rather than by function. Of the methods under analysis, all but Rumbaugh and Martin/Odell do so.

Functional Decomposition

Traditional analysis makes wide use of data-flow diagrams. In object orientation these are found only in Rumbaugh, who uses them in much the same way as any other technique. A system is described by functions and data stores with data flows connecting them. Subfunctions are further broken down until the bottom level is reached. At this bottom level, the connection with the other views is made: bottom-level functions correspond to operations on the data view. This part of Rumbaugh's approach has come in for heavy criticism: and as the method evolves with use, it is likely that the use of data-flow diagrams in this way will change.

The Martin/Odell approach is also functional, but quite different. Object-Flow diagrams (e.g., Figure 6.12) are used to break a system up into activities, but concentrating on the flow of products and resources rather than data. This produces a value-added chain description where each activity takes its resources and adds value to form its product, which in turn acts as a resource for another activity. This approach is extremely useful in high-level strategic analysis where information-technology strategies are prepared for large organizations. It is also a technique that can be combined with such approaches as Porter, SWOT analysis (Strengths, Weaknesses; Opportunities, and Threats), and Soft System modeling for business modeling. While this makes it uniquely suitable among the object-oriented techniques for strategic modeling, it is not as suitable at lower levels.

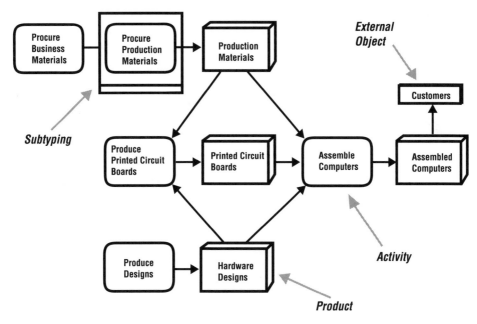

FIGURE 6.12. Martin/Odell's object flow diagram.

Object Decomposition

The object decomposition approach suggests breaking systems down by use of higher-level objects rather than higher-level functions. These higher-level objects then communicate and use each other in roughly the same way that the lower-level objects do. Two principal issues are highlighted in this analysis: communication and visibility.

Communication descriptions are used to determine how objects and higher-level architectural constructs communicate with each other. The Booch object diagram does this at an object level by showing typical objects and the messages that they can send each other. The concurrency aspects of these messages (synchronous, asynchronous) can be shown. Shlaer/Mellor use a similar approach, but separate the messages into two categories: accesses where one object gets information from another in a synchronous manner, and events where objects trigger behavior in other objects through asynchronous sending of events. These two categories of communication are defined on separate diagrams. Objects can be grouped into subsystems and Shlaer/Mellor use the same two communication diagrams at that higher level. Wirfs-Brock introduces the concept of a contract (see Figure 6.13). This acts to combine a number of message calls, and thus abstracts a large number of messages into a single block. This significantly reduces the complexity of tracking module inter-

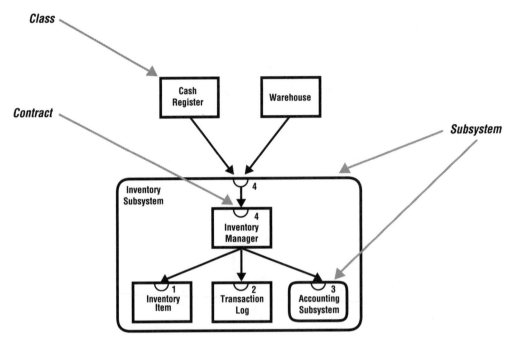

FIGURE 6.13. Wirfs-Brock collaboration graph.

connections. Diagrams are drawn at both class and subsystem level, but no distinction is made between synchronous and asynchronous messaging. Communication between classes is defined in terms of contracts, where a contract is a group of messages. This saves having to mark all messages on the diagram and also permits multiple levels of visibility. Classes may be grouped into subsystems, which may also have contracts.

Visibility is used to show whether classes and subsystems are able to use the facilities of other subsystems. This description shows how a change in the facilities of one system can affect another. No special construct is used in Wirfs-Brock: Visibility is defined and controlled at the contract level. Shlaer/Mellor use diagrams to describe visibility at the highest level of the system only by defining domains such as "user-interface," "timers," etc. Booch switches from a communication-based view to a visibility-based view earlier, and also makes a clear architectural split between logical and physical views. In the logical view, classes are grouped into class categories with visibility relationships between them. In the physical view, classes are broken into modules and subsystems with visibility relationships. It is unclear whether there are any relationships between the architecture of the class categories and that of modules.

Shlaer/Mellor use an entirely different set of notations for design. The class diagrams are used to document a class showing its data and operations with parameters and return values. Other diagrams describe flow of data and control within a class, messages between classes, and inheritance between classes. Personally, I do not like the use of separate design notations and am suspicious of detailed design notations. A very detailed design notation is little different from the code and, unless it can generate code and be generated by existing code (i.e., be used as a dynamic browser for a CASE tool), it is unlikely to be useful as it will not be kept up to date.

Coad/Yourdon (1991a) group the classes on the data view into subjects to provide a view of architecture. The designer is encouraged to base these subject areas by choosing classes toward the top of either the subtyping or aggregation hierarchies. No particular notation is suggested for messages or visibility between them. For design (Coad/Yourdon, 1991b) the analysis model is seen as the Problem Domain component, which is one of four system components, the others being Human Interaction, Task Management, and Data Management.

ANALYSIS AND DESIGN HEURISTICS

Models provide a way of describing the world, but modeling techniques are only part of analysis and design. Each of the methods provides techniques to help analysts and designers to prepare the models. There are no formal techniques to do this. Analysis and design are very much like cooking: The recipe is a first step, but not the whole story. Thus the guidelines provided within the methods act as a way of focusing the modeling. It is difficult to compare and contrast the methods in this context, for much of the advice is brief and informal, and all stress the iterative nature of the process. Most object-oriented writers reject the notion of signed and sealed stages. All say that while a technique is described as if it were stages, the actual route is much more of a spiral where the final model is gradually circled and closed on.

The predominant way of driving the analysis process is through the development of the data view: the data-driven approach. Here, the data view, with its subtyping, associations, and operations, is developed first. The differences between approaches is then quite minor. Rumbaugh indicates that the data model is produced first, followed by state and data flow models. Booch emphasizes developing mechanisms together with the data model. Coad/Yourdon put the priority on aggregation and subtyping to drive the data model before considering associations. The danger in a data-driven approach, found also in traditional data modeling, is the difficulty in knowing where to stop. This inability to know when enough has been done makes data-driven approaches particularly prone to creeping deadlines.

With backgrounds in information engineering, Martin and Odell are very familiar with this problem. Their method describes an event-driven technique for capturing behavior and developing the data view. In this technique, a goal event is determined and formally defined using data view types. The event and its defining types are generalized to an appropriate supertype and the causes of the event are analyzed. These causes are organized according to a logical pattern and described as events. Each event that is thus identified is then used as another source event for the process above. Practitioners find that although this sequence is usually not followed to the letter, the process of modeling events and data simultaneously greatly eases the scoping problems of data-driven analysis. A problem that remains, however, is how to map this data model to the interfaces that users recognize.

The way users interact with the system is the focus for Jacobson (1992) and Wirfs-Brock (1990), with the use of a scenario-driven approach. In this case, typical ways of using a system are walked through. Jacobson formally captures these as use-cases. The use-cases are the foundation of the approach. Each use-case is described textually and then modeled with an analysis model. Use-cases are also used to structure testing.

Wirfs-Brock uses the walkthroughs to identify the responsibilities of the system. These are then assigned to classes. Once a reasonable level of detail is defined (the authors encourage the use of cards to capture this), the interactions between classes to carry out responsibilities are described as collaborations. Both the responsibilities and the collaborations are refined by walking scenarios through the model. This model, unlike most other techniques, is not described by a diagram, but by a collection of index cards. Only once the responsibilities and collaborations have been worked through is a diagram used (e.g., the CRC diagram: an architectural view). The virtue of this approach is that no data structure is indicated at all, and the notion of encapsulation is incorporated into the analysis and design process. There are, as yet, no strong indications to show that it is more useful to approach analysis in this way.

Scenario-driven design keeps ideas close to the usage of the system. However, this can as easily be a disadvantage as an advantage. The danger of scenario-driven approaches is that the system can be built too much around current needs, and this focus will compromise the long-term flexibility. In addition, by concentrating on the way users currently work, the analysis can miss the opportunities for redesigning the business process that the computer system is supporting. Business process redesign can bring far bigger benefits than mere computerization. Data- and event-driven techniques, by focusing on essential process rather than user-interaction, are better able to divorce the designer from inefficient current practice.

The progression from analysis to design is similarly informal. Coad/Yourdon indicates that analysis works on the problem domain component while design considers other components. This is also implied by other writers. Rumbaugh suggests a three-step process of analysis, architectural design, and detailed design. Jacobson has the most structured approach: The analysis model of entity, interface, and control objects is turned into a design model of blocks. Initially, there is a one-to-one correspondence between the two, but as the design develops, changes are made to reflect the demands of the implementation environment. System behavior, using mechanism- and state-based techniques, are used only at this stage — not during analysis. Shlaer/Mellor propose an approach they term *recursive design* which stresses the use of a set of design rules to transform the analysis model into a design in rigorous and repeatable manner. This helps to ensure consistency across large systems. Unfortunately, little material is provided on how these rules are determined and a design notation (rather similar to structure charts) obscures the links between analysis and code.

From all these notes it is clear that there are few firm comments to be made about the heuristics of analysis and design. The most noticeable contrast is the difference between the data-model driven, event-driven, and scenario-driven approaches. The biggest point of agreement is the iterative nature of the process and the demise of the waterfall model of software development.

METHOD SUMMARIES

Booch

Grady Booch is one of the best-known names in the object-oriented design world. His much-referenced paper on object-oriented design was published in 1986. Since then, much of his attention has been focused on Ada, but his recent book (Booch 1991) describes his approach to object-oriented analysis and design. Entity-Relationship diagrams feature in the data view, here called *class diagrams*. Dynamics are shown with a state transition diagram within a class. Timing diagrams and object diagrams show interactions between objects. Logical architecture is shown with object diagrams and class categories that use object decomposition, and the physical design is shown with module and process diagrams. The object diagrams serve both to show object decomposition and to indicate the interobject behavior. Recent papers available from Booch's company, Rational Inc., describe a range of updates to the method. This chapter concentrates on the book, but refers to updates in the text as Booch 1992 notation.

In all, the wide range of techniques in Booch's method give it a lot of flexibility, particularly when dealing with concurrent systems. However, the variety of techniques also makes it difficult to use, since it is not at all apparent how to combine these to best effect for different kinds of problems. The book helps in that five detailed examples are given, but in the end the reader can feel as overwhelmed by the techniques as by the enormous bibliography (Booch 1991, Booch 1992; see also chapter 9).

Coad/Yourdon

Many of those in the object world vigorously criticized Coad and Yourdon's first book on object-oriented analysis. The general feeling was that it lacked rigor, contained confusions over classes and objects, and had little more than Entity-Relationship modeling in it. However, the second edition is in many ways a completely new book and has a great deal to offer.

The heart of the technique still lies in the data view with Entity-Relationship diagrams. These now show aggregation as well as associations and subtyping. Behavior is shown by naming operations on the classes and defining within the class by state-transition charts and flow charts (called *service charts*). Interobject behavior is shown by putting message connections on the Entity-Relationship diagram. Architecture is defined by grouping classes into subjects. These groups are also shown on the Entity-Relationship diagram. Thus, nearly the whole system is described in a single diagram, which is considered to have several layers, so that the reader can choose which views of the system to see. This approach is nicely simple, but may be difficult to work with in larger systems.

The technique for building up the architectural view is worth mentioning. The Entity-Relationship diagram is initially shown with the classes, subtyping, and aggregation relationships, but not with the associations. These relationships are then used to define the subject areas, essentially by equating the subjects with the classes at the top of the subtyping or aggregation trees.

The greatest strength of the method is its simplicity. Unfortunately, that is also its greatest weakness. A common feeling is that while it is an appropriate early start, it is not a method that would be effective in a sizeable project (Coad 1991a; see also chapter 10).

Jacobson (OOSE)

The object field has long known of the existence of Objectory, a software engineering method developed by Objective Systems in Sweden under the leadership of Ivar Jacobson. Unfortunately, getting detailed information about the approach has never been easy, at least not without paying a great deal of money for a license. This situation changed with publication of Jacobson's book, which describes object-oriented software engineering (OOSE), which is presented as a condensed version of Objectory.

The distinguishing aspect of Jacobson's method is the strong focus on use-cases, a scenario in which an actor (e.g., a user) makes use of the computer system. The analysis, design, and testing is entirely driven by the use-case. Upon this, Jacobson builds one of the more structured descriptions of the process of analysis and design.

Another unique feature is the classification of analysis objects into entity, interface, and control objects. This encourages a separated, yet well-integrated way of placing processing and user interfaces into the system design.

The textbook is long, and somewhat long-winded. Its strengths lie in covering areas that are widely neglected (e.g., testing) and descriptions of how the method should be tailored to cover real-time systems and databases. Seen in isolation, the individual techniques are not as strong as other methods, but the strength of the whole is not to be underestimated (Jacobson 1992; see also chapter 15).

Martin/Odell (Ptech)

The book by James Martin and Jim Odell must hold some kind of record for the length of time it has been in production. The book makes wide use of the Ptech method developed by John Edwards and develops it in a form consistent with James Martin's earlier books on information engineering. In many ways, it can be seen as two books. The early parts deal with James Martin's vision of future software development, and the later parts concentrate on the analysis models and methods. Technical readers may find themselves put off by the early chapters, but should not let that discourage them from the later sections.

The data view stresses a binary rather than Entity-Relationship approach to data modeling. The method is significant in that it demonstrates a formal underpinning in class mathematics and a strong philosophical influence. This leads to its elegant way of handling subtyping, support for class expressions, derived associations, and dynamic classification (objects changing class during their lifetimes). Behavior is defined using event diagrams that can express system behavior in a compact diagram. The events are formally linked to the data view, and the CASE tools can compile the event diagrams into executable code. Architecture is handled by object-flow diagrams that use a functional decomposition driven by a value-added chain representation. This is a useful technique for strategic analysis, but does not provide the architectural modeling capabilities of other methods. The analysis approach is notable for encouraging an event-driven approach that identifies events first and then uses these events to define classes.

The Martin/Odell method is unusual in being driven from a philosophical view of analysis and provides much food for thought in the analysis method. Its approach shows a great deal of cohesion between techniques and attention to the semantics. The book does not, however, clearly show how all the ideas should be put together (Martin 1992).

Rumbaugh (OMT)

Rumbaugh's Object Modeling Technique (OMT) was developed at General Electric's research labs in the United States. The method uses three techniques: object diagrams (a dialect of Entity-Relationships diagrams) for the data view, Harel statecharts for behavior, and data flow diagrams for architecture. The Entity-Relationship technique is particularly rich, supporting partitioned and non-partitioned subtypes, derived objects and relationships, and aggregation. The statecharts provide the most powerful state transition modeling in the methods surveyed. The data flow diagrams stress the link to objects by decomposing, so that bottom level bubbles are operations on classes.

Rumbaugh's approach uses techniques that are already found in structured analysis and puts them together well. Those used to structured approaches may find the subtleties of the differences take some getting used to, but overall they will be familiar. The source is a well-rounded book on object-oriented modeling that provides details for implementations in a number of environments, including non–object-oriented ones (Rumbaugh 1991; see also chapter 12).

Shlaer/Mellor

The first book to appear on object-oriented analysis and design was that of Shlaer/Mellor. This first book concentrated on the data view, and was widely considered to be a book on data modeling to which the concepts of object orientation were latterly attached. The second book (*Object Lifecycles*) added behavioral and architectural views. In the Shlaer/Mellor method, classes are modeled in the data view, which provides associations and subtyping. Each class is then given a state diagram, which describes its life cycle. Actions defined on the state diagram are either described by pseudocode or an action data flow diagram that acts as a process precedence diagram. Message connections between classes, divided into asynchronous events and synchronous queries, are defined to begin the architectural view. These message-based models are used again to describe subsystems. At the highest level, domains are defined with visibility relationships (called *bridges*) between them.

A different notation (referred to as OODLE) is used to describe the design side with detailed diagrams for classes and their interactions. This is a disadvantage to the method since one of the key advantages of object-oriented modeling is the clean transition from analysis to design.

Another feature of Shlaer/Mellor is their recursive design notion. This encourages the development of design rules to formally turn a model into a working system. These design rules are dependent upon the analysis method and the development environment. Unfortunately, neither of the books detail this approach (Shlaer 1988, 1991; see also chapter 8).

Wirfs-Brock (CRC, RDD)

The Wirfs-Brock method (also referred to as the *CRC method* — classes, responsibilities, and collaborations — or as *responsibility-driven design*) is certainly the most unusual approach currently published. Unlike all the other methods, which rely on a strong data view, Wirfs-Brock completely abandons data modeling, using only a simple inheritance graph. The technique focuses on describing the system in terms of responsibility, which is taken on by classes. These responsibilities are used to describe collaborations between classes that are eventually formalized in terms of an architectural view. No behavioral view is used. The notion of responsibilities has been well received by most people in the field, and the initial class identification techniques of Wirfs-Brock are widely recommended. One of the key appeals of the technique is that the hiding of the data structure and the use of responsibilities carries the notion of encapsulation into the analysis and design activity. Other techniques see encapsulation more as a detailed design notion.

The question about this approach is whether it is possible to effectively describe systems, particularly larger systems, without defining a data model. This is a point that is particularly relevant when considering that data models stress a data view that should be resilient to changes in its use. In this sense the Wirfs-Brock technique could be seen as similar to process-driven modeling with the attendant danger that a change of requirements could lead to a fundamental change in the model (Wirfs-Brock 1990).

WHICH METHOD TO CHOOSE

There is no easy answer to this question. The software industry is not very good at analyzing its practices objectively. Even now, many years after their introduction, there is no study that proves structured techniques are better than using no methods at all. Much of the rationale for using one method instead of another comes from the gut feelings of those who use them. Statistics quoted by CASE tool companies are generally meaningless. The choice for a technique thus must take into account the environment in which it will be used, and the people who will have to use it.

In this era of rapidly changing techniques (e.g., the Coad/Yourdon method has altered drastically in just two years, and many of the other books have second editions in preparation), there is much to be said for taking the best elements from different methods. The techniques show much similarity, and different features from different methods will suit different practitioners. This approach, of course, puts a great deal of pressure on those putting the methods forward, who have to be familiar with how all the techniques used will hang together. It is best to take a single method as a starting point and introduce features from other techniques gradually as they are required. This approach will need someone who knows the approaches well, who can advise a team when to introduce new features, and knows how they fit into the whole approach.

CASE tools bring in some further questions. These methods are quite new and the CASE tool support for them is not well developed (although CASE tools are now appearing in a rush). The first question is whether a CASE tool is a good investment? What benefit does it offer that a simple drawing tool would not provide? After that question is settled, it is important to be aware of the danger of being locked into a particular vendor. CASE tools sold by the methodologists will only support that particular method, and thus are not likely to support any changes other than that desired by the methodologist in charge. The other approach is to use a flexible CASE tool that supports several methods. Such a tool can reasonably be expected to catch up quickly with new methods, and can be tailored to a particular organization's approach — allowing support for a mix of methods. Customizing a flexible CASE tool is still a difficult task, however, one that will not usually be done by the development team. It is also true that flexible CASE tools will not usually fully support their methods, and will not be as good for a single method as a specific tool.

What To Do

So how does one go about introducing object-oriented methods? The best approach is to begin gently with a pilot project; defining this pilot project is the first stage. The pilot project should have the characteristics of any project used to pilot new technology. It should be a reasonable size, but not be too large. It must be useful. It should not be time critical or carry large risks. Once this is decided, the project team needs to be assigned, and team members should be reasonably enthusiastic about trying new approaches. Only after this has been done should the analysis and design methods be considered. This should be done in the pilot project by considering a number of methods in detail, looking at source books, and by attending a training course. The following guidelines may be helpful:

- Consider the general characteristics of systems developed by the organization as a whole and of this project in particular. Is the method suitable to this sort of system?
- What current expertise is available in the company? If the staff are all trained in a technique that is used by a particular method, a better result can be expected. Beware of subtle differences between dialects that may cause previous experience to be counterproductive. This is especially true in getting staff to think "objects" rather than "functions" in design.
- Look at the support available. What sort of expertise is available, internally or externally, to help introduce a new method?

Much of this analysis is gut feeling. There is a case for some consultancy from those familiar with object-oriented techniques, but it is important to take the particular conditions of your organization into account, rather than just using the consultant's favorite technique.

Once the project is kicked off, monitor it carefully to evaluate the approach. Although the time pressure must not be too great, and it should be expected that the team will go down a couple of blind alleys on their way up the learning curve, an element of the deadline must be used to keep the team focused.

This is where an external consultant can be most valuable but, as in any consultancy, the project must be very carefully controlled. In particular, it is absolutely vital that the consultant not do the work. Rather, the consultant should teach your staff how to do the work. The best way is to use the consultant for design reviews at regular intervals. These design reviews will pick up any inappropriate use of techniques, suggest importing new concepts from other dialects of techniques, and generally encourage the object-oriented way of thinking.

It is important that, even if the aim is to evaluate a design method, the design is to be implemented for something that is needed by the organization. Otherwise, there is a danger that the design will not be judged properly. This system must be both important and visible, but preferably not critical. It is important to allot extra time for the project to allow the team to mount the inevitable learning curve. In the end, object-oriented analysis and design is judged by the quality of the resulting system. This system need not be produced with object-oriented programming systems; object-oriented design is valuable even with conventional implementations.

The most difficult part of all this is the evaluation. Software development is lamentably short of quantitative ways of evaluating software development approaches. The final judgment is inevitably subjective. Remember that there are two things to be judged here. First, there is the obvious factor of how good the delivered system is, and how much effort it took to produce. However, the second factor — what reusable components have been produced — is in many ways the most important. Here, the quality and usefulness of these components must be judged. Consider developing a similar system. How much of the design and the resulting code can be reused? How much does this reduce the effort of further systems development? The problem in evaluating object-oriented approaches is that the greatest benefits occur later as components are reused.

Other Comparative Studies

A report by Alcatel Network Systems is one of the most detailed comparisons. It attempts to develop a scoring system to rate the various methods on a number of different fronts. It concludes by recommending Rumbaugh with some extensions from Wirfs-Brock, Shlaer/Mellor, and Ian Graham. This report is now published by SIGS Books as a White Paper (Cribbs et al. 1992).

A group at Hewlett-Packard produced a useful study that concentrates on identifying the differences using a checklist approach (Arnold 1991).

Two major computing journals have published special issues on analysis and design: the September 1992 (35:9) issue of *Communications of the ACM (CACM)* and the October 1992 issue of *IEEE Computer*. Each contains a number of valuable articles. Over 20 published object-oriented methods are compared in the *CACM* issue. This gives a useful overview, but is rather too brief and research oriented (Monarchi 1992). In *Computer*, Fichman and Kemerer (1992) concentrate on comparing some object-oriented approaches with conventional methods, highlighting the differences between the two approaches.

Berard Software Engineering has developed a comparison that tries to determine a number of discriminators to help people choose between methods. It is a useful and detailed document (66 pages), but expensive (Schultz 1992).

The Object Management Group sponsors a special interest group on analysis and design. The first volume is a framework model that can be used as a basis to compare methods. They plan to survey current methods (volume 2) and compare them (volume 3; Hutt 1992).

Some Recommendations

As indicated above, it is impossible to recommend a particular method for all situations — the specific characteristics of the problem and people involved must be taken into account. The environment in which a method is going to be used is a far more important factor than the often minor differences between methods. However, I do have some recommendations about what choices should be made in the four areas of data, behavior, architecture, and heuristics.

On the data side, there is little to choose from between the methods. Use multiple and dynamic classification (described by Martin/Odell 1992) and in recent *JOOP* articles (by Rumbaugh et al.). While it adds some complexity in implementation, it can greatly simplify analysis. Often the biggest differences between methods is the notation. It is worth making an effort to use as similar a notation to current practice as possible.

In behavior the key issue is the relationship between state- and event-based modeling. Event-based modeling gives a much superior view for considering the whole behavior of a system. Certain cases and classes would benefit from state modeling, so that approach should not be completely rejected. If state-based modeling is to be used, the Harel statecharts used by Rumbaugh (1991) are the most powerful technique. Mechanisms are useful as a supporting act to states.

Architecturally, the functional decomposition approaches are now seen as generally incompatible with object-oriented development and should not be used. The one exception is the object-flow diagrams of Martin/Odell, but only in strategic modeling. Otherwise, object decomposition should be used. Wirfs-Brock's CRC graphs, with the use of contracts, would be my favorite, but Booch's or Shlaer/Mellor's are also valuable.

As far as heuristics are concerned, beware the data-model driven approaches. They can be difficult to scope. Scenario-driven approaches have advantages here, but run the risk of embedding current thinking. This can be a big problem for widely shared systems. In this case, use events and data together, remembering that this approach requires an event-based behavioral technique. Design should be driven by the notion of transforming the analysis model into an implementation environment. The intention should be to keep the code as close as possible to the analysis.

Most important of all is the importance of training and support. This should be a conclusive factor in the choice. Textbooks vary in quality; Rumbaugh gives the best overview of model through to code, and Jacobson addresses many, otherwise ignored, industrial concerns. Coad/Yourdon provides a simple introduction and a method that is easy to get into. With all of this it is important to assess the support you are going to get. In this remember that it is the team, not the company name, that is the key factor.

There is no single best choice. Look at your environment, decide what factors are important, and look at the methods to see which one fits best. Once a method is chosen, do not be afraid to tailor it with techniques and ideas from other methods. Above all, never forget that in five years, none of the methods will be the same.

Notes on This Text

This chapter was originally prepared as a tutorial handout for OOPSLA '92 in Vancouver (based on a tutorial developed for SCOOP '91). It was substantially revised in December 1992 to incorporate Jacobson's method into the comparison and to revise the conclusion.

REFERENCES

Arnold, P., S. Bodoff, D. Coleman, and F. Hayes (1991) An evaluation of five object-oriented development methods, in *JOOP Focus on Analysis and Design*, Richard S. Wiener (ed.), SIGS Publications, New York.

Booch, G. (1991) *Object-Oriented Design with Applications*. Bejamin/Cummings, Redwood City, CA.

Booch, G. (1992) *The Booch Method: Notation*, Rational Inc, Lakewood, Colorado.

Coad, P. and E. Yourdon (1991a) *Object-Oriented Analysis*, Second ed., Prentice-Hall, Englewood Cliffs, NJ.

Coad, P. and E. Yourdon (1991b) *Object-Oriented Design*, Prentice-Hall, Englewood Cliffs, NJ.

Cribbs, J., C. Roe, and S. Moon (1992) *Object-Oriented Analysis and Design Methodologies*, SIGS Books, New York.

Fichman, R.G. and C.F. Kemerer (1992) Object-oriented and conventional analysis and design methodologies, *IEEE Computer*, 25(10): 22–39.

Hutt, A.T.F., J.B. Kain, M. Christopherson, J. Dodd, G. Fine, G. Hoydalsvik, K. Murphy, P. Thomas, and F.G. Wilkie (1992) Object analysis and design, Object Management Group, Framingham, MA.

Jacobson, I., M. Christerson, P. Jonsson and G. Övergaard (1992) *Object-Oriented Software Engineering: A Use Case Driven Approach*, Addison Wesley, Reading, MA.

Martin, J. and J. Odell (1992) *Object-Oriented Analysis and Design*, Prentice-Hall, Englewood Cliffs, NJ.

Monarchi, D.E., and G.I. Puhr (1992) A research typology for object-oriented analysis and design, *Communications of the ACM*, 35(9): 35–47.

Rumbaugh, J., M. Blaha, W. Premerlani, F. Eddy, and W. Lorensen (1991) *Object-Oriented Modeling and Design*, Prentice-Hall, Englewood Cliffs, NJ.

Schultz, R. (1992) A comparison of object-oriented development methodologies, Berard Software Engineering, Gaithersburg, MA.

Shlaer, S., and S.J. Mellor (1988) *Object-Oriented Systems Analysis: Modeling the World in Data*, Prentice-Hall, Englewood Cliffs, NJ.

Shlaer, S., and S.J. Mellor (1992) *Object Life Cycles: Modeling the World in States*, Prentice-Hall, Englewood Cliffs, NJ.

Wirfs-Brock R., B. Wilkerson and L. Wiener (1990) *Designing Object-Oriented Software*, Prentice-Hall, Englewood Cliffs, NJ.

chapter **7**

Contemplating the Universe of Methods

RALPH HODGSON   *IDE EUROPE**

Object technology has revitalized an interest in software methods. Some methods schools advocate the evolution of traditional structured analysis methods, others propose new methods for modeling interactions. Object-oriented modeling goes beyond the traditional notion of clarifying an under-standing of a problem — analyze-before-design — to creating models that are enactable and can form the basis of an implementation — analysis-for-design. The very terms *analysis* and *design* are open to question, and there is a new importance to the role of architecture and design idioms.

In this chapter, the universe of object-oriented methods is explored. Experience with object-oriented development is stimulating a healthy evolution of thinking about methods. Booch '93 is an evolution from Booch '92, itself a development from Booch '91. Rumbaugh '94 will no doubt differ from Rumbaugh '92. It makes little sense to search for "the" method. Like the universe, we have a dynamic cosmos of object worlds in which a method evolves into a bright star or else ceases to be prominent and becomes a red giant before disappearing altogether. Hence, an organization should first understand thoroughly what it means to think in terms of objects. Then, like methodologists, the organization should establish a set of modeling and design principles that combine techniques into a compre-hensive process for doing object-oriented software development.

**Present Affiliation*: IBM Consulting Group, Southbury, Connecticut

INTRODUCTION

Object technology is an expansive — and expanding — universe (Figure 7.1). Indeed, I am motivated by Stephen Hawking's *A Brief History of Time* to draw an analogy with cosmology (Hawking 1988).

A mere atom, representing SIMULA67, depicts the beginning of this universe of object technology. Twenty-five years ago the first object-oriented programming language was invented in Europe. In this sense, object technology has not come to Europe but was born there and has traveled the world to arrive back in Europe alongside continued European developments of the technology. Object technology is today a big universe embracing the worlds of graphical user interfaces, software development environments, libraries, generic application frameworks, operating systems, databases, and software development methods.

Generic application frameworks (GAFs) are ways of building generalized applications that can be specialized to address the concerns of specific applications. Operating systems are becoming object-oriented (e.g., PINK, MACH, CHORUS, and the Object Management Group's CORBA, a common architecture for distributed object systems).

COBOL is included because object-oriented extensions are underway. I credit Larry Constantine with the joke about where the extra *O* should be placed: COOBOL or COBOOL?

Notice another language. The small Challenger space ship is the language SELF, which is an object-oriented language some contend might rival the dominance of C++.

My motivation for showing this universe is to make the point that object technology is developing very quickly. An interest in object technology needs to be understood more precisely. Is the interest in operating systems, object-oriented databases, graphical user interfaces, object-oriented programming languages, or object-oriented methods?

Too numerous to include in the same figure, and deserving their own universe, are object-oriented methods (see Figure 7.5). This chapter looks at the relationship between object-oriented methods and the development process.

THE NATURE OF OBJECT-ORIENTED SOFTWARE DEVELOPMENT

What is an object-oriented approach to software engineering? Before addressing this question, it is useful to compare object-oriented development to other software engineering strategies.

A common approach, which has been the dominant application development paradigm, is function-oriented development. A system is seen as a set of transformations, or computations, creating and modifying information to satisfy functional requirements in the system's environment. Functionality is *decomposed* into smaller and smaller functions.

In event-oriented development, a system is partitioned according to the events that happen in its environment and the desired responses. System analysis precedes by identifying an event list and the set of event responses. The hierarchical structure of the system is *composed* by a middle-out and bottom-up approach. These ideas have their origins in the

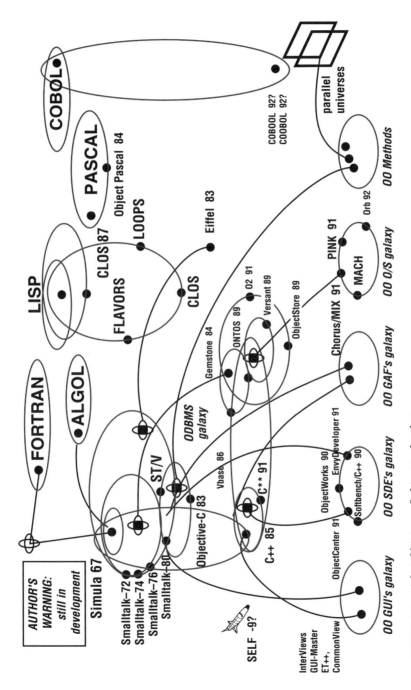

FIGURE 7.1. A brief history of object technology.

essential systems analysis work of McMenamin and Palmer (McMenamin 1984). An event can be seen in a similar way to a message and a response as the invoked behavior of some object. Event-oriented analysis is an appropriate step for clarifying the essential behavior of object-oriented systems.

Data-oriented development focuses on the structure of the data within a system. Functions are built around the abstractions of the data. Many information-based systems follow this approach.

In object-oriented development a system is modeled as a collection of interacting entities that enact the behavior of a domain, some region of interest. Objects represent their domain counterparts and have defined responsibilities for what they know about and what they manage. By exchanging messages, objects make requests for actions and pass information to each other. Classes centralize the descriptions of common properties of objects. A system is built as architecture of distinct subsystems as represented by object instances and domains as represented by distinct class hierarchies and frameworks.

Object-orientation is not a revolutionary phenomena, but an evolution of thought from the traditional viewpoints of function and data. An evolution that can be traced through the principles of information hiding, abstract data types, type inheritance, polymorphism, and invocation by messaging as opposed to a calling paradigm. To relate to objects, I suggest that you see object-orientation as having a strong continuity with the past.

Whatever the continuity we find, objects have caused a shift in the goals of the development process. Whereas the central consideration in structured development is transforming requirements, architecture is the key to structuring object-oriented solutions. In object-oriented development, we are interested in an augmentable model that is capable of evolving to changing requirements.

A key decision in architecture is what might be called the *paradigm step*. Choosing an appropriate model is a matter of viewing subject areas of a system as particular kinds of problems — the essential nature of the subject areas. But the typical (method) strategy of many object-oriented analysis approaches is to take a domain and model its entities and relationships so as to determine object, and then class, structures. Where is the place in this strategy for discovering that we are dealing with a kind of scheduling or optimization problem, or that we can use a constraint-based solver? The paradigm step guides decisions about the boundaries of a model and what reusable frameworks might be applicable.

It is not surprising that object-orientation is bringing about a reappraisal of methods for software engineering. Methods thinkers find it hard to keep pace with the development of object-oriented ideas.

Each methods school has its traditions to observe, and courage is required to make a radical departure from what was taught in the immediate past. So one finds each method religion taking on-board the object-oriented paradigm in interesting ways, some claiming that it was there all the time. While some advocate the use of traditional structured analysis methods for identifying objects, others propose radically new methods for behavioral modeling and system construction.

Many traditional methods, so-called hard systems thinking, are grounded on the view that a problem is "out-there" to be represented by an analysis model and that there is an objectivity about systems thinking. Assumptions that all interested parties will see the system in the same way are managed throughout the development and use of the system. The difficulty for analysis always stems from the variations in the expectations of a proposed system because of misconceptions arising from differences in each of our "appreciative systems" (Checkland 1981, 1990) and in the way systems thinking is allowed to exist as a pluralistic activity involving multiple stake-holders and a so-called critical subjectivity (Flood 1991).

The normative camp posits that systems are created from agreements on what we can envision and as such evolve as we experience their use. Systems are not "out-there" in the real world, but are "brought" into being from our intentions (Ehn 1988; Flood 1991; Winograd 1986).

Here is the dilemma for object-oriented purists. Motivated by the conviction that object orientation is a modeling process, there is a preference to describe the domains that underpin an application or, more often, a family of applications. Functions of an application are highly susceptible to change, and it is better that the computing solution is a working model so that functionality can be evolved.

In the extreme, such a philosophy would deliver no application functionality, in favor of providing enough capability for users to develop their own application environments by interacting through direct manipulation and gesture programming with the delivered models. Of course, such a viewpoint would be inappropriate for building an object-oriented real-time railway signaling system. On the other hand, human-activity systems, so-called soft systems, can be delivered as extensible application frameworks.

However we approach system building, object orientation presents a pragmatic challenge in placing a strong emphasis on promoting existing models for consideration in the analysis and design process, which calls into question what we mean by analysis and design. We should be interested not just in techniques for modeling, but also in how aims and scopes are set for the deliverables of modeling. In other words, how we arrive at a particular modeling boundary and how everything fits together. Central to my thinking is how object orientation relates to the development process — not methods in terms of what techniques to use for abstracting, but the strategies that exist for building systems, how one chooses what to model, and what architectures to employ.

THE DIMENSIONS OF SOFTWARE MODELING

A way to understand the relationship of object-oriented methods to development is to look back to the foundations of software methods. To do that I will use what has been called the *Yourdon footprint*. A system might be described through three viewpoints: a data structure view, a dynamics view, and a functional view. These three viewpoints are illustrated in Figure 7.2.

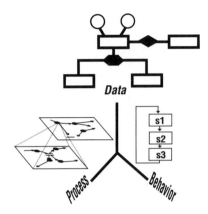

FIGURE 7.2. The Yourdon footprint: three viewpoints of abstraction.

An object, which can be likened to a minisystem, embodies aspects of all three viewpoints, as depicted in Figure 7.3. The object model describes what is present in a region of interest. The dynamics viewpoint looks at when things happen, and the function viewpoint looks at what is being done.

An object also interacts with other objects, using standard protocols as illustrated in Figure 7.4. This interaction characterizes a fourth dimension.

Most object-oriented methods fail to address this fourth dimension. A way of thinking about object interaction is responsibility-driven design — what responsibilities does this object have? How do I see that from the client perspective? Object interaction protocols determine the interfaces of classes and polymorphism, a crucial activity for ensuring malleability and improving reuse.

One further idea that characterizes object-oriented development is "domain abstraction." By *domain*, we mean a subject matter area capable of independent existence — for example, a user interface library, an operating system, a framework of planning strategies, a diagnostics library, an abstraction of scheduling services, or more basic mathematical

Object Structure

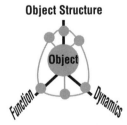

Object model => **what** there **is**
Dynamic model => **when** things happen
Function model => **what is** being **done**

FIGURE 7.3. Objects and abstraction.

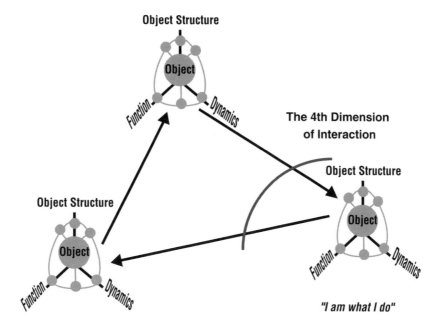

FIGURE 7.4. Object interaction.

abstractions such as queues and sets. Deciding on the domain structure of a system requires viewpoint and scenario analysis. Techniques for achieving domain (or subject) architecture are only now being formulated. For object-oriented development, we must build into these techniques ways of discovering opportunities for large-scale reuse.

A Brief History of Methods

Figure 7.5 attempts to portray the rapidly developing worlds of object-oriented methods. The picture is affectionately called "the cosmic soup of methods."

The big bang of methods happened in the 1960s. I am suggesting that before 1960, there was no methodology anywhere for software engineering other than flowcharts for programming. After the big bang, the three primordial galaxies of the early methods universe formed, the data modeling galaxy, the function modeling galaxy, and the state modeling galaxy. Many object-oriented methods adopted the entity perspective and developed from the Entity-Relationship galaxy. The emergence of object-oriented modeling is depicted as an asteroid belt, with Shlaer/Mellor in 1988 shown as one of the published approaches. For many, this period did not really address object orientation, it only restated entity modeling with the jargon of objects.

Other worlds to consider are Coad/Yourdon (Coad 1991), OMT (Rumbaugh 1991), OSA from Hewlett-Packard in the United States, and a plethora of European methods,

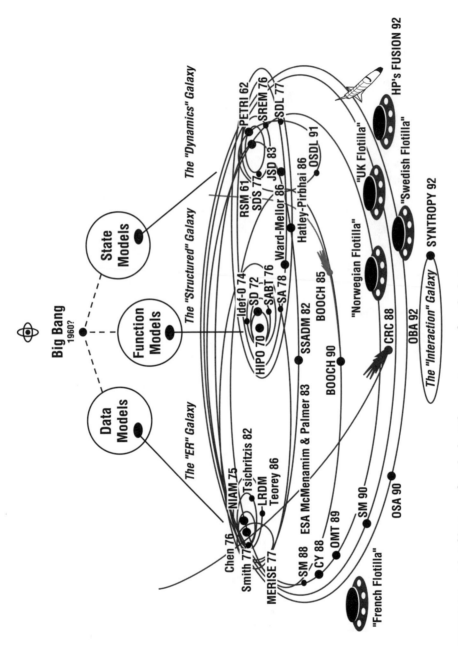

FIGURE 7.5.   A brief history of methods: "The cosmic soup of methods."

shown as flotillas or Unidentified Flying Objects (UFOs). In France, there are about six methods and a similar number in the United Kingdom — SOMA, ORCA, object-oriented SSADM, FUSION, and SYNTROPY. FUSION and SYNTROPY are blends of OMT, Booch, and Class-Responsibility-Collaborators (CRC; Wirfs-Brock 1989). Booch in 1985 is shown as a comet (Booch 1986). We do not know which galaxy it came from, but in 1990 Booch acquired an orbit by embracing a form of Entity-Relationship modeling and state modeling (Booch 1991).

I believe another galaxy is forming, which I call the *interaction galaxy*, where methods are addressing object interaction paradigms, support for polymorphism, and the design of interfaces.

A single object-oriented method is unlikely to cover all requirements of the object-oriented development life cycle. In fact, as each method house discovers weaknesses of its own approach and strengths in other approaches (Monarchi 1992), we witness an evolution of thought as depicted in Figure 7.6.

Underlying all of these methods is a common set of model types. The evolution of methods is a cross-fertilization of ideas, and there is a consensus toward the following set of possible models:

Essential model: anything that unambiguously and rigorously documents the nature and scope of the behavior (in the general sense) of any system-to-be in sufficient detail, but that does not exclude or predicate any particular computing solution.

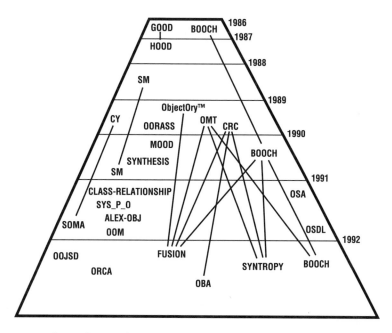

FIGURE 7.6. The evolution of object-oriented methods.

Use scenarios: for every event for which the system has a defined response, a use scenario expresses the thread of control across objects participating in the use scenario.

Object model: the object model expresses relationships between objects within a region of interest.

Interaction model: expresses the totality of communication, without any sequencing, that can occur between objects in terms of requests that objects make of each other.

Event trace model: a model (or view) across objects that expresses the time-ordered messages (invocations) that result from responses to specific events. These requests are the collaborations that support use scenarios, either in full or in part.

Dynamic model: a state transition diagram, or statechart, or Petri-net expressing the dynamic behavior of an object by showing the events it responds to, the actions that it undertakes, the state changes it may undergo, and possibly new events that it may generate.

Use hierarchy: expresses the seniority of control between objects with or without detailing the operations that are undertaken.

Creation hierarchy: a graph depicting the parent-child creation hierarchy for object instances.

Class graph: the lattice of classes that factor out common properties of the domain, expressing the relationships between classes.

Class definition: the implementation details of a class describing unique, overridden, private, and inherited methods and other features. Also captures the design decisions surrounding interclass and intraclass protocols.

Interface specification: the definition of the external view exhibited by instances of a class to their clients. What might be called the promoted or exported interface.

Modeling techniques should be combined to provide an integrated method or process for developing software in an object-oriented way. Rather than take a single method, it is better to understand, as the method houses do, the underlying modeling distinctions and "blend" method techniques into a comprehensive life-cycle coverage.

The process must address the concerns of large systems characterized by many cooperating subject matter areas. While the decomposition of large functional models has had much attention, little work has been done on structuring large object models.

THE IMPACT OF OBJECT ORIENTATION ON THE DEVELOPMENT PROCESS

Development processes, irrespective of implementation technology, are concerned with the breakdown of the work involved in progressing from a perceived need for a new (or altered) system to a delivered system.

Traditionally, system development proceeds by a step-wise transformation from the problem domain (Royce 1970; Boehm 1981; Boehm 1986; Schultz 1985) — analysis then design. Analysis is concerned with the understanding of domains and the elicitation of the requirements of an application. The analysis model expresses the structure of the problem that is being addressed by setting the scope of the system and dealing with what the system will do. The design model expresses how the system implements what is captured in the analysis model.

In the waterfall model, each phase is wholly satisfied before the next begins. Such an idealized model with nothing available until the completion of all development is only appropriate if the specification of our system has a high level of assurance and the delivery conditions are readily achievable. In practice, systems never conform to this ideal model, and discoveries made during development require changes to work done in previous phases. The success of the waterfall model, often construed as schedule adherence, relies on each phase resisting changes so that it can produce its deliverables from the deliverables of the previous phase.

Recognizing the iterative nature of development and the need to plan and assess risks at each iteration has led to the formulation of the Spiral Model of development (Boehm 1986, 1989). The waterfall model is not redundant. There is still the need to progress through phases. In effect, the waterfall model is subsumed within the broader scope of a system delivery model. Within each cycle of the iteration or evolution toward the next release of software, a waterfall process will be found.

Mapping the expression of the problem into a solution using structured analysis and design has been successfully adopted by virtue of the well-defined transformation of a systems functions into implementation modules. Object-oriented analysis and design proceeds by mapping the entities and behaviors of the problem domain into cooperating objects by decomposing the application and its governing domains into classes. The process of mapping models of the problem into solution objects should be facilitated by the direct correspondence of modeling conventions.

A development from the waterfall model is the so-called V model, described in relation with other models in Ould (1990). The V model gives a clearer depiction of the separation of concerns between the user view of the system, the architecture model, and the implementation model. Users relate to the development underway by considering only the upper part of the V model. System architecture need only concern itself with the middle part, where the concerns are focused on mapping an understanding of the problem architecture into a fully tested solution architecture.

At the lowest part of the V model, implementation of our solution proceeds either by the assembly of software components or by coding new ones. What is new for object orientation is the ease with which we can share an understanding of the solution, the effectiveness of prototyping, the opportunity to reuse higher structures of building blocks by considering the role of frameworks at the architectural level, and the possibility of reusing domain understanding at earlier points in the development process.

Object orientation can support very effective rapid prototyping. One way to improve the "trustworthiness" of the process is to employ prototyping at each level. No construction company would contemplate a major building scheme without a model, and the same should be true for systems. The prototype should not be thought of as a quick and dirty feasibility study, but as a model that helps clarify system objectives and survives throughout the lifetime of the development.

Both the waterfall model and V model are examples of development process models and as such represent a process within a broader process of system delivery for which we must agree upon a system delivery model.

Introducing the notion of a delivery model allows us to see each development process as an iteration or evolution toward a satisfactory solution. With iterative models, the accent is on what minimum resource can be expended to ensure the next increment of product, while maintaining consistency with overall project objectives. Each succes-

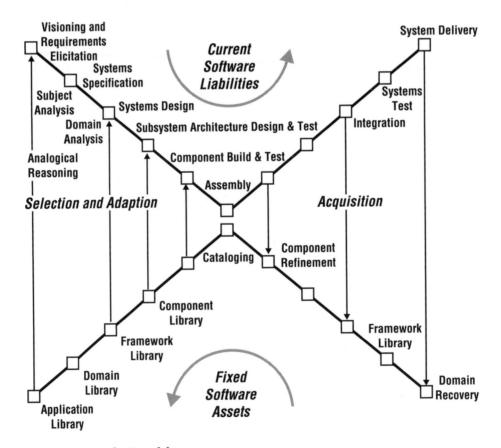

FIGURE 7.7. The X model.

sive delivered product has partial functionality. Minimum resource considerations are formulated alongside other objectives of the product development.

Delivery models are technology-independent. But the nature of the system development process is technology-dependent, and the impact of object orientation on the development process has led me to formulate a new life-cycle model for object-oriented software engineering (Hodgson 1991). Called the X model, it emphasizes current software liabilities in the upper part of the X, and software assets in the bottom part of the X (Figure 7.7).

The upper part of the X is a modified V model expressing how specifications become delivered systems. Just as for traditional development, we have system specification, architectural design, detailed design, coding, unit testing, integration, and system testing. The lower part of the X is an inverted V, to suggest the notion of asset management of reusable repositories either at the component level, the framework level, the domain level, or even the application level.

The X model expresses two broad cycles of activity: a forward activity that synthesizes a new (or modified) system and a reverse activity to acquire systems and their artifacts for cataloging the various models, architectures, and components of the completed work for potential reuse. The forward engineering at each stage in the process tries to reuse by selection, adaptation, and refinement existing work that has been acquired into the library systems.

From a business perspective, all software development in the forward cycle represents current liabilities and in the reverse cycle, fixed software assets. An asset-based attitude to software engineering is a necessary prerequisite for the cultural change that accompanies widespread reuse.

For object orientation, the X model is particularly appropriate. When facing a new application, the development team will devote time to exploring existing domain models to see how they might support the new application. There is considerable emphasis on "what can be brought" to the analysis process.

The X model of software development recognizes that there are different concurrent life cycles to components, applications, and abstract designs. The subject matter of our asset-based libraries is constantly under refinement.

Object-oriented development supports the evolution of systems to meet new requirements resulting from the experience of use. Such evolution might place new demands on existing frameworks and components, possibly requiring their replacement. In object-oriented development, classes are built by a process of continual elaboration. This is an iterative process requiring previous development steps to be revisited as both more specific and more general concepts are found (Wasserman 1991).

The iterative evolution of the system represents new distinctions about the structure and behavior of governing subdomains. In an inheritance-based design, reorganization of the class hierarchies is typical. Reported experiences indicate that a class hierarchy undergoes considerable remelding and refinement as a system and the understanding of its underlying domains evolves (Anderson 1990, Gossain 1990).

For most people, the starting point on software development is not a new system, but an existing system — one that is often poorly understood and has to be re-engineered. That is, it must be brought through some reverse cycle so that there can be forward engineering with the new requirements. However, many organizations do not manage their software as assets, but tend to build only for today's systems.

Object technology, on the other hand, encourages an iteration from an asset base, and this raises new requirements for methods. An asset-based approach to development starts from existing frameworks and components and, by means of an established set of architectures, fabricates these into a system that meets new and changing requirements.

At the implementation level, reuse is possible through components and low-level frameworks (e.g., the NIH library containing collection classes). Reuse at the architectural level is possible through the adoption of higher-level frameworks that provide generalized designs within a domain of interest (a subject area). Higher in the V model, we might reuse domain models by identifying common aspects with the new application. Reuse at the system specification level is facilitated by domain analysis (Prieto-Diaz 1990) and analogical reasoning (Sutcliffe 1989; Vosniadou 1989).

A form of the X model for object-oriented software engineering is shown in Figure 7.8. Starting with some context model, the system-to-be is viewed in its environment to clarify what is inside the boundary and what is outside.

Following decisions about context, subject areas must be determined. Subject architecture expresses the structure of the relationships between domains.

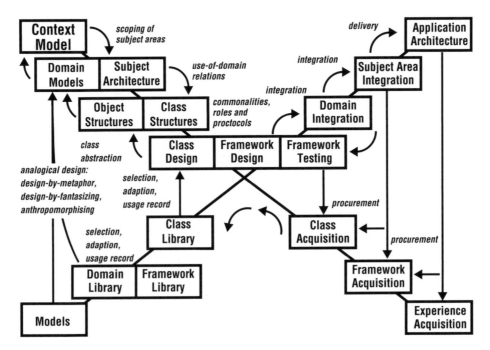

FIGURE 7.8. The X model for object-oriented engineering, envisioning, analysis, and design and assembly with continuous learning.

A short digression into philosophy might provide help on the distinctions between object and subject:

> *Object* is that which we are conscious of, a thing observed, that which is thought of and identified as a type of thing that persists in a region of interest.

> *Subject* is that which is conscious of "thing"; that which regions and contains the thing being observed (used).

Heidegger confronts the nature of the subject-object relation in his essays on the metaphysical foundations of logic (Heidegger 1984). He inquires into the difficulty of speaking about an object being present-on-hand without a subject. Only by dwelling on the intentionality of the relationship between subject and object do we forward our understanding.

In structured methods, we often hear about the subject matter of a system. Analysis is stated by many as the understanding and description of the subject matter of a domain, where *domain* is a viable set of entities that delimit a region of concern.

With these distinctions, we come closer to understanding the subject matter of a system to be a network of domains. In banking, for example, there is the subject matter of customer accounts, bank mandates, and securities. In industrial automation, we have subject matter concerning production scheduling, machine control, job routing, and flow management. A gasoline pump has the subject matter of pumps, fuels, and the activity of dispensing gas and paying for it. Arriving at the class definition even for something as simple as a gas pump needs some consideration for its use. The art of design is in producing something that can be reused in future unanticipated scenarios.

How does the notion of a subject-object relation have meaning for object orientation? We start by considering that objects are not defined outside of scenarios of use. Governed by the intentions of their use, objects have defined responsibilities and needs for associations with other objects. These collaborations give meaning to the nature of a subject-object relation. There is a sense in which the client object of the collaboration, by acting out an intention, is the subject aspect of the subject-object relation.

We have introduced the notion of seeing a system as an architecture comprising a network of domains. By separating the subject matter of the system, we arrive at delineations of domains. A domain is a context of use for other domains. By refining the intentions of use between domains, we express the roles enacted by objects in collaboration. Within a domain, collaborations between objects express how one object is a context of use for other objects.

SUBJECTS AND DOMAINS

Subject orientation may be defined as the process of producing a domain architecture that, through a refinement of intradomain use, supports one or more applications. A subject area is synonymous with the term *domain*, and domain analysis forms an integral aspect of subject orientation.

Prieto-Diaz has written that an application may be thought of as an organized collection of cooperating subject areas operating upon distinct domains (Prieto-Diaz 1990).

First introduced by Neighbors, domain analysis aims to identify the structures of objects and operations that constitute an understanding of the behavior of a region of interest (or activity) general to a number of applications in a problem area (Neighbors 1981).

Doing domain analysis is by no means a well-understood process. There is difficulty in deciding what a region is, and how the subject matter of a problem domain can be separated. Domains are often more discernible after a system is delivered. Domain analysis then becomes the process of breaking down architectures into reusable frameworks of generalized designs, perhaps more correctly called *domain recovery*.

Domain analysis should be done early in the development life cycle. We focus on how the subject matter of the application area is structured by thinking about:

- Event- and action-based behavior
- Logic- or rule-based inferencing behavior
- Algorithmic functionality
- Information structure
- Resource management
- User-interface management

Domains can be:

- Entity domains of real-world objects that capture the characteristic properties of those objects
- Algorithmic domains that capture well-formed theories such as planning, routing, control theory, and scheduling
- Application domains that express the functional abstractions of specific application uses of the entity domains
- Entity domains of a computational nature that provide computing abstractions such as sets, stacks, queues, lists, and trees
- Architectural frameworks that provide the structure of the computing solution such as multitasking operating systems, messaging mechanisms and distributed computing paradigms

If these large-scale structures of the system are factored out, consideration can be made of how the development can be influenced by what already exists in other models or in domain libraries.

A realization of the importance of subjects has come from recent work on object modeling addressing layered abstractions for large entity models (Teorey 1989; De Champeaux 1989; Coad 1991; Rumbaugh 1991).

Teorey's paper states that in any significant problem domain the entity models will easily contain upward of 1,000 entities. It is unreasonable to work with such a large model, and some way of clustering the entities into subject areas is essential to problem comprehension and techniques of decomposition. He proposes modeling techniques for layering large entity models, and he introduced the notion of an entity cluster. An entity cluster groups lower-level entities into a composite entity abstracting away the details of the lower levels. Teorey develops distinctions about groups according to the cohesion that exists within a group. In order of cohesiveness the groupings are dominance, abstraction, constraint, relationship, and convenience groupings.

Entity clusters can still expose lower-level relationships at the clustering level. As a consequence, it is difficult to decide whether a grouping is a new semantic construct or just a navigational aid.

De Champeaux is working with the notion of ensembles that are clusters of objects, but may have their own attributes and dynamics. The difference between an ensemble and a composite object is that an ensemble has internal parallelism and an object is a single state machine. Ensembles encapsulate collections of objects and other subensembles and may be manipulated as single entities. They may have properties that express shared information for all of their constituents. An ensemble also has mechanisms for propagating triggers and events to its constituents. When interacting with other ensembles, requests can be received on behalf of all their constituents. In this way, ensembles help to structure a large model into a hierarchy of layered object models (De Champeaux 1989).

To be strict, ensembles are more of an architectural invention being offered to the system construction process than an implementation-free way of expressing an abstract layered model. Nonetheless, subject areas are evident in the boundaries that appear around ensembles.

Coad has a weaker notion of *subject*, choosing to use the term to refer to any structure that may be collapsed to a single entity depiction in a higher layer. In Coad's notation, this may be an aggregation or generalization. It is unclear how subjects pertain to grouping object structures that are only associations. Rumbaugh expresses the requirement for entity clustering by referencing the work of Teorey, but does not go much further. Shlaer and Mellor have moved from earlier ideas of domain analysis to ideas about layered domain architectures and domain bridges, so-called recursive design (Shlaer 1990).

A common view of subjects as regions of concern within an application area emerges. These are the underlying domains that govern the structure, functionality, and substance of the application. For each subject area, domain models are built by modeling the properties of a domain without constraining the domain to a specific application.

Examples of reusable domains are:

- Networks (graph theory)
- Routers (topology)
- Schedulers (manufacturing)

- Planners (operations research)
- Controllers (control theory)

Common to all of these examples is a model of a well-formed theory from a domain of discourse (suggested in parenthesis). The subject area of graphs can express a domain model that is reusable for applications as diverse as network management, flexible manufacturing, and PCB layout. From operations research, we can capture ideas for planning systems in a framework involving abstract classes.

Domain layers are reusable across different applications having subdomains that decompose the structure of our problem into cooperating class hierarchies. By understanding the anatomy of an application we produce general designs that model the concepts of a domain and express the set of actions predicated in the domain. Subject analysis is the hierarchical leveling of domain models and the structuring of connections between subject-matter areas.

An extensible subject architecture captures the entities and properties of the domain. Provided the protocols of the model are observed, extensibility allows the domain model to evolve in a different life cycle from that of the application and multiple applications to share the same domain models. An inheritance-based architecture has more than one plane-of-use hierarchy, and self-recursion among classes relies on well-defined interclass protocols.

Reusing domains requires creative thought in fitting known models to new problems. It requires us to separate the functionality of differing applications from the domains that govern them. The application is regarded as a use-of-domain layer.

Consider the design of a commodity trading system. One subject area would capture concepts such as commodity, standard contract, spot price, futures price, and exchange rate. Another subject area would capture the notions of a bid and a bidding strategy The application would interface with these models and make use of their protocols. An example of such a framework can be found in the ET++ Swaps Manager (Eggenschwiler 1992).

Another example from the industrial automation industry is a flexible manufacturing system (FMS). An FMS has domain models for equipment, materials, and batches. A subject area might capture the notion of a route as a network of work cells. Generic algorithms for traversing a network could be used to calculate route times by messaging more specific subclasses for processing times at each point on the route. The applications are separated from the models, but comply with the domain protocols.

In functionally decomposed systems subject areas are pervasive throughout the software. The decomposition proceeds without the parallel structuring of object models that support the application functionality. Changes to accommodate new information about a domain are difficult to make. Moreover, the subject areas cannot be shared by another application.

A subject-oriented architecture captures the entities and properties of domains. As long as the protocols of the models are observed, extensibility allows the domain model to evolve in a different life cycle to the application, and multiple applications to share the same domain models.

Subject areas can be found from the essential model and by working with interdomain models. In the essential model, the decomposition of functions will reveal major functional partitions. While some will suggest application objects that "manage" other activities, others will suggest algorithmic domains.

The occurrence of a bubble named *plan AGV route* in an automated factory model might suggest that the routing classes library should be browsed. Further decomposition of the plan-AGV-route process might reveal the usefulness of a class library that knows about graph theory.

Approaching subject matter elicitation bottom-up from domain models might call for the identification of semantically cohesive objects as candidates for including in the domain. These clusters can then be modeled as super-entities with the relationships between other domains containing the composite of relationships found on lower, more-detailed levels, analogous to hierarchical functional decompositions. Whole domains become entities with relationships to other domains decomposable into subrelationships.

CONCLUSION

Over the last decade, thinking on object orientation has progressed from the language level through design idioms to the analysis of problem spaces using domain analysis. Potentially more than any other development in software technology, object orientation is a paradigm shift in every process of the development life cycle. By supporting a separation of architectural concerns in application and domain frameworks, objects challenge the traditional notions of transforming a description of a problem into a homomorphic solution (Daniels 1990).

How is object-oriented software engineering being adopted? Radical changes are rarely the answer and adoption in each industry segment is happening in different ways. Many people will embrace the idea of eventually doing object-oriented development, making a transition from existing designs by re-engineering and using hybrid object-oriented systems.

The information systems community is looking for ways to map the identification of entities and relationships into classes and finding ways of incorporating ideas about business rules into object models. Developers of technical systems are concerned with behavioral models just as much as object models and look for methods that support multiple viewpoints. Builders of interactive systems are looking for techniques that support large-scale reuse, and an iterative approach using application frameworks is becoming popular.

There is no one method for "going object oriented." Across all industries, methods being used for structuring domain models differ from those used for capturing the functional requirements of the application level. While traditional methods might be adaptable, new methods will be called for to support the evolution of domain models, to support the evolution of class hierarchies, and to guide the re-engineering of existing systems using layered domain models.

A strong accent on modeling encourages applications to be viewed as interacting domain models partitioned by subject matter areas, which has been described here as subject orientation. Classes enable component-level and framework-level reuse and domain models enable subject-level reuse.

If I were to choose some areas of deficiency that object-oriented methods should address in the future, this would be my list:

- Precise semantics of the models
- Composability of models
- Support for frameworks
- Dynamic instance interaction views
- Support for polymorphism
- Support for reuse
- Support for frameworks and design patterns (Johnson 1992)
- Model resilience to changing requirements

Methods must help to clarify the abstractions of interconnected systems of class hierarchies so that software can support more than one application. Interfaces are required to be highly stable and as reusable as possible. There is little chance of achieving this if a method does not support polymorphism. Unfortunately, current methods say very little about polymorphism or how to design reusable interfaces.

With few exceptions, current object-oriented methods address the building of software with an emphasis on the creation of new objects as opposed to using or evolving existing objects. This is the key challenge that an organization must face: how to exploit what already exists when considering the next system it has to build.

ACKNOWLEDGMENTS

The author is grateful in various ways to John Deacon, Anthony Wasserman, and other colleagues at Interactive Development Environments. He also acknowledges the many discussions over the years with colleagues in the object-oriented community, especially Steve Cook, Tom Love, Bruce Anderson, Chris Wallace, and John Daniels.

REFERENCES

Anderson, B. and S. Gossain (1990) Software reusability using object-oriented programming, *UK IT 1990*, University of Southampton, UK.

Boehm, B. (1981) *Software Engineering Economics.* Prentice-Hall, Englewood Cliffs, NJ.

Boehm, B.W. (1986) A spiral model of software development and enhancement, *ACM SEN,* 11(3): 14–24.

Boehm, B.W. (1989) Applying process programming to the spiral model. *Proceedings of the 4th International Software Process Workshop,* ACM, New York, 46–56.

Booch, G. (1986) Object-oriented development. *IEEE Transactions on Software Engineering* 12: 211–221.

Booch, G. (1991) *Object-Oriented Design with Applications.* Benjamin/Cummings, Menlo Park, CA.

Checkland, P. (1981) *Systems Thinking, Systems Practice.* John Wiley and Sons, New York.

Checkland, P., and J. Scholes (1990) *Soft Systems Methodology In Action.* John Wiley and Sons, New York.

Coad, P., and E. Yourdon (1991) *Object-Oriented Analysis.* Second ed. Prentice-Hall, Englewood Cliffs, NJ.

Daniels, J. (1990) Object-oriented design: refinement or transformation? *OOPS-30,* Strand Palace, London, 62–63.

De Champeaux, D., and W. Olthoff (1989) Towards an object-oriented analysis technique, *Proceedings, Pacific North-West Software Quality Conference,* 323–338.

Eggenschwiler, T., and E. Gamma (1992) ET++ swaps manager: using object technology in the financial engineering domain. *Proceedings of OOPSLA'92, ACM SIGPLAN Notices,* 27(10): 166–177.

Ehn, P. (1988) *Work-Oriented Design of Computer Artifacts.* Arbetslivscentrum, Stockholm, Sweden.

Flood, R.L., and M.C. Jackson (1991) *Critical Systems Thinking.* John Wiley and Sons, New York.

Gossain, S., and B. Anderson (1990) An iterative-design model for reusable object-oriented software, *ACM SIGPLAN Notices,* 25(10): 12–27.

Hawking, S. W. (1988) *A Brief History of Time: From the Big Bang to Black Holes,* Bantam Press, New York.

Heidegger, M. (1984) *The Metaphysical Foundations of Logic,* translated by Michael Heim, Indiana University Press, Bloomington, IN.

Hodgson, R. (1991) The X-model: a process model for object-oriented software development, *Toulouse '91*: 713–728. *Fourth International Conference on Software Engineering and Its Applications.* EC2, Paris.

Johnson, R.E. (1992) Documenting Frameworks using Patterns, *Proceedings of OOPSLA'92,* ACM SIGPLAN Notices, 27(10): 63–76.

McMenamin, S.M., and J.F. Palmer (1984) *Essential Systems Analysis.* Yourdon Press, Prentice-Hall, Englewood Cliffs, NJ.

Monarchi, D.E., and G.I. Puhr (1992) A research typology for object-oriented analysis and design, *Communications of the ACM,* 35(9): 35–47.

Neighbors, J. (1981) Software construction using components, Ph. D. Thesis, Dept. of Information and Computer Science, University of California, Irvine.

Ould, M.A. (1990) *The Management of Risk and Quality*. John Wiley & Sons Ltd., London.

Prieto-Diaz, R. (1990) Domain analysis: an introduction. *ACM SEN Notes*, 15(2): 47–54.

Royce, W.W. (1970) Managing the development of large software systems: concepts and techniques, *Proceedings of WESCON 1970*, pp 1–9.

Rumbaugh, J., M. Blaha, W. Premerlani, F. Eddy, and W. Lorensen (1991) *Object-Oriented Modeling and Design*. Prentice-Hall, Englewood Cliffs, NJ.

Schultz, D.J. (1985) Standard for the software life-cycle process, ACM SEN, 10(3).

Shlaer, S. and S.J. Mellor (1989) An object-oriented approach to domain analysis, *ACM SIGSOFT SEN* 14(5): 66–77.

Shlaer, S. and S.J. Mellor (1990) Recursive design, *Computer Language,* 7(3).

Sutcliffe, D.A.G. and N.A. Maiden (1989) Analogy in the reuse of structured specifications in a CASE environment, *Proceedings of the Third International Workshop on Computer-Aided Software Engineering*. 148–150. John Jenkins, ed. Imperial College, London.

Teorey, T.J., G. Wei, D.L. Bolton, and J.A. Koenig (1989) ER Model Clustering as an Aid for User Communication and Documentation in Database Design. *Communications of the ACM*, 32(8): 975–987.

Vosniadou, S. and A. Ortony (1989) *Similarity and Analogical Reasoning*. Cambridge University Press, Cambridge, UK.

Wasserman, A.I. and P.A. Pircher (1991) The spiral model for object software development. *Hotline on Object-Oriented Technology*, 2(3): 8–12.

Winograd, T. and F. Flores (1986) *Understanding Computers and Cognition: A New Foundation for Design*, Ablex Publishing Corporation, Norwood, NJ.

Wirfs-Brock, R. and R.E. Johnson (1990) Surveying current research in object-oriented design. *Communications of the ACM*, 33(9): 104–124.

part 4

PERSPECTIVES ON SPECIFIC OBJECT-ORIENTED METHODS

chapter 8

The Shlaer/Mellor Method: A Formalism for Understanding Software Architectures

COLIN B. CARTER AND CHRISTOPHER H. RAISTRICK   *KENNEDY CARTER*

This chapter presents recursive development (Shlaer 1990) as a uniform approach to the study of problem domains and software architecture domains. The underlying assertion is that the performance and maintainability of a system will be improved more significantly by the selection of a set of rules to be applied globally across all software components than by any amount of low-level tinkering with individual code modules.

INTRODUCTION

Those who would peddle the benefits of object-oriented design (OOD) often cite as a strength the fact that the stand-alone quality of classes means that each one can be subjected to its own development process, allowing an approach based on the notion of "analyze a little, design a little, code a little, test a little." This assertion, while clearly true, has two significant implications:

- Each component is subjected to its own design phase; consequently the amount of effort expended on design is proportional to the number of software components delivered.

- Each component may be structurally different from all other components.

It is a central idea in OOD that the internals of a class are not visible to the users of that class (an idea violated by the provision of the **friend** keyword in C++). This can easily lead the designer of a class to conclude that the internals can be implemented in his own idiosyncratic style and, provided the class fulfills its contract with its clients, nobody will care. This is clearly an unsafe conclusion. Anyone who has ever been given the task of maintaining a piece of software will realize that the amount of time expended in trying to understand why the software looks the way it does typically exceeds that expended in making the required changes. This phenomenon is simply a consequence of the decision to iterate the design process over all software components, effectively making every component a special case.

We will describe an alternative to this iterative approach to development, namely recursive development. It is founded on the principle that the rules defining how to construct each software component are expressed once only and are applied globally to all components. The rules are expressed in the form of a software architecture. The key issues to be addressed when developing a software architecture will be presented in the context of recursive development (Shlaer 1990), which provides a framework for system development, and object-oriented analysis (Shlaer 1988, 1992), which offers a formalism for describing a particular domain. Therefore, before discussing software architectures in detail, the principles of recursive development and object-oriented analysis (OOA) will be introduced.

RECURSIVE DEVELOPMENT

Recursive development is a system development process that can be summarized as in Figure 8.1.

Domain Partitioning

Domains are distinct subject matter areas that can and should be analyzed separately. Each domain to be analyzed comprises a number of individual components, or objects in the OOA sense, but the domain can be reused *as a whole*, not on a component-by-component basis. The benefits of reuse at such a high level are clear. The cost of cataloging and the time taken to integrate domains to form a complete system are significantly lower than those associated with component-level reuse. The domain chart shown in Figure 8.2 provides a graphical summary of the chosen domains and their dependencies.

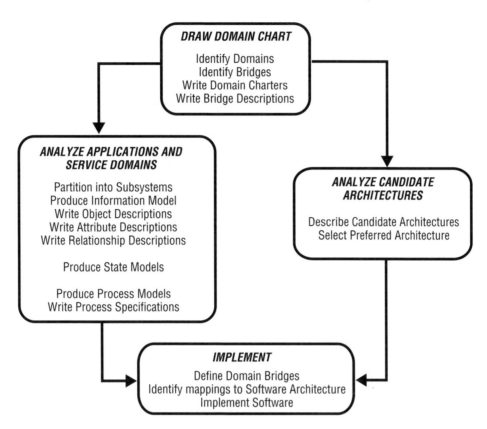

FIGURE 8.1. The recursive development life cycle.

Domain Analysis

The formalism chosen for the analysis can be selected on the basis of indigenous expertise within the organization, available CASE tools, and other constraints. In this sense, recursive development represents a clear decoupling of method from notation, two distinct ideas that are often jumbled together. There is, however, a constraint on the quality of the chosen analysis formalism, in that it must be sufficiently precise to allow mappings to be defined from the components of the analysis notation onto components of the chosen software architecture. This immediately rules out a number of historically popular analysis formalisms, notably narrative English text and data flow diagrams. For the purposes of this chapter, it is assumed that object-oriented analysis is the chosen analysis formalism.

For the purposes of performing recursive development, domains are categorized into four groups:

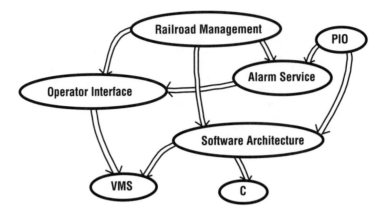

FIGURE 8.2. The domain chart.

- Application domain
- Service domains
- Software architecture domain
- Implementation domain

APPLICATION DOMAIN

The analysis of the application domain is comparable to the ideas of logical or essential models from earlier analysis and design methods (Ward 1985; DeMarco 1978). The purpose of the analysis of the application domain is to capture knowledge and an understanding of the problem being considered. The subject matter is that of the end user and not the system developer.

SERVICE DOMAINS

Service domains represent subject matters that are largely independent of the application, but that are required to support the application. Examples of common service domains include:

- **Operator interface.** It is possible and desirable to formalize the characteristics and behavior of screens, windows, icons, scroll bars, and so on without alluding to the application to be supported.
- **Physical input/output.** At a low level, this domain typically comprises input and output registers, and analog-to-digital and digital-to-analog converters. At a higher level, communications protocol standards are covered, including the OSI seven-layer model for telecommunications and data bus standards for military applications.
- **Alarms.** Many systems have a requirement to inform operators of alarm conditions.

- **Recording and playback.** This domain provides services to permit recording of transactions, events, and user interactions for later playback and analysis.

From this set of examples, it can be seen that service domains provide potential for reuse at a high level. This is because they are not polluted with knowledge of the application that will use their services. The purpose of analysis in the service domains is not always the same as in the application domain. Analysis of the application domain develops an understanding of the real world, whereas analysis of a service domain may require the creation of an abstract world. The analysis in these circumstances states the policies of that abstract world for others to understand. The development of an innovative operator interface would fall into this category. Of course, the subject matters of some service domains (e.g., communications protocols) are clearly defined and creativity is neither required nor permitted.

SOFTWARE ARCHITECTURE DOMAIN
This domain will be considered in detail later.

IMPLEMENTATION DOMAINS
Implementation domains typically include programming languages, run-time systems, and operating systems. These are rarely subjected to a formal analysis, as they are usually detailed in reference manuals and standards. It is important, however, to have a good understanding of the facilities provided by the implementation domains because elements of the other domains will use these domains.

By convention, the domain chart (Figure 8.2) has the application domain at the top, then service, architecture, and implementation domains proceeding down the chart in that order. The top of the chart then represents the most specialized and real-world notions within the system and the bottom represents the most reusable and computer-oriented notions. The arrows connecting domains represent bridges and indicate that the higher (client) domain requires services of the lower (server) domain. The bridges formalize the mappings between domains and will be discussed later.

Object-Oriented Analysis

Object-oriented analysis (OOA) is a formalism for analyzing the content of any domain. It is founded upon the well-established notion of three viewpoints, but these viewpoints are more convincingly integrated than has been the case in previous methods. The organization of the three viewpoints within OOA is based upon the information model (Figure 8.3).

Each object (analogous to an *entity* in other methods) that has dynamic behavior will have a state model (or entity life history). The Moore finite state model is used, which specifies processes to be executed on entry to each state (rather than on transitions à la Mealy). Therefore, a process model can be developed for each state showing the data

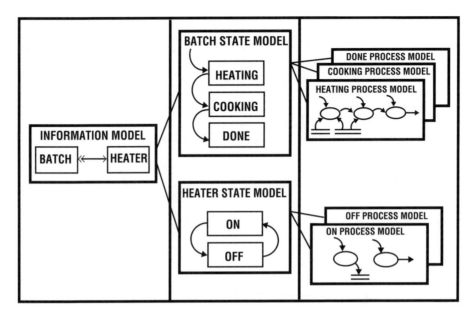

FIGURE 8.3. Object-oriented analysis model organization.

dependences between the processes in that state. In many cases, however, the actions specified in the state models require no further elaboration.

The relative importance of the three viewpoints is quite clear: The information model takes priority, the state model is second, and the process model is relegated to third place. This simply reflects the capacity of the notations to describe large and complex subject matters clearly. Note that the analyst does not have the discretion to build or organize the models in any other way. This contributes significantly to the precision of the analysis models.

SPECIFICATION OF SOFTWARE ARCHITECTURE

The software architecture domain proclaims and enforces the system-wide rules regarding the organization and access of data and the overall control of the system as a whole. The software architecture can also be viewed as a virtual machine layer that isolates the application and service domains from the implementation domains. This viewpoint can be seen on the domain chart (Figure 8.2).

The architecture domain is not real-world based. It is largely created by proficient designers and is potentially very reusable. By stating and enforcing system-wide policies, it is possible to create uniform, coherent, and consistent designs. Architectures can be compared, contrasted, measured, and subsequently tuned to ensure compliance with performance and resource requirements. The system developer can have a set of architectures to choose from, each with particular characteristics: some highly fault tolerant, some optimized for high-speed responses to stimuli. Architectures can be developed to exploit the features of programming languages from BASIC to Eiffel. Architectures avoid the temptation to slide into unproductive arguments about whether object-oriented design is better than structured design.

Off-the-shelf architectures are already available. A key element of methods like Modular Approach to Software Construction, Operation and Test (MASCOT), and Hierarchical Object-Oriented Design (HOOD) (CRI 1989) is that they are packaged with a software architecture. The weakness of these approaches is that they propose a single architecture that may not be appropriate to particular applications. For example, HOOD proposes an architecture that exploits Ada tasking — which is fine if you are able to use Ada tasking to the extent that HOOD requires. If the designer can't afford that many tasks, HOOD ceases to be an appropriate architecture.

Much of system development today is performed without any formal notion of architecture. Each designer uses his or her own understanding of what is required and then individually creates a design to implement it. Each component is lovingly handcrafted. The resulting system has two undesirable qualities:

- The components do not fit together properly, giving rise to the need for a software integration phase.
- Each component has a different internal structure, making the system harder to understand and, therefore, more costly to maintain.

The first aspect of a software architecture to consider is the organization and access of data. The concern here is specifically with persistent data, that is, data that must survive beyond the execution of a single module, but not necessarily beyond the execution of the program.

Persistent Data

ORGANIZATION OF PERSISTENT DATA

In defining the policies to be adopted in terms of the structure and storage of persistent data, there are obviously many possibilities. One widely used policy is that "all persistent data shall be stored as records in a database." Another approach is to use the persistent data features of programming languages, such as FORTRAN common block and C static. Although the use of programming language features specifies a mechanism for storing persistent data, it does little to specify the organization of that data, and most programming languages leave the developer free to choose one of myriad possible approaches. Many common problems stem from the fact that each developer does choose "one of the myriad" — unfortunately it is usually different from the one chosen by his or her colleagues.

One of the benefits of a formalized analysis method like object-oriented analysis is that it identifies the data that needs to be persistent. For example, the formalism identifies the following sources of persistent data:

- The attribute values of object instances
- The state transition table for each object
- The set of allowable events for each object
- The set of creation states and events for each object
- Current time
- Timers

Access to Persistent Data

The next stage is to establish the policies to be adopted for access to persistent data. Again, there are many possibilities, some of which are clear-cut and others vague. If the policy on data organization is to use a database, then access is likely to be through an appropriate query language. If the persistent data features of a programming language are being used, then there will be some restrictions on access due to the scoping and visibility rules of the language, but in general little guidance is offered to the designer. The key concept in programming languages that provides control over organization and access to data is encapsulation.

The use of the term *encapsulation* here simply refers to the grouping of the operations with the data they access. This must be achieved by some mechanism that ensures only access to the data is via the access operations. This mechanism is provided by, but is not exclusive to, object-oriented programming languages. Page-Jones (1980) introduced an encapsulation mechanism, the information cluster, into structured design. Encapsulation is possible in languages like C and in some versions of Pascal. The benefits of encapsulation, abstraction, and information hiding have been elaborated many times. This chapter will focus on the effective application of encapsulation and will not seek to justify it yet again.

It is important to note that a decision to abandon encapsulation in favor of holding all persistent data in a global data area is still an architecture, since rules can be specified for mapping the persistent data elements of the analysis onto structures in the global area.

If a decision is made to use encapsulation, perhaps to exploit the features of the chosen implementation language, then the basis of encapsulation must be stated. Again the OOA formalism helps. The analysis models comprehensively define the structure and organization of data within each domain. From the sources of persistent data listed in the previous section the encapsulations in Table 8.1 can be identified.

These basic encapsulations act as building blocks and can be used over and over. It is practical to consider their implementation in the chosen language and specify them as

TABLE 8.1. Encapsulation operations.

Data	Encapsulating Operations
Attribute values of object instances	Instance operations
State transition table for each object	State machine operations
Allowable events for each object	Event validation operations
Creation states and events for each object	Creation state operations
Current time	Current time operations
Timers	Timer operations

templates. Better still, they can be implemented as generics in languages like Ada and Eiffel. This is illustrated with an Ada generic for the state transition table (Figure 8.4).

HIGHER LEVEL ENCAPSULATIONS

It is quite reasonable to specify an architecture using these basic encapsulations. However, the architecture can be further refined to exploit the fact that in object-oriented analysis there are only three different sorts of object, namely active, passive, and monitor (Shlaer 1992). To consider just one of them, an active object has a state model that characterizes its dynamic behavior, and an instance of that state model (called a *state machine*) is associated with each instance of the object. Active objects interact by sending and receiving events. An active object would typically contain at least the first four basic encapsulations identified above. It is therefore possible to develop a higher encapsulation that is a template for an active object. This encapsulation will use the basic encapsulations and provide the template operations on the active object as a whole.

Again, the mapping from elements of the analysis models to elements of the architecture can be specified. The arrows from application and service domains to the software architecture on the domain chart (Figure 8.2) summarize this mapping. The arrow from software architecture to programming language summarizes the mapping elements of the architecture to elements of code as illustrated by the Ada example (Figure 8.4).

Overall Control of the System

The rules defining organization and access of data form the first part of the software architecture. The second part addresses flow of control through the system. There are two separate but linked aspects to this:

- Communication between objects (in the OOA sense)
- Tasking and concurrency

COMMUNICATION BETWEEN OBJECTS

The OOA formalism identifies two forms of intercommunication between objects:

- An asynchronous form in which objects can send and receive events
- A synchronous form in which an object can access the attributes of another object without sending an event

```
generic

  type EVENT_SET is (<>);
  -- the generic actual parameter is to be an enumerated type containing
  -- all of the events the given object responds to.

  type CELL is (<>);
  -- the generic actual parameter is to be an enumerated type containing
  -- all of the states of the given object
  -- plus cant_happen and event_ignored.

  type STATE is (<>);
  -- the generic actual parameter is to be a subtype of cell containing
  -- all of the states of the given object
  -- but not including cant_happen and event_ignored.

  CANT_HAPPEN : CELL;
  EVENT_IGNORED : CELL;
package STATE_TRANSITION_TABLE is

  type STT-CELLS is array (STATE range <>,EVENT_SET range <>) of CELL;

  procedure CREATE (STT_FRAME : STT_CELLS);

  procedure ADD_TRANSITION ( EVENT :           in EVENT_SET;
                             CURRENT_STATE :   in STATE;
                             NEXT_STATE :      in CELL    ) ;

  procedure FIND_TRANSITION ( EVENT :          in EVENT_SET;
                              CURRENT_STATE :  in STATE;
                              NEXT_STATE :     out CELL    ) ;
                              IS_A_NEW_STATE : out BOOLEAN    ) ;
end STATE_TRANSITION_TABLE,
```

FIGURE 8.4. Ada generic package for encapsulated state transition table.

```
package body STATE_TRANSITION_TABLE is

  STT_STATES : STT_CELLS(STATE,EVENT_SET);

  procedure  REPORT_EVENT_CANT_HAPPEN ( EVENT :  in  EVENT_SET;
                                       CURRENT_STATE : in STATE)
                                       is separate;

  -- the state transition table can be set up by writing the whole table
  procedure CREATE STT_FRAME : STT_CELLS) is
  begin
    STT_STATES := STT_frame;
  end CREATE;

  -- or by adding individual transitions : for this to be used the table would
  -- have to be initialised as all can't happen or all event ignored

  procedure ADD_TRANSITION (EVENT;             in EVENT_SET;
                            CURRENT_STATE;     in STATE;
                            NEXT_STATE;        in CELL   ) is
  begin
    STT_STATES (CURRENT_STATE, EVENT) := NEXT_STATE;
  end ADD_TRANSITION;

    --This procedure indexes into the table with event and current state and
    -- returns the new state if there is one.

  procedure FIND_TRANSITION (EVENT:             in EVENT_SET;
                             CURRENT_STATE:     in STATE;
                             NEXT_STATE:        out CELL;
                             IS_A_NEW_STATE:    out BOOLEAN  ) is
  begin

    if STT_STATES (CURRENT_STATE, EVENT) = EVENT_IGNORED  then
      IS_A_NEW_STATE:= FALSE;
      NEXT_STATE := STT_STATES (CURRENT_STATE, EVENT);
    elsif STT_STATES (CURRENT_STATE, EVENT) = CANT_HAPPEN then
        IS_A_NEW_STATE:= FALSE;
        NEXT_STATE:= STT_STATES (CURRENT_STATE, EVENT) ;
        REPORT_EVENT_CANT_HAPPEN (EVENT , CURRENT_STATE) ;
    else
        IS_A_NEW_STATE:= TRUE;
        NEXT_STATE:= STT_STATES (CURRENT_STATE, EVENT) ;
    end  if;
  end  FIND_TRANSITION;
end  STATE_TRANSITION_TABLE;
```

Object-oriented analysis defines rules relating to event ordering and data consistency. The architecture must provide mechanisms that support both forms while preserving the rules of the OOA formalism. Interestingly, it is not necessary for one mechanism to be asynchronous and the other synchronous to preserve the rules. Both forms can be mapped onto fully synchronous communication, such as a normal subprogram call.

Possible mechanisms within the architecture for event communication range from the subprogram call mentioned above, through encapsulated event queues, to using features of the underlying operating system. Each of the mechanisms can be measured, in terms of storage required to implement and time taken to send an event. This information can be fed into the consideration of the resource and performance requirements at all early stage. The appropriate architecture can then be chosen to meet the resource and performance requirements.

TASKING AND CONCURRENCY

The software architecture also defines the policy of the extent to which concurrency will be exploited. The whole system implemented as a single thread of control (single program) is obviously the simplest case. In the more general case elements of the analysis can be allocated to different tasks to a very fine level of granularity. Rather than listing dozens of tasking strategies, we shall consider a small number and look at their consequences.

- **A task for each instance of each object.** This approach mirrors the concurrency of the real world as accurately as possible, but even for fairly small problems it could result in hundreds or thousands of tasks!
- **A task for each object.** By handling all of the instances of a single object in a single task, the number of tasks required drops drastically while preserving the essence of the concurrency in the real world. This is a popular approach.
- **A task for some of the instances of each object.** In this architecture, the instances of a single object are distributed over several tasks. If those separate tasks are then run on separate processors, the architecture exhibits graceful degradation. If a processor fails, then only a subset of the instances are lost and it may even be possible to reestablish those instances on the remaining processors.
- **A task containing some states of many objects.** This further distribution strategy allows for optimized stimulus response performance. If the relevant states of all the objects in a stimulus response thread are placed in a single task the architecture will deliver the minimum response time.

There are obviously many others. The key point is to notice how formalizing the idea of architecture permits discussion of various characteristics of a system without reference to an application. Effort can be focused on optimizing and tuning the architecture rather than interfering with individual code units. This is more cost-effective and retains the uniform and coherent end result.

This chapter has introduced some of the primary features of software architectures, but by no means all of them. Architectures are to some extent chosen to exploit features of the selected implementation language. So architectural features that make use of inheritance, for example, would be pertinent for implementations using object-oriented programming languages. An example of such an architecture is described in Shlaer (1992).

THE IMPACT OF RECURSIVE DEVELOPMENT

The recursive development life cycle varies significantly from the traditional life cycle models. This is primarily a result of the distinction between analysis and design. Most traditional methods distinguish between these in a number of similar ways, for example:

- Analysis has to do with *what*, design has to do with *how*.
- Analysis has to do with the problem, design has to do with computers.

Recursive development makes the distinction by stating that analysis is the study of any subject matter, and design is the specification of a software architecture and mappings onto the components of that architecture. This is simply a recognition of the fact that any subject matter that needs to be understood is a candidate for analysis. Therefore, a developer using recursive development treats all subject matter, computer-oriented or otherwise, in a uniform way.

With existing methods, which for comparison's sake we refer to as *iterative development*, the phases of design and coding involve taking each element of the analysis and manually transforming it into its corresponding design element and then into code. In recursive development, the structure of the design is formalized as a set of blueprints in the software architecture domain. Of course, this domain must be specified, but the process of design is effectively reduced to that of specifying the mappings between domains. A comparison of iterative development and recursive development, in terms of phases and effort, is presented in Tables 8.2 and 8.3.

TABLE 8.2. **Summary of life cycle phases.**

Iterative Development	Recursive Development
FOR each requirement	FOR each requirement
Analyze	Analyze
Design	Execute analysis model (test)
Code	END FOR;
Execute code (test)	Define design rules
END FOR;	Test rules
Integrate software	Apply rules to generate code

TABLE 8.3.   Summary of effort required.

Phase	Effort for Iterative Development	Effort for Recursive Development
Analysis	≈ Complexity of requirements	≈ Complexity of requirements
Design	≈ Complexity of requirements	Fixed (decreasing each project)
Code		
Production	≈ Complexity of requirements	Fixed (potentially automatic)
Testing	≈ Complexity of requirements	≈ Complexity of requirements

When performing iterative development, the effort required for the phases of analysis, design, coding, software integration, and acceptance is always proportional to the size and complexity of the problem. In the early use of recursive development there will be no existing service domains, so the analysis effort will still be proportional to problem size and complexity. However, the effort to specify the mappings from application and service domains to the architecture varies little with problem size and the mapping into code is considerably faster because it is template-based. The rigor of domain analysis and specification of bridges will reduce software integration effort massively. The effort required for acceptance test clearly remains proportional to problem size, since we still have to demonstrate compliance with each requirement.

With the repeated use of recursive development, an organization can expect to build up a set of mature and reusable service domains, a set of well-understood and quantified architectures, and an established set of mappings between the lower-level domains. This will greatly reduce the system development effort and significantly reduce the elapsed time to complete a project. Experience has shown that the identification of service domains can even produce significant savings in the first project because a set of work packages that have traditionally been partitioned across teams were found by domain analysis to share a common underlying behavior.

CONCLUSION

This chapter has introduced the recursive development process involving the use of object-oriented analysis. It has concentrated on the new and powerful idea of specifying software architectures. The combination of a rigorous analysis formalism, the specification of an architecture, and the specification of mappings between domains opens up the possibility of a new dimension of CASE tool support. If the CASE tool understands the semantics of the domains and mappings then the potential is there for code generation to be elevated to system generation.

REFERENCES

CRI-CISI-INGENIERIE-MATRA (1989) Hierarchical Object Oriented Design (HOOD) Manual, Issue 3.0.

DeMarco, T. (1978) *Structured Analysis and System Specification*, Prentice-Hall, Englewood Cliffs, NJ.

Page-Jones, M. (1980) *The Practical Guide to Structured System Design*, Prentice-Hall, Englewood Cliffs, NJ.

Shlaer, S. and S.J. Mellor (1988) *Object-Oriented Systems Analysis — Modeling the World in Data*, Prentice-Hall, Englewood Cliffs, NJ.

Shlaer, S. and S.J. Mellor (1990) Recursive design, *Computer Language*.

Shlaer, S. and S.J. Mellor (1992) *Object Lifecycles — Modeling the World in States*, Prentice-Hall, Englewood Cliffs, NJ.

Ward, P.T. and S.J. Mellor (1985–86) *Structured Development for Real-Time Systems*, Vol. 1, "Introduction and Tools" (1985); Vol. 2, "Essential Modeling Techniques" (1985); Vol. 3, "Implementation Modeling Techniques" (1986), Yourdon Press, Prentice-Hall, Englewood Cliffs, NJ.

chapter 9

The Booch Method:
Process and Pragmatics

GRADY BOOCH   *RATIONAL*

The use of object technology has wide-reaching implications for any development organization that undertakes to use this relatively new paradigm. Fortunately, sufficient experience with this technology has developed for us to be able to draw conclusions about practices that distinguish successful from unsuccessful endeavors. In this chapter we examine some of these pragmatic implications

INTRODUCTION

Software development is hard work. Any significant piece of software requires the intense and cooperative intellectual effort of a focused team of developers. No programming language, tool, or method can magically replace the basic human creativity needed to successfully design, implement, and deploy a complex software system. Indeed, this complexity is inherent. It results from the combinatorial explosion of component interactions and the multitude of degrees of freedom that exist in all nontrivial software systems.

The ever-growing capabilities of our hardware and an increasing social awareness of the utility of computers create tremendous pressure to automate more and more applications of ever greater complexity. As computer professionals, we strive to build systems that are useful and that work; as software engineers, we confront the task of creating these complex systems with scarce computing and human resources.

Object-oriented technology has evolved in diverse segments of the computer sciences as a means of managing this inherent complexity. More recently, the theory of object-oriented technology has matured sufficiently to influence the practice of software development. In turn, there has been an accumulation of experience in the practice that allows us to be more prescriptive about the theory.

Over the past ten years, we have developed, contributed to, and influenced many different and complex software systems worldwide. We don't claim to have all the answers with regard to the many issues of software development. However, we have observed a number of practices that can be correlated to successful systems, as well as many practices that generally lead to failure, however that failure may be measured.

In this chapter, we explain the essence of these recommended practices.

ASSUMPTIONS

As pragmatic developers, we are primarily interested in building industrial-strength software. This means that we are largely uninterested in simpler software systems, which in general are those that can be constructed by one or two developers, represent a relatively small investment of time, have deliverables typically consisting of little more than the generated code, and have a short useful lifespan. This is not to say that such software systems are utterly insignificant; indeed, each may involve a novel intellectual contribution. However, they generally are not pivotal to any business concern, and their production is highly dependent on the unique individual skills of their developers, requiring little if any discipline in their creation. Indeed, many such software systems can be developed using very sloppy techniques without any material impact.

The kinds of projects in which we are interested are dominated by issues of scale, requiring a mature, repeatable process to generate a family of programs (Humphrey 1989). Such projects can be characterized by a number of common properties:

- Their size and complexity requires the involvement of a team of developers.
- The generation of a production-quality release involves a year or more of effort.
- In addition to the generated code that forms the production release, there are many ancillary products, including the documentation of strategic and tactical design decisions, end-user documentation, prototypes, development, test and release scaffolding, and components that may be reused in generating other systems.
- Their useful lifespan typically transcends the original development team. Indeed, most critical software systems are never thrown away because they represent a significant capital investment. Such systems tend to evolve over time, as part of what is typically — but inaccurately — called *software maintenance*.

All such projects require the use of sound software engineering principles to intelligently balance the competing, sometimes contradictory, and usually incomplete requirements that frequently tend to change over the lifetime of the project.

It is to these kinds of problems that we turn our attention.

FIRST PRINCIPLES

A successful project is one whose deliverables satisfy and possibly exceed the customer's expectations, is developed in a timely and economical fashion, and is resilient to change and adaptation.

By this measure, we have observed that three fundamental principles are common to virtually all the successful complex software systems we have encountered:

- The use of object-oriented decomposition
- The existence of a strong architectural vision
- The application of a well-managed iterative and incremental development lifecycle

We acknowledge that many simpler systems have been successfully deployed using other approaches. However, let there be no misunderstanding: The approaches to simple system development do not scale well to more complex applications. On the other hand, the principles we describe herein do scale down to smaller systems and, hence, are applicable to a very wide range of problems.

Object-Oriented Decomposition

In traditional structured approaches to development, the algorithm serves as the fundamental unit of decomposition. This paradigm is supported and encouraged by the fact that in many older programming languages, the primary structural element is the subprogram.

In contrast, the fundamental unit of decomposition in the object-oriented paradigm is the class, which represents the structure and behavior common to a logical collection of objects. This paradigm is directly supported by the facilities of object-based and object-oriented programming languages.

In the object-oriented paradigm, we view the world as a collection of objects that cooperate with one another to achieve some desired functionality. These collaborative structures form the basic mechanisms of the system that together yield its outwardly observable behavior. Similarly, we organize the classes of these objects into hierarchies, so as to exploit the commonality in their structure and behavior and to achieve an intelligent separation of concerns.

An object-oriented decomposition allows us to view a system from several different yet unified perspectives. Its logical model allows us to consider the existence of the system's key abstractions and mechanisms; its physical model describes how these elements are packaged. Similarly, the static view of these elements captures the structural aspects of the architecture, whereas the dynamic view indicates how these elements behave individually and collectively to satisfy the functional requirements of the system under development.

Object-oriented decomposition is based on the principles of abstraction, encapsulation, modularity, and hierarchy. Object-oriented analysis applies these principles to describe the requirements of a system from the perspective of the classes and objects found in the vocabulary of the problem space. Similarly, object-oriented design applies these same principles to craft the architecture necessary to satisfy these requirements.

It is important to realize that, in object-oriented systems, the class is a necessary but insufficient element of decomposition. For all nontrivial systems, the problem is not to devise individual classes; rather, the problem involves inventing societies of classes, whose instances collaborate with one another. This indeed is the problem of scale: We must focus on building categories of classes and mechanisms as well as subsystems of modules, not just individual classes and files.

Recommended practices include:

- Apply object-oriented decomposition, using the principles of abstraction, encapsulation, modularity, and hierarchy. Such decomposition yields architectures that consist of collections of cooperative objects whose classes are organized into hierarchies.
- Recognize that the class is a necessary but insufficient element of decomposition. This means that development must involve crafting societies of classes, not just individual abstractions.

Architectural Vision

The architecture of an object-oriented software system encompasses the individual classes, objects, and modules from which the system is composed, together with the coherent organization of these elements into higher-level structures.

The architecture of a software system is largely irrelevant to its end users. However, as Stroustrup points out, having a clean internal structure is essential in constructing a system that is understandable, can be extended and reorganized, and is maintainable and testable. It is only through having a clear sense of a system's architecture that it is possible to identify common abstractions and mechanisms. Exploiting this commonality leads to systems that are simpler and therefore smaller and more reliable.

Given the degrees of freedom inherent in software, there is no "right" way to build any system. For any given application domain, there are certainly some profoundly stupid ways, and occasionally some very elegant ways, to develop a solution. How then do we distinguish a good architecture from a bad one?

Fundamentally, good architectures tend to be object-oriented. This is not to say that all object-oriented architectures are good or that only object-oriented architectures are good. However, it can be shown that the application of the principles that underlie object-oriented decomposition tend to yield architectures that exhibit several desirable properties of organized complexity.

In short, good software architectures tend to have several attributes in common:

- They are constructed in well-defined layers of abstraction. Each layer represents a coherent abstraction provided through a well-defined and controlled interface, and is built on equally well-defined and controlled facilities at lower levels of abstraction.
- There is a clear separation of concerns between the interface and implementation of each layer, making it possible to change the implementation of a layer without violating the assumptions made by its clients.
- The architecture is simple. Common behavior is achieved through common mechanisms.

We make a distinction between strategic and tactical architectural decisions. A strategic decision involves the organization of the higher-level structures of an architecture. Approaches to error detection and recovery, user-interface paradigms, database access, and real-time scheduling of activities all represent strategic architectural decisions. Correspondingly, a tactical decision involves the details of a layer's interface and implementation. The types, function signatures, and algorithms of a layer all represent tactical architectural decisions.

We cannot say it strongly enough: To be successful, a software-development project must have a clear vision of the system's strategic and tactical architecture. As Stroustrup observes, "It is a recipe for failure not to have an individual or group with the explicit task of maintaining the integrity of the design."

Recommended practices include:

- Seek to craft systems that are constructed in well-defined layers of abstraction, for which there is a clear separation of concerns between the interface and implementation of each layer. Build simple architectures in which common behavior is achieved through common mechanisms.
- At all times, maintain a clear vision of the system's strategic and tactical architecture.

Iterative and Incremental Life Cycle

The process that leads to the construction of object-oriented architectures tends to be both iterative and incremental in nature. The process is iterative in the sense that it involves the successive refinement of an object-oriented architecture, through which we feed the experience of each prototype back into the analysis and design of the problem. The process is incremental in the sense that each pass through the analysis/design/implementation cycle leads us to gradually refine the elements of our architecture, ultimately converging on the strategic and tactical design decisions that meet the end user's real (and usually unstated) requirements and yet is simple, reliable, and adaptable.

Prototyping plays a fundamental role in this life cycle. As viewed from outside the development project, a stream of prototypes emerges as a major product of the process. Some model the external behavior of the system; others model the internal architecture. The more comprehensive prototypes integrate the results of these others and ultimately evolve into the released production system. This incremental evolution of prototypes into the production system thus becomes the focus of most of the development activities and serves as a means of continuously integrating and measuring the products of the design.

The construction of a prototype must never be allowed to become a veiled form of hacking. Rather, each prototype must be undertaken for well-understood reasons. The best prototypes allow the development team to:

- Obtain deeper information and understanding about the requirements of a system
- Determine whether certain functionality can be achieved
- Assess the risk associated with a certain design
- Serve as a vehicle for communicating the design within the team and to customers
- Assess performance, cost, reliability, and adaptability

For a few limited application domains, the problem being solved may be well defined, with many different implementations already crafted. Here, it is possible to codify the development process: The designers of a new system in such a domain already understand what the important abstractions are. They already know what mechanisms ought to be employed, and they generally know the range of behavior that is expected of such a system. Creativity is still important in such a design process, but here the problem is sufficiently constrained as to already address most of the important design issues.

Most industrial-strength software problems are not like this: most involve the balancing of a unique set of functional and performance requirements, and this task demands the full creative energies of the development team. Furthermore, any human activity that requires creativity and innovation ultimately involves an iterative and incremental process and relies on the experience, intelligence, and talent of each team member; it is impossible to provide any cookbook recipes (Booch 1991).

Clearly, however, we desire to be prescriptive. Otherwise, it would be impossible for us to ever evolve a mature, repeatable development process for any organization. It is for this reason that we earlier spoke of having a well-managed incremental and iterative development process — well-managed in the sense that the process can be controlled and measured, yet still free enough to encourage creativity. It is to this topic that we turn our attention in the next section.

Recommended practices include:

- Apply an iterative and incremental life cycle to successively refine the object-oriented architecture, feeding the experience of each prototype back into the analysis and design of the problem.
- Focus most of the development activities on the creation of a stream of prototypes, through which the products of the design are continuously integrated and measured. Certain prototypes should ultimately evolve into the released production system.
- Undertake each prototype for well-understood reasons.

THE DEVELOPMENT LIFE CYCLE

Any organization that desires to be successful in crafting complex software systems must have a mature, repeatable process for development. At first, this may seem to conflict with our recommendation to embrace an iterative and incremental life cycle: Ultimately, software design is indeed neither a top-down nor a bottom-up activity. However, if we are to ever control our software-development projects, we must reconcile this round-trip gestalt design approach with more rigid management practices.

For this reason, we distinguish between the macro and the micro process of software development. The macro process is more closely related to the traditional waterfall life cycle, and it serves as the controlling framework for the micro process. The micro process is more closely related to Boehm's spiral model, and it serves as the framework for an iterative and incremental approach to development.

We must emphasize that every project is unique, and hence project managers must strike a balance between formality and informality in the development process. For less complex applications, developed by a tightly knit team of highly experienced developers, too much formality would be constraining. For very complex applications, developed by a large team of developers who probably are distributed geographically as well as chronologically, too little formality will lead to chaos.

Macro Process

The macro process of software development generally commences with the acceptance of the system's requirements. Good requirements should specify the system's:

- External behavior
- Constraints
- Responses to undesirable events

and little more. Requirements that specify the details of a design have gone beyond their scope.

We do acknowledge that requirements are, by their very nature, incomplete. Users are generally unable to articulate their true and detailed requirements until they can observe a running system. For this reason, we recommend the successive refinements of prototypes as a means of focusing the user's requirements and directing the ongoing analysis activity. Domain analysis, through which we discover the vocabulary of the problem space, and scenarios are particularly effective in elucidating the user's real requirements. From this point, the macro process tends to track the following activities:

- Devise and prototype a preliminary software architecture
- Release intermediate architectural and behavioral prototype(s)
- Assemble production release(s)

During this macro process, many more prototypes will be produced, focused on the design of specific behavioral and architectural aspects of the system.

The major products of the macro process are the comprehensive prototypes that ultimately evolve into the production system, together with formal reviews of these prototypes and design documentation. Progress is measured through these formal reviews relative to the degree to which each prototype's goals were met.

Micro Process

The micro process of software development is largely driven by the requirements of the stream of prototypes and releases that emerge from the macro process. This micro process tends to track the following activities:

- Identify the classes and objects at a given level of abstraction
- Identify the semantics of these classes and objects
- Identify the relationships among these classes and objects
- Specify the interface and then the implementation of these classes and objects

This process is by its very nature iterative and incremental.

The major products of the micro process include prototypes, as well as architectural and implementation design documents. Each of these products feeds into the next cycle of the micro process. Progress is determined by informal reviews and measures of completeness and stability.

Recommended practices include:

- Institute a well-defined macro and micro process of software development. Strike a suitable balance between formality and informality, adjusted to the nature of the problem as well as the development team.

- Employ requirements that specify the system's external behavior, constraints, and responses to undesirable events.
- Apply the following canonical macro process: Devise and prototype a software architecture, release intermediate architectural and behavioral prototypes, and assemble production releases.
- Apply the following canonical micro process of software development: Identify classes and objects at a given level of abstraction, specify their operations, identify their relationships, and then specify their interfaces and implementations.

PRAGMATICS

The successful development and deployment of a complex software system involves much more than just generating code. In this section, we examine the issues associated with the infrastructure of software development.

Management and Planning

Especially in the presence of an iterative and incremental life cycle, it is of paramount importance to have strong project leadership that actively manages and directs the project's activities. Foremost, this involves establishing concrete deliverables (mainly prototypes and documentation), measuring the results of these deliverables, and adjusting tasks, resources, and schedules to address the greatest risks to the project's success.

Externally, the major milestones that must be managed include the delivery of comprehensive prototypes and production releases, the production of documentation, and the conducting of formal reviews. Internally, many more prototypes, internal design documents, and informal reviews should be scheduled.

Walkthroughs of the architecture as well as the implementation are essential in building confidence in the quality of the products and in communicating the vision of the architecture to the entire team.

Recommended practices include:

- Establish concrete deliverables (mainly prototypes and documentation), measure the results of these deliverables, and be willing to adjust tasks, resources, and schedules according to the project's current risks.
- Conduct many formal as well as informal reviews of the architecture as well as the implementation.

Staffing

It is important to remember that development is ultimately a human endeavor. Developers are not interchangeable parts, and the successful development of any complex system requires the unique and varied skills of a focused team of people.

When staffing a development project, the following roles and responsibilities should be considered:

- *Project manager.* Responsible for the active management of the project's deliverables, tasks, resources, and schedules.
- *Project architect.* Responsible for evolving and maintaining the vision of the system's architecture. This typically is the responsibility of one or two particularly insightful individuals, but sometimes may be the shared responsibility of a larger group.
- *Requirements analyst.* Responsible for evolving and interpreting the end user's requirements; must be expert in the application domain; must not be isolated from the rest of the development team.
- *Subsystem lead.* Responsible for the design of an entire subsystem; devises, defends, and negotiates the subsystem's interface and directs its implementation; as the ultimate owner of the subsystem, is responsible for its testing and release.
- *Application engineer.* Responsible for the implementation of a subsystem, under the direction of the subsystem's lead; may do some class design but generally is responsible for implementing and unit-testing the classes and mechanisms designed by others on the team.
- *Reuse engineer.* Responsible for managing the project's libraries of components and designs; through participation in reviews and other development activities, must actively seek out opportunities for commonality and cause them to be exploited; often produces and adapts components for general use within the project or entire organization.
- *Quality assurance.* Responsible for measuring the products of the development personnel process; generally directs system-level testing of all prototypes and production releases.
- *Integration/release.* Responsible for assembling compatible versions of released personnel subsystems to form the delivered prototypes and production releases; responsible for maintaining configurations of released products.
- *Documenter.* Responsible for producing end-user documentation of the product and its design.
- *Toolsmith.* Responsible for creating and adapting software tools that facilitate the production of the project's deliverables, especially with regard to the generated code.
- *System administrator.* Responsible for managing the physical computing resources, including networks.

Not every project requires all of these roles. For small projects, many of these responsibilities may be shared by the same person; for larger projects, each role may represent an entire organization.

Recommended practices include:

- Always remember that development is a human activity, developers are not interchangeable parts.
- When staffing a project, consider all of the varied roles and responsibilities needed to populate the development team. For smaller projects, many of these responsibilities may be shared by the same person. For larger projects, each role may represent an entire organization.

Integration and Release Management

Real projects require the development of a family of programs. At any given time in the development process, there will be multiple prototypes and production releases, as well as development and test scaffolding. Most often, each developer will have his or her own executable views of the system under development.

The use of an interactive and incremental life cycle also means that there should never be a single "big bang" integration phase. Instead, integration should be continuous over the life cycle. There generally will be many smaller big bang events, usually marking the creation of another prototype or external release, but each of these events is generally incremental in nature, having evolved from an earlier release. This strategy actually reduces development risk, because it tends to accelerate the discovery of architectural and performance problems early in the development process.

Recommended practices include:

- Plan for the creation of a family of programs.
- Use the practice of continuous integration, whereby there is never a single "big bang" integration event.

Reuse

Reuse within a project or even an entire organization doesn't just happen; it must be institutionalized. This means that opportunities for reuse must be actively sought out and rewarded. Typically, this is best achieved by making certain individuals responsible for a reuse activity. Such an activity involves identifying opportunities for commonality, usually discovered through architectural and implementation reviews, and exploiting these opportunities, usually by producing new components or adapting existing ones. The reuse of these components then tends to suggest further improvements and generalizations.

Ultimately, reuse costs resources in the short term, but pays off in the long term. A reuse activity will be effective only in organizations that take a long-term view of software development and optimize resources for more than just the current project.

Recommended practices include:

- Institutionalize a reuse activity. Commission this activity to actively identify and exploit opportunities for reuse.
- Optimize resources for the entire organization, not just the current crisis. Only in this manner will a reuse activity have any impact.

Testing

Similar to the principle of continuous integration, testing also should be a continuous activity during the life cycle. In the context of an object-oriented architecture, testing must encompass at least three dimensions:

- *Unit testing.* Involves testing individual classes and mechanisms; is the responsibility of the application engineer.
- *Subsystem testing.* Involves testing a complete subsystem and its behavior; is the responsibility of the subsystem lead.
- *System testing.* Involves testing the system as a whole; is the responsibility of the quality-assurance team. System tests also typically are used as regression tests by the integration team when assembling new releases.

Testing should address not only the system's external behavior but the quality of the system's architecture as well. Recommended practices include:

- Conduct unit, subsystem, and system testing continuously throughout the development life cycle.
- Perform tests to address the system's external behavior as well as the quality of the system's architecture.

Quality Assurance and Metrics

The gathering of software metrics ultimately serves as a tool for the development team and end users to measure the progress of a project, together with the quality of the resulting products. Certain traditional metrics are directly applicable to object-oriented decomposition, and some new metrics are suggested.

In particular, the collection of defect-discovery rates is a most useful measure of the maturity of the architecture. "Bug hunts" should be scheduled, together with a formal alpha and beta testing program that exercises the prototypes and releases in the context of real users. Another important measure is the rate of change of class and subsystem interfaces; interfaces that are changing frequently are unstable and indicate that the design is not yet mature.

Certain other metrics are valuable, including counting classes and subsystems, measuring class and subsystem coupling, and computing complexity measures of individual classes and methods.

Recommended practices include:

- Actively gather software metrics to measure the progress of the project and the quality of its products. Defect-discovery rates and measures of stability, size, coupling, and complexity are generally useful metrics.

Documentation

The documentation of a system's architecture and implementation is important, but the production of such documents should never drive the development process (Parnas 1986). Documentation is an essential, although secondary, product of the development process. Another important principle to remember is that documents are living products that should be allowed to evolve together with the iterative and incremental evolution of the project's prototypes and releases. Together with the generated code, delivered documents serve as the basis of most formal and informal reviews.

What must be documented? Obviously, end-user documentation must be produced, instructing the user on the operation and installation of each release. In addition, architectural and implementation documentation must be generated to communicate design decisions to the development team and customers and to preserve information about all of the strategic architectural decisions, so that the system can be adapted readily.

In practice, the essential documentation of a system's architecture and implementation should include:

- Documentation of the high-level system architecture
- Documentation of the key abstractions and mechanisms in the architecture
- Documentation of scenarios that illustrate the behavior of key aspects of the system

The notation of the Booch method (1991) is particularly well-suited to expressing many of these details. Recommended practices include:

- Treat documentation as an essential, but secondary, product of the development process. The production of documentation should never drive the development process.

- Provide documentation of the system's architecture, key abstractions, mechanisms, and scenarios.

Tools

The rapid development of prototypes and releases requires development tools that offer rapid turnaround, especially for the edit/compile/execute/debug cycle. In addition, support must exist to capture, review, and browse the architecture. Configuration management and version control is also a key item in the tool suite, and it is necessary to keep track of the rapidly evolving configurations of a project's family of programs.

It is important to choose tools that scale well. A tool that works for one developer writing a small stand-alone application will not necessarily scale to production releases of more complex applications. Indeed, for every tool, there will be a threshold beyond which the tool's capacity is exceeded, causing its benefits to be greatly outweighed by its liabilities and clumsiness.

A programming language is in fact just a tool, but unfortunately the selection of a particular language for a given project is usually more of an emotional or political issue than a technical one.

Recommended practices include:

- Apply tools that scale well and offer rapid turnaround for the edit/compile/execute/debug cycle.
- Use tools to capture, review, and browse the architecture, as well as to manage the evolving configurations of a project's family of programs.

Technology Transfer

The effective use of the principles described in this chapter requires a change in attitude relative to traditional development techniques. This change will not happen overnight within a project, nor will it happen through a short training course. Furthermore, it is likely that some members of the development team will be unable to make the transition to these practices. This does not mean that these people are incompetent: They may indeed prove to be superior application engineers, but perhaps will be less effective as subsystem leads or architects.

Making the transition to these principles takes experience and talent. Plan on at least half a year for a developer to gain the skills necessary to become an adequate class designer. It generally takes a few years of experience in a given domain to become an adequate architect. Within any given company, there may be only a handful of master architects.

The most attractive feature of the division of roles and responsibilities described earlier is that this perspective acknowledges that development is a human activity and that different developers indeed have different skills. By institutionalizing these roles, the organization offers a meaningful career path for its technical personnel. Having senior members play the role of mentor to junior members is perhaps the most effective way to retain the organization's software-development experience. Recommended practices include:

- Recognize that applying these principles requires a change in attitude. Allow sufficient time for the team members to mature in their roles.

SPECIAL TOPICS

Certain development topics warrant special treatment, primarily because these issues tend to arise in every complex system.

User-Interface Design

The design of an effective user interface is still much more of an art than a science. For this domain, the application of prototyping is absolutely essential. Feedback must be gathered early and often from end users so the gestures, error behavior, and other paradigms of user interaction can be evaluated. The generation of scenarios is highly effective in driving the analysis of the user interface.

Database Design

Some applications involve a major database component; others may require integration with existing databases whose schemas cannot be changed, usually because of the existence of large amounts of data already populating the databases. For such domains, the principle of separation of concerns is directly applicable. It is best to encapsulate the access to all such databases inside the confines of well-defined interfaces. This principle is particularly important when mixing object-oriented decomposition with relational database technology. In the presence of an object-oriented database, the interface between the database and the rest of the application can be much more seamless, but it must be realized that object-oriented databases are more effective for object persistence and less so for massive data stores.

Real-Time Design

Real-time means different things in different domains. Real-time might denote subsecond response in user-centered systems and submicrosecond response in certain data-acquisition and control applications. It is important to realize that even for hard real-time systems, not every component of the system must (or can) be optimized. Indeed, for most complex systems, the greater risk is whether the system can be completed, not that it will perform within its performance requirements. For this reason, we warn against premature optimization. Focus on producing simple architectures, and the generation of prototypes will illuminate the performance bottlenecks of the system early enough to take corrective action.

Legacy-System Design

The strategy for coping with legacy systems is much like that of databases: Encapsulate access to the facilities of the legacy system within the confines of well-defined interfaces.

SUMMARY OF RECOMMENDED PRACTICES

- Apply object-oriented decomposition, using the principles of abstraction, encapsulation, modularity, and hierarchy. Such decomposition yields architectures that consist of collections of cooperative objects, whose classes are organized into hierarchies.
- Recognize that the class is a necessary but insufficient element of decomposition. This means that development must involve crafting societies of classes, not just individual abstractions.
- Seek to craft systems that are constructed in well-defined layers of abstraction, for which there is a clear separation of concerns between the interface and implementation of each layer; build simple architectures in which common behavior is achieved through common mechanisms.
- At all times, maintain a clear vision of the system's strategic and tactical architecture.
- Apply an iterative and incremental life cycle to successively refine the object-oriented architecture, feeding the experience of each prototype back into the analysis and design of the problem.
- Focus most of the development activities on the creation of a stream of prototypes, through which the products of the design are continuously integrated and measured. Certain prototypes should ultimately evolve into the released production system.
- Undertake each prototype for well-understood reasons.
- Institute a well-defined macro and micro process of software development. Strike a suitable balance between formality and informality, adjusted to the nature of the problem as well as the development team.
- Employ requirements that specify the system's external behavior, constraints, and responses to undesirable events.
- Apply the following canonical macro process: Devise and prototype software

architecture, release intermediate architectural and behavioral prototypes, and assemble production releases.

- Apply the following canonical micro process of software development: Identify classes and objects at a given level of abstraction, specify their operations, identify their relationships, and then specify their interfaces and implementations.
- Establish concrete deliverables (mainly prototypes and documentation), measure the results of these deliverables, and be willing to adjust tasks, resources, and schedules according to the project's current risks.
- Conduct many formal and informal reviews of both the architecture and the implementation.
- Always remember that development is a human activity. Developers are not interchangeable parts.
- When staffing a project, consider all of the varied roles and responsibilities needed to populate the development team. For smaller projects, many of these responsibilities may be shared by the same person. For larger projects, each role may represent an entire organization.
- Plan for the creation of a family of programs.
- Use the practice of continuous integration, whereby there is never a single "big bang" integration event.
- Institutionalize a reuse activity. Commission this activity to actively identify and exploit opportunities for reuse.
- Optimize resources for the entire organization, not just the current crisis. Only in this manner will a reuse activity have any impact.
- Conduct unit, subsystem, and system testing continuously throughout the development life cycle.
- Perform tests to address the system's external behavior as well as the quality of the system's architecture.
- Actively gather software metrics to measure the progress of the project and the quality of its products. Defect-discovery rates and measures of stability, size, coupling, and complexity are generally useful metrics.
- Treat documentation as an essential, but secondary, product of the development process. The production of documentation should never drive the development process.
- Provide documentation of the system's architecture, key abstractions, mechanisms, and scenarios.
- Apply tools that scale well and offer rapid turnaround for the edit/compile/execute/debug cycle.
- Use tools to capture, review, and browse the architecture, as well as to manage the evolving configurations of a project's family of programs.
- Recognize that applying these principles requires a change in attitude. Allow sufficient time for the team members to mature in their roles.

REFERENCES

Booch, G. (1991) *Object-Oriented Design with Applications*, Benjamin/Cummings, Menlo Park, CA.

Humphrey, W. (1989) *Managing the Software Process*, Addison-Wesley, Reading, MA.

Parnas, D., and P. Clements (1986) A rational design process: how and why to fake it. *IEEE Transactions on Software Engineering* SE-12(2).

chapter 10

The Coad/Yourdon Method: Simplicity, Brevity, and Clarity — Keys to Successful Analysis and Design

MARTIN RÖSCH   RÖSCH CONSULTING GMBH

Companies considering the adoption of object-oriented methods and tools face a considerable dilemma. Will a radical change in practice and approach, even if proven effective in the long-term, cause short-term problems in the initial projects that adopt it? Will the communication problems between old and new ways of thinking cancel out the perceived benefits?

Our experience in applying Coad/Yourdon object-oriented analysis and design, supported by OOATool and more recently by ObjecTool, indicates that the simplicity, brevity, and clarity of the approach enables it to overcome the problems of adoption in the shortest possible time. The focus on communication — between team members and between the team and users — is the essential element in obtaining benefits from a radically new approach, even in the very first project. Complexity is inherent to the application and the software; it should not be compounded by the choice of method, by multiple layers of models, or by unnecessary complexity of notation.

This chapter covers the discussion of both method and tool: OOATool and ObjecTool from Object International Inc. and the Coad/Yourdon method for object-oriented analysis and development (Coad 1991a, 1991b, 1993). OOATool and its successor ObjecTool (which covers object-oriented analysis, object-oriented design, and now object-oriented programming with C++ and Smalltalk code generation) is more than just a documentation tool. OOATool implements a specific method to support its notation and its underlying rules and to provide help with strategy. Both method and tool are needed since a method without a tool results in bureaucracy. A tool without a method, on the other hand, can lead to chaos. Using a tool with object-oriented analysis helps you to learn an object-oriented way of thinking — what Peter Coad refers to as "object think." It has proven its value, firstly for getting people acquainted with object orientation, and then for finding and documenting a stable architecture for the development of information systems.

The same notations, concepts, and approach are used for both analysis and design, and — most importantly — the model is consistent across these activities. While many methodologists ignore the border line between object-oriented analysis (OOA) and design (OOD), the Coad/Yourdon method makes a clear distinction between the two. Analysis is understanding and documenting the problem domain as it will be modeled by and known to the information system. Design, on the other hand, means inventing the mechanisms: adding the human interaction elements, specifying how and where (on which processors, processes or threads) processing will be carried out, and the choice and description of data management. This is reflected in the four-component model of object-oriented design in the method (Coad 1991b): human interaction component, problem domain component, task management component, and data management component.

Keys to Successful Analysis and Design

Simplicity, Brevity, and Clarity

The first goal of object-oriented analysis ranks far above all others: to achieve simplicity, brevity, and clarity in describing the problem domain.

Note that analysis describes the problem domain, not the intended information system itself. Turning away from the system may look like a step off the road at first glance, but the opposite is true. By focusing attention on the problem domain and describing it class by class, we make sure that the structure of the system will reflect the discovered structure of the problem domain.

Stable Architecture

Attention to the problem domain is the most important precondition for the stability of the architecture of the information system. Problem domain concepts are much more stable than data structures and functions. Take bookkeeping as an example. Bookkeeping as we know it today, with double-entry records, was invented by the Fugger family several hundred years ago. The basic structure of bookkeeping has not changed since then — now that's stability in problem domain concepts!

Stability of this kind is found in most business applications. Underlying the volatile elements that are system-dependent, the nature of the problem itself is relatively stable — at least over decades, if not centuries!

Avoid Structure Clashes

In an object-oriented analysis, we create a description of the problem domain that, at the same time, forms the basis of the architecture of the information system. In the next phases of design and programming, the goal is not to change this architecture, but to expand it and fill in the implementation detail. This results in direct traceability of concepts discussed and agreed on with customers and users in the implementation of the solution.

Reduction of Maintenance Efforts

The stability of the architecture — from analysis to programming — eases the orientation of developers. The system is not reinvented in the design phase as has occurred with previous approaches. The transition from analysis to design remains visible and understandable and can be traced in both directions. Maintenance work becomes easier because the structure of the system is the same in analysis, design, and programming.

"Don't Touch the Whiskey" — Take Your Time and Do It Right

In the past, analysis of business systems has often been taken lightly, since it was not until the design phase that the structure of the information system was created. The results of the analysis were often put aside when the first design steps had been taken — never to be picked up again or kept current during maintenance.

This must change with object-oriented analysis. The structure of the problem domain becomes the template for the structure of the information system. As a consequence, the structure of the information system emerges early in the life cycle, during the analysis phase. So don't let yourself be rushed into design or coding. A thorough analysis is the foundation for all further work.

"Don't touch the whiskey" is the distillation of ancient (Scottish?) wisdom, which perhaps surprisingly has application to object-oriented development today (Coad 1993). One who starts coding too early spoils it all. A good whiskey takes 12 years to mature. But don't worry — an object-oriented analysis can be done a little faster. Based on our consulting experience, you should average about one class per day. Given the relatively low complexity of today's commercial environments, this amounts to a time frame of 1 to 2 months (20 to 40 classes) for typical analyses of management information applications.

Easily Understandable

Object-oriented structures are closer to our human thinking than anything we have used in the past for building information systems. This is why object-oriented analysis models are easier for humans (users and customers included) to understand. This does not mean that object-oriented anaysis models are automatically more correct. Errors can always be made, but they are easier to detect because the documentation is more accessible.

Criterion for Assessing OOA Models

There is one essential criterion for judging the results of an object-oriented analysis, that is, the OOA model. "How well does the model support the communication between the team members, and between the team and users?"

The final authority in any discussion about the correctness of an OOA model rests with the intended users of the information system. This principle can make many problems and conflicts refreshingly simple.

THE OBJECT MODEL

The development of an object model, working with OOATool, consists of discovering and documenting classes, objects, and their interrelation. The object model contains the part of the problem domain that will be known to our information system.

Classes and Objects

Figure 10.1 shows an example of a ***Class&Object*** symbol in object-oriented analysis. We describe classes rather than single objects so the description of a class applies to all objects of that class (and its subclasses). The description applies to what the objects "know" (their attributes) and what they can "do" (their services).

Books in this model know their title, author, and ISBN. Books can lease themselves and register the fact that they have been returned. The physical representation of the data does not matter in analysis. It is not important how a book remembers its title or whether the title is 20 or 30 characters long. The parts that make up a postal address are equally unimportant at this stage. For the purposes of analysis it is sufficient to document the fact that a book remembers the name and address of the person who borrowed it.

How Much Detail Is Needed?

So does this mean you should never record details in an object-oriented analysis? Not at all; you should record as much detail as is needed for a clear and understandable documentation of the problem domain. No less —

FIGURE 10.1.   A simple object.

but also no more. If, to come back to our example, it is not important what an address looks like, it is sufficient to use the word *address* as the name of an attribute. Simplicity, brevity, and clarity is the most important principle of object-oriented analysis. Any surplus detail disturbs the whole picture, bores the reader, and detracts from more essential things.

The Responsibility of Objects

In our example we have made books responsible for being able to lend themselves and to register the fact that they have been returned. We can go one important step further. If the book is past due, it should be able to write a reminder or at least initiate some action — all from within itself, without any further triggering by anybody or anything.

This is an unusual capability for a simple book. How can it be done? The principle we use here is that the objects in our object-oriented analysis can be seen as being active representatives of the real-world objects. We assign responsibilities to these representatives that the real objects themselves would never be able to take over. Thus we can make objects of type **book** responsible for writing a reminder to the renter if they have not been returned after, say, 30 days. How this capability is implemented is a decision that will be made during the design phase.

In the same way other objects, like invoices, can be assigned useful responsibilities. For example: "Invoice, alert me if you have not received your payment within 20 days after delivery." This is what the invoice object does if it has not received full payment by the given date. How this is carried out is a design decision, so during analysis we can simply assume the capability will be achievable. This makes analysis easier — it is hard enough anyway — and allows us to focus on the essentials of the problem domain.

FIGURE 10.2. An object with a long-term responsibility. The service "watch over timely return" will alert us after 30 days.

Book

Title
Author
ISBN
Date of lease
Name of renter
Address of renter

Lease
Register return
Watch over timely return

Classes and Objects from the Inside or from the Outside?

When OOA and OOATool were first applied, the data structure of objects was of primary interest. This is why attributes were included in the earliest stages of developing the object model. Our view on this has changed in the recent past. Some critics argue that the inclusion of attributes is a violation of the encapsulation of data by classes. They argue that attributes are part of the internals of an object, and from the outside, it should not even be known that they exist.

FIGURE 10.3. Attributes accessed by two services each.

Theoretically, this criticism is correct although what it means in practice is that many more services must be added to the model to access the information an object knows. Our consulting practice has shown that both points of view — the original of Peter Coad and Ed Yourdon, as well as the responsibility-driven approach (Wirfs-Brock 1990) — can well be combined. For example, if we make objects of type *book* responsible for remembering their authors, titles, and ISBNs and for returning this knowledge to any requester, then — using the original Coad/Yourdon approach — we need three attributes.

If we did not show attributes on the exterior description of the object, we would instead need six services, as illustrated in Figure 10.3.

Needless to say, we did not like this alternative. The goal of encapsulation is not in this case aiding the goal of communication. However, it is clear we can achieve both goals by using something in between. We *think* in terms of object responsibilities — the services provided by a class to other objects — but we use attributes to record the accessible knowledge of the object. This works very well. Instead of using two services, *accept title* and *output title*, we use an attribute called *title* and imply from it that this is knowledge that can be accessed and updated; that is, a new title can be accepted and the current title output by any object of type *book*.

FIGURE 10.4. This is simpler, shorter, and clearer.

This reduces the number of properties that we have to document from six to three and brings us closer to our stated goal of simplicity, brevity, and clarity. This interpretation is also in accordance with the OMG's CORBA standard, which has standardized exactly on this usage of attributes.

Memory, Behavior, Identity

To summarize: We use the attributes of a class to describe what each object belonging to that class is able to remember; the services of a class describe each object's *behavior*.

It is also important to note that the *identity* of objects is taken as given in the analysis phase. We assume that each object is uniquely identifiable irrespective of the values of its attributes. How this is done — for example, that in a relational database key attributes are used to guarantee uniqueness — will be specified later in the design phase. Once again this aids simplicity, brevity, and clarity in the analysis phase, as it is not important to find "keys" for every class during analysis. Users can relate to the natural identity of real-world objects and discuss the problem of unique representation only in as much as it is a genuine part of the problem domain.

Structures

Objects in the problem domain are related to each other in a variety of ways. These connections are discovered and documented in object-oriented analysis. In doing so we distinguish between three kinds of connections that have been used by people to organize knowledge and thinking for centuries. They are:

- Whole/part structures
- Generalization/specialization
- Associations

In addition, there is the possibility in the method and tool to add message connections that document specific message communications between objects.

We refer to associations as *object connections*, and we will deal with these structures first.

Object Connections

For our example library it may be useful to document the renter separately from the book. Thus, we can modify our model by creating a new *Class&Object* and showing an object connection between them (Figure 10.5).

Note that the cardinality of the connection is shown on the link. A renter may have rented zero or more books, so 0–1 is placed next to the *Renter* class; a book may be rented by zero or one renter so 0–1 is placed next to the *Book* class.

The *Renter* object knows her or his name and address and is able to rent a book, return

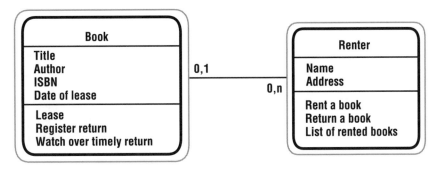

FIGURE 10.5. Two objects that know each other.

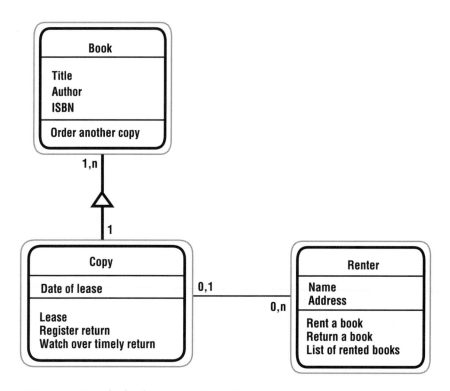

FIGURE 10.6.   Popular books suggest themselves to have more copies ordered.

it, and present us with a list of books currently on loan to this renter — again, a capability of our electronic object that may be hard to get from the its real-world counterpart.

Whole/Part Structures

We will now add another development step to our library's object model. A book should be able to distinguish its potentially many copies and order another copy of itself if it finds that it is more popular than anticipated. We may consider the copies of a book to be parts of the book object and so show them with a whole/part link. The copies can be rented by the renters of our library (Figure 10.6).

For each book, there are one or more copies. Each copy in this model plays the role that was filled by books in the previous models. A renter may have rented zero or more copies of some books while each copy can be rented by zero or one renter at a time.

Generalization/Specialization

For the purposes of this example, the library model can be enriched once again. Suppose the library now rents videos, and magazines in addition to books. The result is that we now have three different kinds of lease objects: books, videos, and magazines. For each of these, there are one or more copies, as the specializations inherit the link from *Lease-Object* to *Copy*. Thus, for example, there are one or more copies of each video object.

Figure 10.7 shows that *Book*, *Video*, and *Magazine* are regarded as specializations of *Lease-Object*. All the different kinds of lease object share the attributes, services, and connections already defined for *Lease-Object*. In addition, as *Book*, *Video*, and *Magazine* are themselves classes, multiple instances of the class (i.e., multiple titles or issues) may be remembered.

Note that the class *Lease-Object* in this example is different from other classes in that

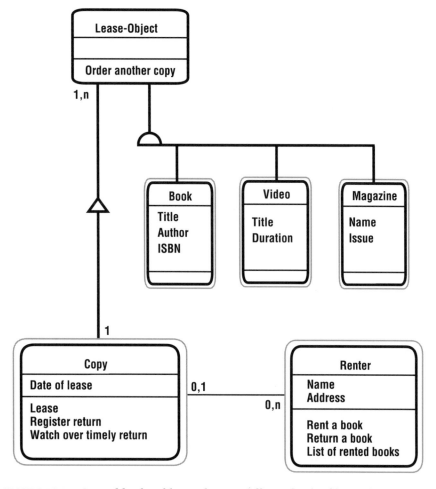

FIGURE 10.7. General lending library showing different kinds of lease-objects.

it has no objects — all the instances are explicitly *Books* or *Videos* or *Magazines*. The class's purpose is to bundle common attributes, services, and connections of its specializations and to make these available (via inheritance) to *Book*, *Video*, and *Magazine*. The notation to show this class has no objects is to display only the inner border of the *Class&-Object* icon, making it a *Class* icon (Figure 10.7).

Messages

During object-oriented analysis, it is also possible to enter message connections that document the use of one class's services by another. However, our consulting practice has shown that it is only in rare cases that the simplicity, brevity, and clarity of the object model can be improved by the explicit documentation of message connections.

The reason for this is that object models abound with messages. If we add all these message connections to the drawing, it almost certainly reduces clarity instead of providing more information. Message connections are nearly always parallel to existing object connections or whole/part structures that, in any case, both imply messages — potentially in both directions. We therefore use message connections only rarely, and only when it will improve the understandability of the model.

PRESENTING THE INFORMATION

The information contained in an OOA object model becomes valuable to humans only through a well-organized and understandable presentation. OOATool offers a range of capabilities that can be used to present the various parts of an object model to different audiences, giving each audience only the information it needs and understands, while maintaining the coherent representation in the underlying object model. In this section, we consider some of the techniques for doing this.

Subject Areas

Subject areas are divisions of the object model that group together logically connected *Class&Objects*. So with the help of subject areas, it is possible to group *Class&Objects* visually to show they belong to a common area of interest, by enclosing the icons with a bold border showing the subject area boundary.

If we only want to look at the library part of our object model, for example, we can use OOATool to reduce the representation of another part of the model to a single icon so it won't distract from our current focus. Subjects are a simple, easy, and fast technique to guide a reader's attention when looking at a drawing, and they help us partition large models to manage their scale.

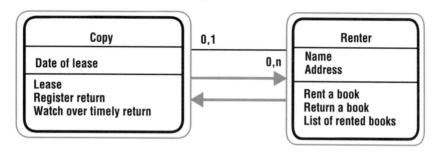

FIGURE 10.8. Message connections document the use of another class's services.

Multiple Drawings Per Object Model

For nontrivial models (i.e., with more than 7 ± 2 classes) it is advantageous to present them in multiple drawings instead of one. Each drawing shows one aspect of the object model. It has proven useful to limit the size of drawings to 7 ± 2 classes and one sheet of A4 paper each. The multiple drawings are connected through their common object model stored in the tool's database. If anything is changed in any of the drawings, the changes automatically become visible in the other drawings of the model. By "hiding" classes and by using filters (see below), users of the tool can control which *Class&Objects* appear on which drawings.

Hiding

The "hide" function may be applied to *Class&Objects* on individual diagrams. As its name implies, it prevents the "hidden" *Class&Object* from appearing on the specified drawing. However, the *Class&Object* remains in the model and is still visible on other drawings. The combination of multiple drawings with hiding is sufficient for most object models, but for some projects it is also useful to define "filters."

Filters

If more detailed control over the contents of drawings — particularly if, for example, different types of users wish to see different amounts of detail from the same diagrams — filters may be used to control which attributes and services appear on the drawings. Filters may also be used for classes.

Documentation Production

The drawings and descriptive text that results from the object-oriented analysis form the basis of the complete documentation for the work and eventually the system. Drawings are printed as they were designed on the screen. Descriptive texts are collected by OOATool from all the components of the object model and combined into one text that may be printed or saved as a file for further processing by documentation or desktop publishing systems.

GUIDANCE TO THE ANALYST

There is little doubt that the best guidance for analysts is to be obtained from those who have carried out object-oriented analyses successfully before. Unfortunately, such guidance is not always available in person, and in such cases it is useful to be able to obtain it from a tool itself. There are principally two ways in which such information can be supplied.

Strategy Cards

Guidance information, project specific strategies, and development procedures can be included on-line using *strategy cards*. Some of the tips and tricks from Peter Coad and Ed Yourdon (Coad 1991a) have been included on-line in OOATool. For some activities, such as finding **Classes&Objects** in the problem domain — a common inquiry in first projects — information is included on these strategy cards, and users can adapt them according to their needs. They also can add their own strategy cards to guide developers in following the standards set up for their companies.

Model Critique

The experience of expert analysts can also be translated into rules for checking complete or partially complete object models. The completeness of documentation and the thoroughness in the use of the techniques supplied by the tool is readily amenable to automated checking. Thus, developers can have their object models checked by OOATool for compliance with a number of these rules. This is helpful both to the developers themselves and to reviewers of the object model.

CONCLUSION

We have seen that the Coad/Yourdon approach to object-oriented development is based on a straightforward goal: simplicity, brevity, and clarity as the key to communication. Object-oriented principles change many of the ground rules of analysis and design. The object model is applicable to both phases, and the model provides both the foundation for implementation and an accessible model for users to understand the problem domain and the system. The object-oriented analysis and design requires both a method and a tool to avoid bureaucracy on one hand and chaos on the other. Again, users should be guided by the principle of simplicity, brevity, and clarity to ensure that tool support helps the learning process in "object think" — the communication process within the team and with users — and the development process in seeing a single model transformed from an understanding of the problem domain into an automated system in the simplest possible fashion.

REFERENCES

Coad, P., and E. Yourdon (1991a) *Object-Oriented Analysis*, 2nd Edition, Prentice-Hall, Englewood Cliffs, NJ.

Coad, P., and E. Yourdon (1991b) *Object-Oriented Design*, Yourdon Press, Prentice-Hall, Englewood Cliffs, NJ.

Coad, P., and J. Nicola (1993) *Object-Oriented Programming*, Yourdon Press, Prentice-Hall, Englewood Cliffs, NJ.

Wirfs-Brock, R., B. Wikerson, and L. Wiener (1990) *Designing Object-Oriented Software*, Prentice-Hall, Englewood Cliffs, NJ.

chapter **11**

The Texel Method: A Pragmatic and Field-Proven Approach

Putnam P. Texel   *P.P. Texel and Company Inc.*

The Texel method represents an amalgamation of features from other principal object-oriented methods, driven by clients' requests from both the scientific and MIS communities. Table 11.1 details the specific mixture of techniques implemented by the Texel method — a true blend of event- and data-driven philosophies that attempts to provide the best of both approaches to the community — a simplified user interface above a rigorous definition and collection of Object Classes.

The Texel method is well documented, in terms of a process description and an accompanying management guide, and is supported by state-of-the-art tool technology, the meta-CASE capability of VSF Ltd. The package therefore represents the potential for an organization to increase its Software Engineering Institute's (SEI) Capability Maturity Model (CMM) rating to a level 2 at least, if not to a level 3.

The Texel method has been successfully employed in the scientific and MIS communities, both in the United States and in the United Kingdom. Its success is based on a pragmatic approach to transitioning an organization to the successful incorporation of object-oriented technology.

The Method — An Overview

Table 11.1 shows the techniques from other methods that are used within Texel. Figures 11.1–11.5 illustrate the next level of detail. These figures provide an overview of the major activities in the method, as well as the specific processes that are required to support the activity. The activities and processes are well defined and articulated, both graphically and textually.

Requirements Engineering

As shown in Figure 11.1, the first major activity is Requirements Engineering using Jacobson's Use Case model (Jacobson 1993). The use case definition becomes the basis for all Requirements Generation and Trace. Both a static and dynamic Requirements Trace are performed and supported by the VSF Texel-SF Tool. Specifically, Use Cases are traced to the Subsystems that participate in the implementation of the Use Case, to the Object Classes within the Subsystems, to the methods within the Object Class. That relationship is kept both as a static view and as a dynamic view, with the dynamic view supporting sequencing of actions.

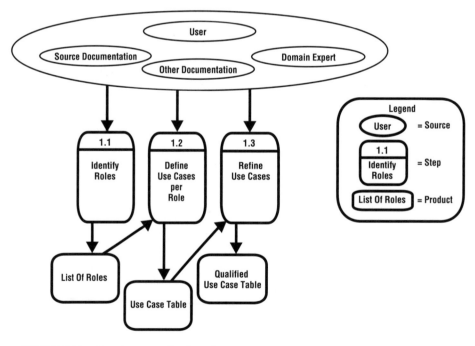

FIGURE 11.1. Requirements Engineering.

TABLE 11.1. The Texel Method "Mixture."

Activity	Adapted From	Enhancements
Requirements Engineering		
Requirements generation	Jacobson – Objectory	Qualified subject of Use Case
Requirements trace		
Static trace	Unique to Texel	Use case traced to: Subsystem Object class Method
Dynamic trace	Unique to Texel	Use case traced to: Event Method
Object-Oriented Analysis (OOA)		
Static view	Unique to Texel	COCL DL BOCL SCM Shared object classes
	Shlaer/Mellor	Aggregation List attributes Leveling of graphic representation No RSD (incorporated in OCSD)
Dynamic view	Schlaer/Mellor	Guidelines
	Jacobson – Objectory	Use case as external event Interaction diagram
	PTech	Substates
Object-Oriented Design (OOD)		
Object class architecture	Booch – Concepts Separation of declaration and implementation	No "blob"
	GTE – notation	Real time extensions Exceptions Access rights
Object class structure	Booch – concepts GTE – notation	No "blob" Requires/required by

Object-Oriented Analysis

Figures 11.2 and 11.3 focus on the activity of performing object-oriented analysis. Figure 11.2 presents the static view activity, while Figure 11.3 presents the dynamic view activity.

Static View

A unique feature of the Texel method is its formal Candidate Object Class List (COCL) that is refined, using predefined Disposition Keys, to a Baseline Object Class List (BOCL). The BOCL becomes the basis for Subsystem identification. The major benefits of a formal COCL are described below:

- The formal COCL provides an open system, whereby Texel can be linked quickly and efficiently with other front ends (e.g., IDEF) or any other process description method or tool.

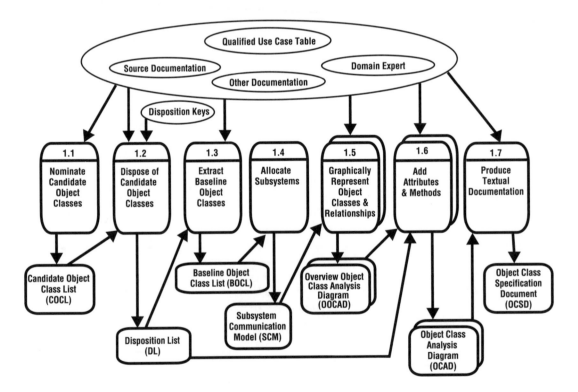

FIGURE 11.2.   OOA – static view.

- The combination of the Use Case technique (Jacobson 1993), the COCL, and associated Disposition Keys provides power not present in any other method today. The Roles, Subjects, and Qualifiers from the Use Cases are automatically entered into the Candidate Object Class List and disposed of as Object Classes, ensuring their consideration for Subsystem selection, but, more importantly, providing an earlier identification of Subsystems.

Shlaer/Mellor Information Structure Diagrams (Shlaer 1988) (renamed *Object Class Analysis Diagrams*) form the heart of the static view of object-oriented analysis. One major change from the Shlaer/Mellor method is the addition of List Attributes, which are permitted and encouraged (specifically within MIS systems). Aggregation and multilevel views are supported by Texel and further strengthen the Shlaer/Mellor concept. Notation from OMT further clarifies the static view (Rumbaugh 1991). The Object Class Specification Document (Shlaer 1988) has been expanded by the addition of methods identification and method descriptions, Ancestor/Descendant and Composite/Part descriptions — all of which are then captured by the Texel-SF tool and automatically contribute to the draft of the graphical representation of the object-oriented analysis solution and the accompanying Program Design Language (PDL).

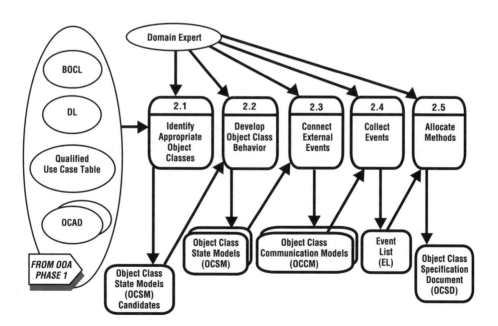

FIGURE 11.3. OOA – dynamic view.

Dynamic View

The dynamic view represents an enhancement to the traditional state model (Shlaer 1992) by applying Use Cases as External Events and the addition of substates, à la PTech (Martin 1993), to support reuse across application domains. Finally, Jacobson's interaction diagram (Jacobson 1993) begins to form a bridge between object-oriented analysis and design. This bridge appears to be particularly useful within the MIS community because the application domain is less "concrete," and state models can be categorized resulting in object classes that have similar state models. Finally, many Object Classes have trivial or, perhaps, no applicable state model at all, permitting a more efficient transition to the design activity.

OBJECT-ORIENTED DESIGN

Object-Oriented Design (OOD) (Booch 1993) comprises two major activities: the overall software system architecture described first graphically and then textually, as well as the architecture of each individual Object Class, also described graphically and textually. The processes required to implement the two major activities of OOD are described in Figures 11.4 and 11.5, respectively.

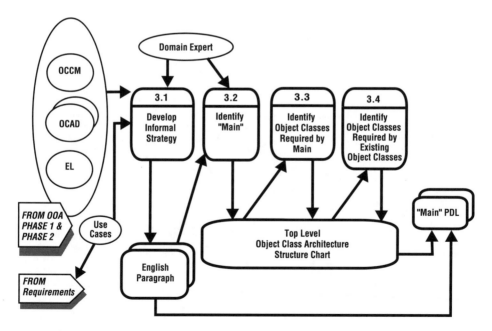

FIGURE 11.4. OOD – Software System Architecture.

The graphic representation is based on symbology initially created by GTE for a representation in Ada, and expanded and refined by Texel & Company Inc. to be a language-independent representation of the resulting software architecture based on an Object-Oriented Design.

The textual representation, or language-specific PDL, is dropped automatically from the tool in Ada83, Ada9X, or C++, using the language as its own PDL. This provides the well-documented benefits of

- Early identification of design errors
- Early initiation of interface testing

due to the compilation of files to

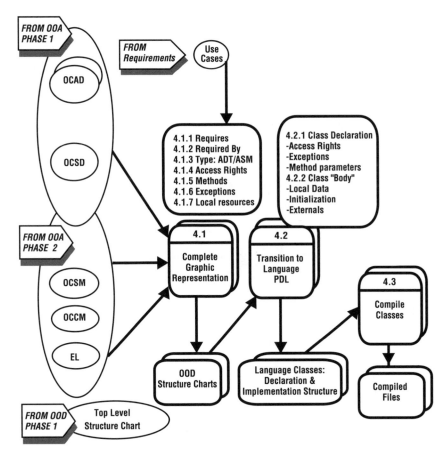

FIGURE 11.5. OOD – Object Class Architecture.

- Verify visibility between Object Classes
- Ensure calling conventions are adhered to between Object Classes

Language-specific Object Class declarations and implementation (structure only) are output by the tool Texel-SF, and are customizable with respect to file templates, Database Integration, and test tool selection to form the beginning of a complete integrated development environment. Currently, Texel-SF is linked to the POET Object-Oriented Database Management System and IPL's Cantata and AdaTest testing tools.

FUTURE ENHANCEMENTS

Plans are to link the methodology and the Texel-SF workbench to RTM and a repository of reusable components, at both the Object Class and Instance Levels.

REFERENCES

Booch, G. (1993) *Object-Oriented Design with Applications*, Benjamin Cummings Publishing Co., Redwood City, CA.

Jacobson, I., M. Christenson, P. Jonsoon (1992). *Object-Oriented Software Engineering: A Use Case Approach*, Addison-Wesley, Reading, MA.

Martin, J. (1993) *The Principles of Object-Oriented Analysis & Design*, Prentice-Hall, Englewood Cliffs, NJ.

Rumbaugh, J., M. Blaha, W. Premerlani (1991) *Object-Oriented Modeling & Design*, Prentice-Hall, Englewood Cliffs, NJ.

Shlaer, S. and S. Mellor (1988) *Object-Oriented System Analysis: Modeling the Real World in Data*, Prentice-Hall, Englewood Cliffs, NJ.

Shlaer, S. and S. Mellor (1992) *Object Life Cycles: Modeling the Real World in States*, Yourdon Press, Prentice-Hall, Englewood Cliffs, NJ.

chapter 12

The Rumbaugh Method (OMT): The Selection of an Object-Oriented Analysis Method

STUART FROST   *SELECT SOFTWARE TOOLS LTD.*

Select Software Tools Ltd. is a vendor of PC-based CASE tools. The range currently supports a variety of structured methods. Early in 1992, we decided to add an object-oriented analysis and design method to the range of tools. This chapter discusses the reasons Select chose to support OMT (Object Modeling Technique) out of all the possible object-oriented analysis and design methods. An overview of the method is given, together with a discussion of Select's own use of OMT during the development of the toolkit. This is followed by a consideration of the level of success in using the method and a comparison with previous projects that used Yourdon and SSADM.

HOW DID WE CHOOSE THE METHOD?

There is currently a plethora of object-oriented analysis and design methods in the marketplace. Clearly, there is a need for a shakeout to reduce confusion among users. We feel that one of the prime motivating factors will be the availability of low-cost CASE support. Given that Select's aim is to provide such support, we felt that it was vital to spend time considering the various methods to make an informed choice.

But before considering the choice, it is perhaps useful to ask a very important question.

Does the Method Matter?

Many people get very evangelistic about methods. After several years of using and supporting a variety of methods, we have come to the conclusion that the actual method being used is not that important.

The most important factors in the use of any method are that it gives visibility to the analysis and design stages of the life cycle and that it smooths the path through the life cycle as much as possible. This means that the method chosen must support the paradigm being used by the developers. For example, you might choose MASCOT for task-oriented projects, Yourdon for structured projects, SSADM for projects using relational databases, and HOOD for package-oriented projects.

In fact, one of the key benefits of using object-oriented methods is the smoother life cycle when compared with earlier techniques. This is often overlooked.

Criteria Used

We began by setting out various criteria by which to assess the effectiveness of each method:

- The method should support all of the main object-oriented semantics: the inheritance (is-a-kind-of), aggregation (is-a-part-of), and association (is-related-to).
- It must cover both analysis and design to a reasonable extent and provide a smooth transition between the various stages of the life cycle.
- It should provide support, or at least form a good basis for providing support, for real-time and MIS systems.
- It should not be overly complex.
- It should, where possible, use familiar techniques to reduce the learning curve for users experienced in structured methods.
- It should be an open standard, that is, it should be published, public, and well known.
- The book in which the method is described should be readable and reasonably complete and consistent.
- Training courses and consultancy should be available on both sides of the Atlantic from a variety of sources.
- Other CASE vendors should be supporting, or considering support of, the method.

Out of all of the current object-oriented methods, only four were regarded as being worthy of consideration against the above criteria: Booch, Shlaer/Mellor, Coad/Yourdon, and OMT.

Booch

The Booch method (Booch 1991) stands out from the other three because it is not based on the Yourdon structured method. This is seen as a weakness because, when combined with the complexity of the method, the learning curve is quite high.

In addition, Booch provides minimal support for analysis, although it is very strong for the design phase, especially for real-time systems. Unfortunately, this strength is insufficient to outweigh the disadvantages.

Shlaer/Mellor

Shlaer/Mellor (1988, 1990) uses techniques very similar to the Yourdon structured method (Yourdon 1990). In fact, it could be argued that it is too similar and tends to give a relational view of the world, as opposed to an object-oriented one.

The method is, in fact, quite widely used and is supported by a few CASE vendors. However, many aspects of the method are not adequately described by the books, and users are, therefore, reliant on courses developed by the authors of the method. This tends to give a proprietary flavor that mitigates against using the method as a basis for a low-cost CASE tool.

Coad/Yourdon

Coad/Yourdon (1990, 1991) is more loosely based on Yourdon than Shlaer/Mellor, with a stronger distinction between relational and object-oriented views. In fact, it is very similar to OMT in many respects.

However, Select felt that the method was rather more superficial than OMT and lacked the expressive power of the latter method. It was also our view that Coad/Yourdon did not provide a sound basis for real-time systems.

OMT (Rumbaugh)

As is clear by now, OMT (Rumbaugh 1991) was the final choice. This was due to the following factors:

- **Support for both analysis and design for a wide variety of application areas.** The combination of the object, dynamic, and functional models gives OMT the ability to support many different kinds of applications, including real-time systems (although the authors don't make any claims for this area). In addition, the transition between analysis and design is smooth and fairly well defined.
- **Small learning curve.** OMT is based on Yourdon, but with a strong object-oriented bias.

- **Well-written book.** The book by Rumbaugh et al is reasonably clear and complete. Some aspects, especially those relating to integration between the three models are not presented very consistently, but such criticisms can be levelled at most software engineering books.
- **Several third-party training courses and consultants.** OMT is supported by several training and consultancy organizations in Europe and the United States. This is extremely important for vendors of low-cost CASE tools, since it removes the risk of customers feeling that they are entirely dependent upon the developer of the tool.
- **Widely used.** OMT was developed in the General Electric Research and Development Center, New York, and has been used for some time in that environment. In the United Kingdom, companies such as Object Designers Ltd. have been using OMT as the basis for their object-oriented developments over the last two years. In addition, we have found several major clients who are starting OMT pilot projects (e.g., British Aerospace and Serco).

OMT OVERVIEW

OMT uses three integrated models to describe a system: the object, dynamic, and functional models.

The Object Model

The object model is central to the method and uses a diagram similar to the entity-relationship diagrams used in Yourdon. Classes and their attributes and operations are shown, together with relationships between classes. Relationships that can be drawn include inheritance, aggregation, and association. The modeling syntax is rich enough to represent most of the object-oriented constructs in common use.

Figure 12.1 shows the symbol for a class in OMT notation. The attributes and operations correspond to C++ data and function members.

Figure 12.2 illustrates single inheritance. The *land* and *water* vehicle classes are subclasses of *vehicle*.

In Figure 12.3, we have added multiple inheritance by introducing an amphibious vehicle.

Figure 12.4 illustrates the diamond symbol, used to show aggregation or part-of relationships.

Figure 12.5 shows how the notation would be used for design of gas station control systems. Note that we have

CLASS NAME
ATTRIBUTE LIST ...
OPERATION LIST ..

FIGURE 12.1. Symbol for a class in OMT notation.

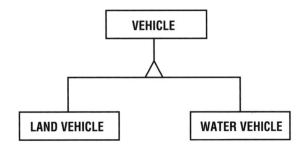

FIGURE 12.2. Single inheritance.

also used the association notation (e.g., between the console and the pump), which is similar to a relationship in entity relationship notations.

Dynamic Model

The dynamic model consists of a state transition diagram (STD) for each of the classes in the object model.

The STD notation is that defined by Harel (1987), which allows for decomposable states. This is richer and more powerful than that commonly used in Yourdon (Figure 12.6).

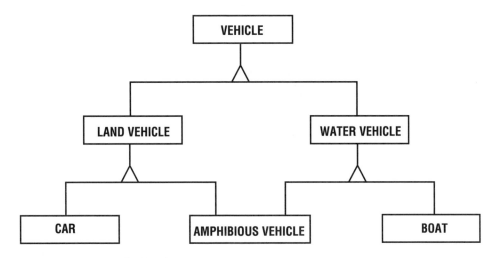

FIGURE 12.3. Multiple inheritance.

Functional Model

The functional model uses a hierarchy of data flow diagrams (DFDs) in a similar fashion to the Yourdon method. However, the DFDs are not very well integrated with the object and dynamic models, and it is difficult to imagine many projects making extensive use of the functional model.

Some aspects of the functional model are, however, quite useful. For example, the context diagram is vital for defining the scope of the system. Also, it may be possible to strengthen the real-time aspects of the method by introducing the concept of a processor and task model using DFDs (Ward-Mellor 1985).

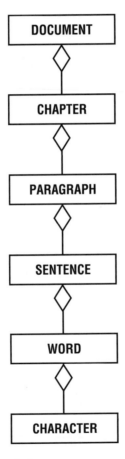

FIGURE 12.4. The diamond symbol.

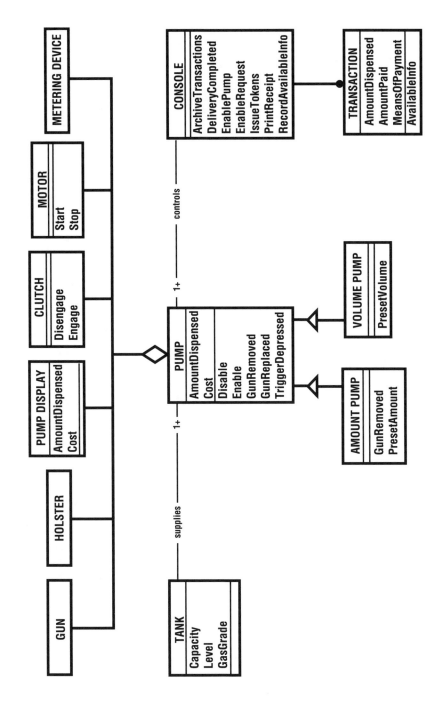

FIGURE 12.5 Design of a gas station control system.

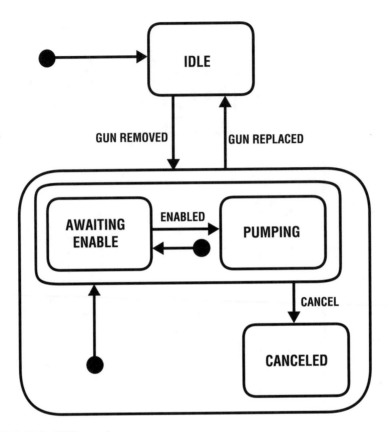

FIGURE 12.6. STD notation.

SELECT'S USE OF OMT

In the past, Select has used both Yourdon and SSADM to develop its range of CASE tools. However, for the OMT toolkit, we thought it might be useful to actually use the method. Since we didn't really want to use anyone else's CASE tools, we decided to adapt our Yourdon toolkit to support the main constructs (i.e., inheritance and aggregation). This involved extending the Chen-style entity-relationship diagrams. The state transition diagrams, which do not support decomposable states, and the data flow diagrams were used without modification.

All of our staff are experienced Yourdon practitioners, and no one encountered any significant problems using OMT.

The object model was used quite extensively, with only a few state transition diagrams being drawn. We did not find it necessary to use the functional model to any great extent, although it is felt that drawing a context diagram could be useful in order to scope the system being designed.

Select is implemented in TopSpeed Modula-2, which now supports multiple inheritance. The combination of Modula-2 and OMT was found to work particularly well, with a good mapping between the analysis, design, and implementation phases.

OMT Compared with Yourdon and SSADM

In Select's view, Yourdon and SSADM are very similar methods that use closely related techniques (e.g., DFDs, ERDs, etc.). However, whereas Yourdon is best suited to real-time projects, SSADM is oriented toward MIS.

OMT vs. Yourdon

As stated earlier, Yourdon has reasonably good real-time features. However, these are by no means perfect and there is no reason why the same features should not be used with OMT. In fact, most of them are described in Rumbaugh's book (e.g., events, event traces, etc.). With the addition of timing diagrams and perhaps the use of data flow diagrams to show processor and task models, there is no reason why OMT should not be as strong as Yourdon for real time.

The transition between analysis and design is much smoother with OMT since there is no change of notation. Yourdon moves from data flow diagrams to structure charts.

Given the above, together with the increasing availability of cross-embedded C++ compilers, it is our view that OMT will replace Yourdon as the general-purpose real-time method.

OMT vs. SSADM

SSADM's main strengths are its support for relational databases and its strong life cycle (many would say that it's far too strong). SSADM is also about to become a British Standard and is very widely used in U.K. government. In addition, some vendors are experimenting with object-oriented extensions based on entity life history diagrams. SSADM will stay with us for some time to come.

However, given such developments as Object Designers' Syntropy, which gives OMT a stronger life cycle and a general, though slow, move toward object-oriented databases and languages, SSADM will be steadily displaced by methods such as OMT — especially in commercial environments.

CONCLUSION

It now seems that OMT will be one of the leading object-oriented methods over the next few years — although this is not to say that it will be the only one! As history has shown, there is room for more than one method in mainstream software engineering. We certainly don't regret our decision to support OMT within the Select range, especially given the success in using the method for our own development.

REFERENCES

Booch, G. (1991) *Object-Oriented Design*, Benjamin/Cummings, Menlo Park, CA.

Coad, P., and E. Yourdon (1990) *Object-Oriented Analysis*, Yourdon Press, Prentice-Hall, Englewood Cliffs, NJ.

Coad, P., and E. Yourdon (1991) *Object Oriented Design*, Yourdon Press, Englewood Cliffs, NJ.

Harel, D. (1987) Statecharts: a visual formalism for complex systems. *Science of Computer Programming*, 8: 231–274.

Rumbaugh, J., M. Blaha, W. Premerlani, et al. (1991) *Object-Oriented Modeling and Design*, Prentice-Hall, Englewood Cliffs, NJ.

Shlaer, S., and S.J. Mellor (1988) *Object Oriented Systems Analysis: Modeling the World in Data*, Yourdon Press, Prentice-Hall, Englewood Cliffs, NJ.

Shlaer, S., and S.J. Mellor (1990) *Object Life Cycles: Modeling the World in States*, Yourdon Press, Prentice-Hall, Englewood Cliffs, NJ.

Ward, P.T., and S.J. Mellor (1985) *Structured Development for Real-Time Systems*, Yourdon Press, Prentice-Hall, Englewood Cliffs, NJ.

Yourdon Inc. (1990) *Yourdon Structured Method Reference Manual*, Yourdon Inc., Raleigh, NC.

chapter 13

The SOMA Method: Adding Rules to Classes

IAN GRAHAM   SWISS BANK CORPORATION

Most methods for object-oriented analysis and design offer a means of describing computer-based systems in terms that will be implementable in object-oriented programming languages. All current methods have various omissions and weaknesses. Some fail to cover such issues as requirements capture, reuse management, or the project life cycle. Most, as is well known, are weak in terms of modeling global dynamics (Graham 1993a). Others are just not expressive enough for the higher-level tasks of systems analysts, in that information supplied by users must be converted into code-like forms of expression in a mostly irretrievable fashion.

Even simple things like database triggers are hard to describe, and complex statements of system control strategy, business policy, and environmental constraints are almost impossible. This chapter describes an extension that may be made to most object-oriented analysis methods and that enriches their semantic content. This is done by adding rule-sets or policies to objects. The extension is part of the SOMA method filter, documented in order of increasing detail (Graham 1991a, 1993b, 1993c, 1994). The effect of this innovation is that:

- More information is captured and less is lost in transcription.
- The end result is more traceable and reversible.

- Users find the form of expression more natural, and analysis deliverables are more readily traced to requirements and business objectives.
- Human activity systems can be described as easily as computer systems, leading to applications in business process re-engineering.
- It is as easy to describe a non-object-oriented system as it is to describe an object-oriented one, leading to useful results for people migrating to object technology.
- Knowledge-based systems can be described.

Other methodologists who have experimented with the idea of adding rules to their methods miss the point when they write "the rules are written on the diagrams" (Martin 1993). Rules should be added in a properly object-oriented manner. They should be encapsulated by objects, and they should be inheritable. Of course, this does not prevent a rule-set or policy from being an object in its own right; such an object's rules would be meta-rules. Other methods have no other constructs. SOMA allows both policy objects and policies about objects. Other writers such as Nerson (1992) use rather otiose logical formalisms to express rules, thus dividing themselves from the user community as soon as they put pen to paper (or mouse pointer to CASE tool).

We will present the policy extension using the SOMA notation, but the reader is encouraged to apply it on top of any other base notation. I should also state that SOMA includes a fairly complete coverage of all life cycle issues from requirements capture to coordination and reuse. These are not presented here, and we will be dealing purely with the representational part of SOMA. (The complete method is described in Graham 1994.) Before getting down to the business of rules, I will introduce the remainder of the SOMA notation as briefly as possible.

OBJECT MODELING

Before we can capture knowledge, we need some form of representation. An object-oriented approach dictates that the representation should be in the form of objects, so we begin with a summary of the SOMA representation. Some authors have observed that an object-oriented approach to analysis and *a fortiori* requirements capture is nonsense on the grounds that analysis should be independent of technology. These people assume that object technology is the same as object-oriented programming and deduce that object-oriented analysis is a tool and that representing knowledge with this tool is therefore implementation-dependent. A philosopher would be able to deduce from this that representation in natural language is also forbidden because language is a tool, albeit a very fundamental one. This argument, and there are many variants on it (e.g., Bryant and Evans 1993), is errant nonsense. First, object orientation is a representational metaphor quite independent of object-oriented programming languages per se. Second, representation in terms of objects (including concepts) is fundamental to human cognition. Provided that

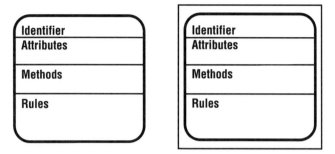

FIGURE 13.1. *(a)* A class or object-type. *(b)* A class with instances.

the semantics are rich enough (and not all methods are ideal yet), there should be nothing that is not representable in this way. Note that I deliberately refuse to tie the semantics of SOMA to one formal logical representation.

This chapter offers a suggested notation and method framework that will support the objectives of requirements capture. If a CASE tool is used it may restrict the notation available, but most object-oriented notations will be compatible with the approach described herein.

Objects are displayed in the form shown in Figure 13.1(a). If the icon has square corners it represents an instance, if round, as illustrated, a class. Thus, an object has an identifier and three lists: attribute names, method names, and rule names. Each of these has additional information attached.

Surrounding a class icon with a box as in Figure 13.1(b) says that the class is not an abstract class. In other words, the class may have concrete instances that are not classes. This also tells us that any subclasses do not form an exhaustive list of possible subclasses.

Layers

Layers are not just a convenient way to decompose the problem domain; they are bona fide objects in their own right with the semantics of objects. Layers differ from other objects in two ways: (1) They exist at the top of a composition structure; and (2) each of their methods must be implemented by a method of some object within that structure. This means that layers can be arrived at top-down or bottom-up. Further, the requirement that every method must have a properly terminated implemented-by link assists in completeness checking during top-down design. Equally, the analyst can ask, during a bottom-up analysis What does this method implement for the layer?

For example, a commercial system might have the following layers: marketing, sales, accounts, and production. The accounts layer is an object representing the accounts department as a whole and may have a method called *ProduceSalesInvoice*. *Accounts* is composed of three objects or layers: *PurchaseLedger*, *SalesLedger*, and *NominalLedger*.

The *ProduceSalesInvoice* method is implemented-by the *ProduceInvoice* method of the *Sales* object, denoted: *Sales.ProduceInvoice*.

Structures and Data Semantics

Structures to be identified are of three main kinds: use, classification and composition structures.

Use structures record the message-passing topology of the system or, equivalently, the visibility or client/server relationships. As shown in Figure 13.2, writers may ask a printer to print a draft, and editors may ask them to print a final copy. Writers can release text to an editor, and editors check changes with the author, who can approve them. Not all attributes, methods, and rules are shown.

Classification, inheritance, or generalization/specialization structures permit the analyst to record the semantics of classification. Inheritance is used only in this sense and any kind

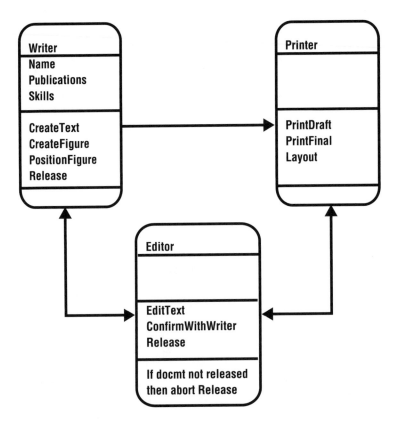

FIGURE 13.2. A fragment of a use structure.

of ad hoc polymorphism or inheritance merely for the purpose of code sharing is banned. The notation for these structures follows the Chen style of entity-relationship modeling. Thus, a diamond connector marked AKO (a kind of) indicates that the objects attached participate in a classification structure. A bar on a connector indicates a link to a superclass and its absence, a link to a subclass. The bars can be named if desired. In the case of multiple inheritance, there will be two or more such bars. Normally, multiple inheritance is conjunctive; that is, the subclass is a kind of all its superclasses. In rare cases, disjunctive inheritance is useful. In this case, where the subclass is a kind of one of the superclasses, a double bar is used. This, too, can be named and annotated.

Any composition structure is a layer. Classification structures are viewed as orthogonal to these. They are not layers, and they are not usually shown on the same diagram as composition. Messages arrive at the outside of layers and are delegated to subobjects via implemented-by links. Messages can arrive anywhere in a classification structure, but do so most often at instances. Thus, in use structure diagrams, classification structures are expanded, but composition structures are not.

Classification or AKO diamonds may be annotated with two letters as follows: E/O, E/M, I/O, or I/M. E/O stands for *exclusive/optional* and I/O means *inclusive/optional*. The term *exclusive* indicates that each subclass's intersection with the other subclasses is empty, and *inclusive* indicates that the subclasses may overlap. *Optional* indicates that the list is not exhaustive, and there may be more, as yet unidentified, subclasses. An M, for *mandatory*, indicates that a member of the superclass must be in at least one of the subclasses; that is, the subclasses are an exhaustive list or *partition* of the class.

Other kinds of associations and their static semantics must be catered for. Data semantics in most entity modeling methods are annotated only at the instance level. It has been found useful to permit class-level connections of this type. This serves to enrich the semantics. For example, at the instance level, for every wheel there is at most one bicycle that it is part of. However, at the class level, for every wheel type many bicycle types may incorporate it. Connections of this sort may be thought of as associations; that is, a structural relationship other than use, classification, or composition. In some cases, these associations have properties and should be expanded into objects in their own right. In others, the association may be so important for the application (e.g., kinship in anthropology) that a fourth or fifth structure needs to be added to the model. Data semantic links indicating multiplicity and modality may be used on composition structure links.

In Figure 13.3 *E/O* indicates that there can be no overlap of subclasses (exclusive) and that there may be other subclasses not shown. *E/M* indicates that **interest bearing current account** is the only subclass of current account.

Attributes and Operations

Attributes are discovered using standard data modeling techniques. Two special list-valued attributes are used: **AKO:** and **Parts:**. The **AKO:** attribute is list-valued and contains the superclass names for the object. The **Parts:** attribute contains a list of objects that

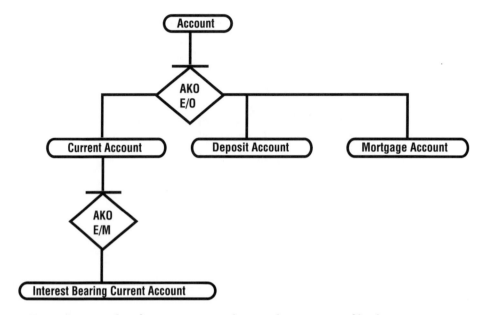

FIGURE 13.3.   A classification structure showing the semantics of bank accounts.

compose the object. Where automated support is available, the dual attributes, **Members:** and **APO:**, may be employed to aid navigation through the model, but these must be updated automatically, otherwise reuse is compromised.

Every attribute has a type, which must be a valid user-defined or primitive class in the system. The analyst is free to decide which classes are primitive, but must list these. Typical primitives include real, integer, string, list, date, and so on. Attributes also store associations. For example, if we have the semantic relationship that says that employees must work for exactly one department while departments may employ zero or more

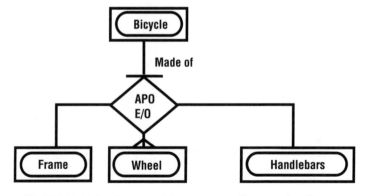

FIGURE 13.4(a).   A composition structure (instance level).

employees, then we might record *WorksIn:(DEPT,1,1)* as an attribute of *EMPLOYEE* and *Employs:(EMPLOYEE,0,n)* as an attribute of *DEPT* or produce the equivalent crow's foot diagram.

The extent to which such associations compromise reuse has been widely debated, but the requirements of commercial systems development seem to have brought the consensus round to their acceptance, and associations are even part of the OMG abstract object model.

This concludes the presentation of the representational aspects of SOMA. We now turn to the policy extension implicit in this notation.

RULES AND ASSERTIONS

Rule sets provide second-order information about object behavior and will inevitably be discovered in the course of the discussion with users. They should not need to be thrown away as a result of an inexpressive notation. Rules may be of several different types. For instance, we may have triggers, business policies, environmental constraints, and control rules. Business rules typically relate two or more attributes and triggers relate attributes to methods. For example:

Business rule:
    If Service_length > 5 then Holiday=25
Forward Trigger:
    When Salary + SalaryIncrement > 20000 run AwardCoCar

Business rules specify second-order information such as dependencies between attributes, (e.g., a dependency between the age of an employee and her holiday entitlement). Lastly, global assertions that apply to all methods may need to be specified. A typical business rule in a personnel application might include "change holiday entitlement to

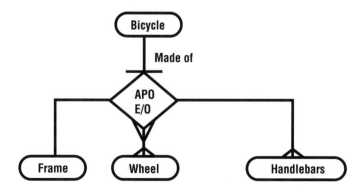

FIGURE 13.4(b). A composition structure (class level).

five weeks when service exceeds 5 years" as a rule in the rules window of the *Employee* object. With this extension the notation can cope with analysis problems where a relational or deductive database with object-oriented features is envisaged as the target environment. Quite complex rules can be expressed simply as rule sets. For example, the *InsuranceSalesman* class might contain the rules for giving the best advice to a customer in the form:

> *If client is retired and Client.RiskAverse: is false*
> > *then BestProduct: is "Annuity"*
> *If client is young and Client.RiskAverse: is false then*
> > *BestProduct: is "Endowment"*
> *If Client.RiskAdvser: is true then*
> > *BestProduct: is "Bonds"*
> *If Client. Children: > 0 then*
> > *Client.RiskAdverse is true*

The rules fire when a value for **BestProduct:** is needed. Note that these rules do not compromise the encapsulation of **Client** by setting the value of **Risk.Averse** in that object. The **Salesman** is merely making an assumption in the face of missing data or prompting the **Client** for that information. If the **Client.RiskAverse:** attribute is already set, these rules never fire.

More interesting is what happens with control rules. Rules may be specified not only to disambiguate multiple inheritance, but to define priority rules for defaults and demons. A demon is a method that wakes up when needed; that is, when a value changes or is added or deleted. In other words, these rules can determine how to resolve the conflict that arises when an attribute inherits two different values or perhaps specify whether the default value should be applied before or after inheritance takes place or before or after a demon fires. They may also specify the relative priorities of inheritance and demons. These rules themselves may have defaults.

An example I have often used to illustrate this idea is the description of an adventure game where a jeweled sword is a kind of weapon and a kind of treasure. **TREASURE** has no operation for killing trolls, but weapons do. Clearly in this case, though not in every case, the jeweled sword must inherit the method from weapon. This can be expressed as a rule for jeweled sword or as one for "takable" items in general, perhaps in the form: *If KillTroll* and not *KillTroll then KillTroll*. Similarly, the jeweled sword gets 10 points from **TREASURE** and 0 points from **WEAPON**. The rule here is to take maxima.

These control rules are encapsulated within objects, instead of being declared globally as is the case with all current implementations in object-oriented programming languages. They may also be inherited and overridden. The benefit of this is that local variations in control strategy are possible. Further, the analyst may inspect the impact of the control structure on every object — using a browser perhaps — and does not have to annotate convoluted diagrams to describe the local effects of global control. If such a global view is desired, state-transition diagrams may be used. Genuinely global rules are contained in a top-level object, called *object*, and will be inherited by all objects that do not override them. Just as state-transition or state-change diagrams may be used to describe the procedural semantics of methods, so decision trees may be found useful in describing complex sets of rules.

Integrity rules are regarded as part of the data semantics and stored as part of the type information.

One must also be aware of the need to decide whether rules belong to individual methods or to the object as a whole. Rules that relate several methods do not belong within those methods, and rules that define dependencies between attributes also refer to the object as a whole. Conversely, rules that concern the encapsulated state of the object belong within one of its methods. The most important kind of "whole object" rules are control rules, which describe the behavior of the object as it participates in structures that it belong to; these are rules that control the handling of defaults, multiple inheritance, exceptions, and general relationships with other objects.

Everything that can be expressed as rules can, in principle, be expressed as a combination of pre-, post-, and invariance conditions. However, doing so can be complex and unreadable. The advantage of rules is clarity and conciseness. The analyst will be able to judge which is best in individual cases. As an example, the rule about holidays could be expressed as a post-condition on the length of service attribute, so that whenever its value changes in any way, a method that updates *Holidays:* is called. This is really a post-condition on the method for updating length of service, not on the attribute. Since this standard method is not usually exhibited, this adds to the difficulty of maintaining its conditions, and the rules approach seems much cleaner on balance. In implementation, this decision may be easily reversed. Where formal correctness is an issue, rules should be avoided because of the possibility of side effects and the lack of a formal proof theory. I find that this is rarely an issue for commercial systems where rules are usually the best form of clear expression for analysis purposes.

BUSINESS POLICY AND PROCESS MODELING

One of the advantages of encapsulating policy in objects is that the same representation that is used for describing computer systems may be used for describing business processes. The current fashion in management science is to denigrate functional descriptions of businesses, emphasizing instead descriptions of business processes. This can be traced to the recent work of Hammer (1990) and Davenport and Short (1990), but also to the much older work of Checkland (1981) on soft systems analysis. Functional descriptions tend to inhibit change and reproduce models of organizations with deep hierarchical structures and excessive functional specialization within the divisions. This leads to difficulties in responding to competitive pressures and restructuring the business. The process-oriented view emphasizes flat organizational structures, project-oriented work groups and, tangentially, the use of information systems to empower employees at all levels in terms of decision-making. The only question left, if you accept the wisdom of building process models, is how this can best be done.

It is obvious to me, and to some other practitioners, that processes are goal-oriented tasks carried out by communicating networks of actors and other objects. Thus, object-oriented analysis ought to be a useful tool for business process re-engineering. One would build an object-oriented model of the processes and use it to simulate changes in a what-if manner. The difficulty here is that many business processes take place in an environment where rules apply: legislation, company policy, psychological constraints, and so on. Current object-oriented analysis methods are primarily designed to model crisp, precisely specified requirements and are not good at process modeling for this reason. Adding rules to objects addresses this problem head-on. Worse still, much business reasoning is perfectly fuzzy — and with good reason. Consider, for example, the trading policy for a futures and options house. One of the rules might include "when market is *moderately bullish* to *very bullish*, buy a call or a vertical call spread" and "when market is *moderately bullish*, buy a butterfly call or a vertical call spread" (Saint-Peter 1984). The terms in italics are irreducibly fuzzy; there is no gain to be had from defining *bullish* exactly because the precision would be self-defeating in terms of complexity alone. Further, how is one to decide which rule applies when the market is moderately bullish? Fortunately, a simple answer is provided by fuzzy set theory. In the latter, *bullish* is represented as a fuzzy set; a vector of truth values between 0 and 1. *Very* and *moderately* are fuzzy modifiers within the fuzzy logic, usually defined by x^2 and $x^{0.5}$. A fuzzy rule system will automatically compute the compatibility between the input data and the rules and fire the rule that is "truest." Thus, the second of our two rules should be weighted higher in a moderately bullish market. (For the details see Graham and Jones 1988.)

SOMA copes with both crisp and fuzzy business rules. Since I have argued that policies should be inheritable as well as encapsulated, this must apply to the fuzzy rules, too. This presents no additional technical difficulties, especially since there are several existing languages in which the aforementioned fuzzy rules could be encoded directly. In ICL's REVEAL (Graham and Jones 1988; Graham 1991b) they would be actual source code with no syntactic changes needed. However, in business models, there is a further difficulty. Suppose, for example, that we have a rule for the accounts department object that says "all accountants must be literate and numerate" (an impossible dream, I realize). Now suppose that within the firm there are specialist accounts departments. By inheritance, the employees of these departments must be literate and numerate, too. The tax department is an accounts department quite unlike the others and because of the nature of the work the requirements for literacy and numeracy (in this imaginary context) are less stringent. Our model may show that *the tax department is an accounts department* **only to a certain extent.**

Suppose we model this by saying that our certainty about the last italicized statement is 0.8. What can we then say about the literacy and numeracy of the tax people? Fortunately, SOMA has a technique for dealing with the problem. When inheritance takes place along AKO links with certainty factors, we attach the certainty to the rules inherited and interpret these rules using the Dempster-Shafer certainty calculus used in MYCIN (Buchanan and Shortliffe 1984). When the rules are fuzzy rules, a mathematical technique is applied that reduces the impact of the fuzzy predicates according to the certainty factors through as many levels of inheritance as necessary. This technique is too complex to describe here, but is described in detail in Graham (1991a and 1993c). The result in this case is a rule that is interpreted as "tax accountants must be fairly literate and fairly numerate."

The practical import of these rather abstract observations is that all the factors and processes within a business can be directly modeled within SOMA or any other similarly extended method. Of course, the fuzzy extensions will be used rarely, but like multiple inheritance, they provide great power on the rare occasions when they are necessary. My observations also imply that one can move from mere passive object-oriented modeling of a business to active simulations based on (fuzzy) rule-based languages.

Conclusion

Object-oriented methods give us a very good way of representing knowledge about systems, businesses, or computers. Extending them to capture policy in a direct, readable fashion provides a number of benefits and opens up new applications in business process re-engineering and soft systems analysis. Permitting encapsulated, inheritable policies embeds the rule idea naturally within the object-oriented metaphor and leads to a uniform style of expression and a clear understanding of the status of rules within the model. Using the same modeling techniques for both business and systems analysis enhances traceability and enables better communication between the analysts and the users.

References

Bryant, A., and A. Evans (1993) OO Oversold, *Proceedings of OT'93*, British Computer Society OOPS Specialist Group, Cambridge, England.

Buchanan, B. G., and E. H. Shortliffe (1984) *Rule-Based Expert Systems: The MYCIN Experiments of the Stanford Heuristic Programming Project*, Addison-Wesley, Reading, MA.

Checkland, P. (1981) *Systems Thinking, Systems Practice*, Wiley, Chichester, UK.

Davenport, T. H. and J.E. Short (1990) The New Industrial Engineering: Information Technology and Business Process Redesign, *Sloan Management Review*, Summer, 11–27.

Graham, I.M. (1991a) *Object-Oriented Methods*, Addison-Wesley, Wokingham, UK.

Graham, I.M. (1991b) Fuzzy Logic in Commercial Expert System Shells: Results and Prospects, *Fuzzy Sets and Systems*, 40(3): 451–472.

Graham, I.M. (1993a) OOPS-59 Conference Report, *Object Magazine*, 2(6).

Graham, I.M. (1993b) Migration Using SOMA: A Semantically Rich Method of Object-Oriented Analysis, *Journal Of Object-Oriented Programming*, 5(9).

Graham, I.M. (1993c) *Object-Oriented Methods*, 2nd Edition, Addison-Wesley, Wokingham, UK.

Graham, I.M. (1994) *Migrating to Object Technology*, Addison-Wesley, Wokingham, UK (in press).

Graham, I.M., and P.L.K. Jones (1988) *Expert Systems: Knowledge, Uncertainty and Decision*, Chapman and Hall, London.

Hammer, M. (1990) Reengineering Work: Don't Automate, Obliterate, *Harvard Business Review*, July–August: 104–112.

Martin, J. (1993) *Principles of Object-Oriented Analysis and Design*, Prentice-Hall, Englewood Cliffs, NJ.

Nerson, J. (1992) Applying Object-Oriented Analysis and Design, *Communications of the ACM* 35(9): 63–74.

Saint-Peter, N. (1984) *How to Make Money in Stock Options*, Prentice-Hall, Englewood Cliffs, NJ.

chapter 14

Requirements Analysis with the Object-Oriented Software Development Method

Edward Colbert   *Absolute Software Co.*

By integrating object-oriented requirements analysis with object-oriented design, the Object-Oriented Software Development method (OOSD) allows a practical focus on the objects of a problem throughout. OOSD requirements analysis clearly represents problem requirements and leads smoothly to design, creating a single, consistent abstract model with strong validation and verification that is easy to maintain and closely follows the "real world." This chapter applies OOSD to a sample problem and shows how OOSD achieves its goals.

INTRODUCTION

OOSD seeks to identify the objects in a problem, to understand the structural and behavioral modularity and properties of each object, and to recognize objects that are members of a common class and so share modularity, behavior, and properties, in a single consistent abstract model. In requirements analysis, this model identifies the *what*: the required objects, classes, functions, behavior, and properties of the problem. In design, this model determines the *how*: it is refined into an architecture for software components with a smooth transition to code. The model is developed and viewed through graphic and textual representations that provide ready communication.

OOSD formally defines the properties of objects, describing the system as an object. The system is then refined into its component objects. Classes are methodically identified by generating them from objects in the system. A particularly thorough verification procedure establishes that the system is correctly implemented and achieves the required properties. Objects are treated uniformly, including the system object. By performing the same essential activities in analysis, preliminary design, and detailed design, an unusually consistent model is built that closely follows the real world, can be tested early, and is easy to modify and reuse.

OOSD can be applied in a variety of development models including evolutionary, spiral, waterfall, prototyping, and market-driven (Royce 1970, Boehm 1981, Boehm 1988, Gilb 1988, Sodhi 1991, Summerville 1992). In this chapter, I will use the waterfall model, which is relatively linear and suitable for written exposition. I will discuss OOSD requirements analysis, with an overview of how OOSD is applied to design.

OOSD REQUIREMENTS ANALYSIS

Our goal during requirements analysis is to understand what the customer needs us to build. We build a model of the application and validate that our model will actually meet the customer's needs. OOSD recognizes the system itself as an object.

In OOSD requirements analysis, four activities are performed on the system object to create the model of the application. Graphic and textual representations produced by these activities are used to validate the model. The four activities are:

- Object-interaction specification
- Object-class specification
- Behavior specification
- Property specification

These activities can be performed in almost any order once an initial object-interaction specification has been done (and they are discussed in a different order below). An iterative approach is recommended, since the performance of each activity generally suggests refinements in the others.

Two different strategies for requirements analysis have been found to be useful. When starting a new development (*green-field development*), we begin by identifying, in the context of the system object, the objects and classes that are required. When reworking an existing system (re-engineering a system, or restructuring an organization or business), we apply an approach described by Ken Orr (Orr 1981) as *middle-up-down*, where we describe the objects and classes that are components of the current system or organization ("middle"), abstract away the details of the implementation and define the boundary of the new system or organization ("up"), then design the new components ("down").

In this chapter, I will show how OOSD is used in a new development, analyzing a temperature-monitoring problem given in an early book by Booch (Booch 1986)[1].

Temperature Monitoring Problem

There exists a collection of ten independent sensors that continually monitor temperatures in an office building. Initially, all of the sensors are disabled. We may explicitly enable or disable a particular sensor, and we may also force its status to be recorded. Furthermore, we may set the lower and upper limits of a given sensor. In the event that any of the enabled sensors registers an out-of-limits value, the system must immediately post an alarm condition. In addition, it must request and record the status of all the sensors every 15 minutes (set by a timer hardware interrupt). If any sensor does not respond within 5 seconds after this time, we must assume that the sensor is broken and immediately post another alarm. Asynchronously, a user command may order us to enable or disable a specific sensor, set the temperature limits, or force the status of a given sensor to be recorded. In any case, failure of the user interface must not affect the monitoring of any currently enabled sensors.

The sensors are located in the lobby, main office, warehouse, stock room, terminal room, library, computer room, lounge, loading dock, and cleaning room. They use memory-mapped I/O ports to write integer values to the ten 16-bit words starting at address 16#0100#. Each value when multiplied by the precision of the sensor (0.5°) results in the external temperature value. When a fault is detected or a sensor goes out of limits, the system will turn on a warning light, which the user must manually clear. To activate a warning light, the system must place all 1's (16 bits) in the memory-mapped I/O ports: 16#0010# (address of fault warning); 16#0011# to 16#001A# (address of out-of-limits warning).

Object-Interaction Specification

Object-interaction specification identifies the objects that are required to communicate with our system, and the interactions between our system and these objects, using an object-interaction diagram (OID) and a dictionary. Object-interaction diagrams describe a set of objects and the interactions between the objects (see Figure 14.1). The object-interaction diagram is the fundamental representation of the model of the application; the

---

[1]Although a later edition of the book has appeared, the problem as stated in the edition I cite has certain useful features for this chapter. The following discussion will find various inadequacies in the problem statement. This process is typical of software development; it is nearly inevitable, given human limitations, and should not be seen as a reflection on the original author.

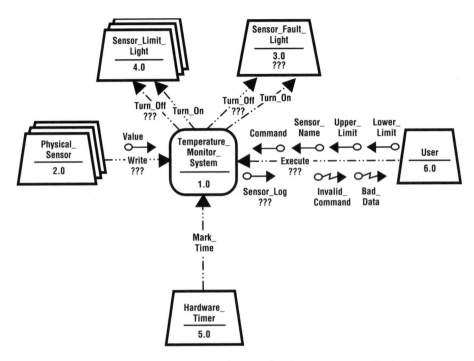

FIGURE 14.1. Context object-interaction diagram for the *Temperature_Monitor_System*.

top-level OID, called a *context diagram* or *external view*, describes the system object in the context of those objects, outside the system, which the system object interacts with. The dictionary lists every part of the system model (e.g., objects, classes, interactions), giving the purpose, requirements, and any other useful information.

OBJECT-INTERACTION DIAGRAM

OOSD considers an object *active* if it displays independent motive power. A *passive* object, by contrast, can only perform work, and can only change its state, while performing one of its operations in response to a request by another object, ultimately under the motivation of an active object. An active object need not exercise its motive power (e.g., a human being sometimes acts in response to requests or commands). A printer demon would be represented as an active object, even though it does not perform any work until it receives a print request from another object; when the demon receives the request, the demon releases the other object and performs the actual printing on its own power. External objects are outside the scope of the system to be implemented.

In an object-interaction diagram (Figure 14.1), active objects are shown by round-cornered rectangles (e.g., *Temperature_Monitor_System*), passive objects are shown by

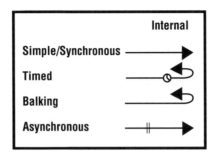

FIGURE 14.2. Types of request.

square-cornered rectangles (e.g., in Figure 14.9), and external objects are shown by trape-zoids (e.g., **User**). Shadowing (e.g., **Physical_Sensor**) indicates multiple objects of the same class, which are distinguished by some form of mapping (e.g., an address). The names of objects should be nouns.

An interaction describes a request by one object to another that the requested object perform one of its operations, along with any objects or data that are exchanged as part of the interaction. Interactions are shown in an object-interaction diagram by arrow-shaped arcs connecting the objects that interact. Interface interactions, (i.e., with an external object) are shown by lines with a dash-dot-dot pattern. Often their implementation involves hardware and has special properties. The arc is labeled with the name of the operation being requested, which should be a verb or verb phrase.[2] An operation is *requested by* the object shown at the tail of the arrow in the interaction, performed by the object shown at the head of the arrow.

The arc is annotated to distinguish four kinds of requests, according to the way the request is issued (Figure 14.2). In a *synchronous* request, the two objects will remain syn-chronized throughout the interaction (like a telephone conversation).[3] In an *asynchronous* request, the requesting object issues its request, but does not wait to see if the request is received or the requested operation is performed (like mailing a letter). *Timed* and *balking* requests are essentially synchronous, but the requesting object can give up (i.e., stop wait-ing). In a timed request, the requesting object gives up if the performing object does not start performing the requested operation in a specified period of time. In a balking

---

[2]If this convention is not strictly enforced, people accustomed to Structured Analysis tend to treat requests as data flows, and people accustomed to languages using a message and method scheme, like SmallTalk [Goldberg 1989; Wegner 1990] tend to treat requests as messages. OOSD views methods as ways of implementing opera-tions, and messages as ways of implementing requests.

[3]If either object is internally concurrent, then possibly only a component is actually synchronized with the other object. If both are internally concurrent, only components of each may be synchronized. This will be clarified by the behavior descriptions of each object.

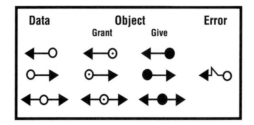

FIGURE 14.3. Flows.

request, the requesting object gives up if the performing object does not start performing the requested operation immediately. In this chapter I take up only synchronous requests. The other types are typically introduced during the refinement of analysis and design.[4]

Four kinds of arrows show exchanges of objects or information during an interaction. The arrowhead on the couple indicates the direction of flow (see Figure 14.3). OOSD distinguishes data flows, grant object flows, give object flows, and error flows. For example, in Figure 14.1 the *Execute* interaction between the *User* object and the *Temperature_Monitor_System* object consists of the *Execute* operation request; four data flows, namely *Command*, *Sensor_Name*, *Limits*, and *Sensor_Log*; no object flows; and two error flows, namely *Invalid_Command* and *Bad_Data*. The *Execute* operation is requested by the *User* object, and performed by the *Temperature_Monitor_ System* object.

By *data flow*, OOSD means a transfer of information between two communicating objects about one or more objects. By *object flow*, OOSD means that one of the communicating objects actually hands over a measure of control of some object, either granting access only while retaining ultimate control (grant object) or giving over control entirely (give object). An *error flow* is a kind of data flow that reports that an object failed to perform a requested operation, with the reason. The error flow is given a name that describes the failure. Other data flows and object flows are given the names of the data or objects to be transferred from the perspective of the performing object.

In all OOSD diagrams, question marks signal an issue that needs to be discussed with the customer (or system engineer). The issue is described in the dictionary entry for the entity marked with a question.

IDENTIFYING OBJECTS AND INTERACTIONS

Many object-oriented methods that identify objects during requirements analysis perform what Shlaer and Mellor call an "object identification blitz" (Booch 1991; Coad and Yourdon 1991; Rumbaugh et al. 1991; Shlaer and Mellor 1992). In OOSD requirements analysis, we consider the system as an object, and we only need to identify the other

---

[4]OOSD users sometimes call a synchronous request "simple," because its semantics are equivalent to a message in SmallTalk, a member function call in C++, or a subprogram or entry call in Ada. An asynchronous request needs some form of mailbox.

objects that are either required to communicate with the system or are exchanged (or about which data is exchanged) during interactions. For example, in Figure 14.1 the *Temperature_Monitor_System* is our system object, *User, Hardware_Timer, Physical_ Sensor(s), Sensor_Limit_Light(s)*, and *Sensor_Fault_Light* are all objects that communicate with the system, *Command, Sensor_Name, Lower_Limit, Upper_Limit, Sensor_Log*, and *Value* are all objects about which data is exchanged during interactions.

We should be able to identify the interactions between the system object and external objects from what is said, in whatever oral or written statements we are given, about communications between objects. For example, we were given the requirement "when a fault is detected or a sensor goes out of limits, the system will turn on a warning light." We represented this as the two interactions where the *Temperature_ Monitor_System* requests the *Turn_On* operation of a *Sensor_Limit_Light* or of the *Sensor_Fault_Light*. Interactions between external objects are by definition generally outside our problem.

In deciding what external objects and interactions to represent, we need to balance two concerns. We want a complete and consistent model, and if our model lacks these qualities it will probably not be correct (see "Validation of the Requirements" later in this chapter). We also want to represent exactly what the customer specified, so we can discuss our model with the customer. In OOSD, we strive for these potentially contradictory goals by adding objects or interactions to those in the problem statement as needed for completeness, flagging new or inconsistent objects and interactions with question marks, and annotating our questions in dictionary entries.

For example, our problem statement said "the system will turn on a warning light which the user must manually clear." Plainly, the *Temperature_ Monitor_System* should request the *Turn_On* operations of the *Sensor_Limit_ Light(s)* and the *Sensor_Fault_Light*, but should it request the *Turn_Off* operation? Turning off (clearing) the lights was not one of the user commands given in the problem statement. Also, we are told of multiple *Sensor_Limit_Light(s)*, but only one *Sensor_Fault_Light*. In our model (Figure 14.1) we included two interactions showing the *Temperature_Monitor_ System* requesting the *Turn_Off* operation of both *Sensor_Limit_Light(s)* and the *Sensor_Fault_Light*. We noted the two interactions and the *Sensor_Fault_Light* with question marks, and described our question in the dictionary entries for the *Turn_Off* interactions and the *Sensor_Fault- _Light*.

In representing external objects and interactions, any given diagram should be kept at a consistent level of abstraction, from the perspective of our system. Usually the problem statement will be found to contain one or more design decisions expressed as requirements. For example, our statement says the system must post an alarm condition when a sensor registers an out-of-limits value, but this is really a design decision implementing a requirement that the system warn the user when a sensor is out of limits. Furthermore, we are given a requirement that "posting an alarm condition be implemented by turning on a warning light," and that "turning on a warning light" be implemented by "placing all 1s (16 bits) in a memory-mapped I/O port." While we must represent what the customer specified, we must also determine the level of abstraction we currently need to work at, and stick with it so long as we are there. If some other level of abstraction appears useful, it should be given another diagram, and possibly deferred to a later activity.

In Figure 14.1, we have represented *Sensor_Limit_Light* and the *Sensor_Fault_Light* as external objects, and have shown the *Turn_On* and *Turn_Off* interactions. To be consistent, we should show a user-interface device rather than the *User*, and we should show how the device interacts with the system. However, since no particular device was required, this ideally should be deferred to design. Figure 14.4 is a view of the system at a more uniform level of abstraction. We have abstracted away the lights, and represented the *Warn_Sensor_Out_Of_Limits* and *Warn_Sensor_Faulty* interactions between the *Temperature_Monitor_System* and the *User*. At the other extreme, we could draw another diagram showing the memory-mapped I/O ports instead of the lights as external objects, and representing *Write* interactions between the *Temperature_Monitor_System* and the ports. In this diagram, we would also represent the sensor ports, which were specified in the problem statement, and ports needed to support the user interface device, which were not specified. Such a diagram would obscure *what* we expect to accomplish (e.g., warning the user that a sensor is faulty or out of limits), while clarifying *how* we expect to accomplish it (e.g., by writing to certain ports).

As a general rule, I recommend drawing a problem view of the context of the system (e.g., Figure 14.4) as a requirements-analysis activity, and drawing a system engineering

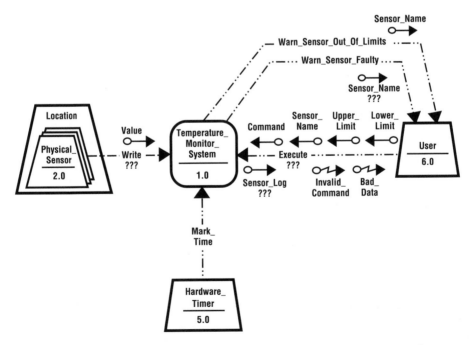

FIGURE 14.4. Context object-interaciton diagram for the *Temperature_Monitor_System* (problem view).

view (e.g., a refined version of Figure 14.1) as a design activity. The problem view better illustrates the communications that must occur; while the system engineering view better illustrates the devices, such as the lights in our example, used to implement the required communications. In addition, because the problem view is more abstract, it leaves us more flexibility to meet system engineering design changes, and is more reuseable and portable.

In most cases the requester and the performer of an interaction, and thus its direction, are obvious from the problem statement. Sometimes the direction is not obvious, especially during design, or during requirements analysis if the context of the system has not been well defined. We then select the direction that seems most natural and study the impact of the choice. Usually setting one direction instead of the other will simplify the behavior of the two objects or otherwise promote software engineering goals. For example, one direction may make polling unnecessary, improving the efficiency of one or both of the objects or ease adding operations to one of the objects, making it more adaptable.

Objects that only request services from the system are not as critical to identify as the services they request. The system does not care which object makes the request; as long as the proper information or objects are supplied, the system will perform the service. However, showing the objects that issue requests is useful for talking to the customer or system engineers, and facilitates communication among reviewers and developers.

Behavior Specification

The object-interaction diagram gives a static view of the behavior of each object in the system. Object-interaction diagrams show which objects interact, but not under what conditions. For example, Figure 14.1 does not show what conditions cause **Temperature_ Monitor_System** to request **Turn_On** from **Sensor_Fault_Light**.

The behavior specification activity identifies the dynamic behavior of the system object. OOSD uses statecharts (Figures 14.5 and 14.6), derived from Harel (Harel 1987, 1988), to represent behavior; however, other graphic representations could be used.

Harel statecharts are based on traditional state transition diagrams that describe "behavior in ways that are clear and realistic, and at the same time formal and rigorous, sufficiently so to be amenable to detailed computerized simulation [or other analysis techniques]" (Harel 1987). The behavior of a system is described in terms of states, stimuli that cause changes of state, and any actions that are performed in response to a stimulus in addition to the change of state. Harel extended traditional state transition diagrams by formalizing the representation of hierarchical states ("depth"), that is, states nested within other states, simultaneous ("orthogonal") behavior, and communication between simultaneous behaviors. As Harel puts it (Harel 1987):

In a nutshell, one can say:

statecharts = state-diagrams + depth + orthogonality
+ broadcast-communication

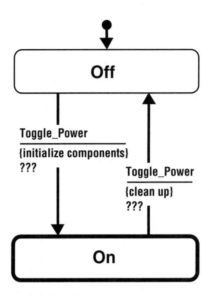

FIGURE 14.5. Top-level behavior diagram for the *Temperature_Monitor_System* (external view).

OOSD statecharts integrate Harel's basic notation with the object-oriented concepts of objects, classes, and operations, and can be used to describe any object.

OOSD Statechart Notation

In an OOSD statechart, a basic state is represented by round-cornered rectangles (e.g., *Off* and *On* in Figure 14.5). The label of a basic state contains the name of the state, and a description of any work performed while in the state (except work that for accuracy must be shown by decomposing the state). If work is mentioned, its description is placed under a horizontal line.

A state may summarize more detailed behavior, in which case it is drawn with boldface lines when collapsed and normal lines when expanded (e.g., the *On* state in Figures 14.5 and 14.6). A state may have substates, shown by drawing their rectangles inside its rectangle. A state may also be drawn with separate, dashed rectangles to represent *orthogonal components*.[5] A state (and any orthogonal component) may contain substates or orthogonal components, but not both.

In Figure 14.6, we have expanded the *On* state of the *Temperature_Monitor_System*

---

[5]Harel draws dashed lines across the rectangle to show these components, but drawing the components as separate parts, so they can be treated independently (e.g., by selecting them with drawing programs), making it easier to manipulate the diagram.

and all of its substates and orthogonal components, illustrating how the system behaves when it is on. The *On* state has three orthogonal components, indicating that when the *Temperature_Monitor_System* is on, it simultaneously exhibits *Recording*, *Sensor_ Management*, and *Command_Processing*, and that *Sensor_Management* simultaneously exhibits *Value_Monitoring* and *Testing*. The shadowing on the orthogonal component *Sensor_Management* indicates multiple occurrences of this behavior; the number of occurrences is part of the dictionary entry for *Sensor_Management*. *Command_Processing* consists of three states, *Wait*, *Wait_for_Acknowledge*, and *Record_Status*. *Record_Status* has four substates, *Wait_for_Sensor*, *Sensor_Responded*, *No_Response*, and a *termination state* represented by a bull's-eye.

In representing behavior, we first note the state in which the behavior starts. The diagram shows a solid circle called the *start* or *default marker*. A change-of-state arc points from the start marker to the *start state*. In Figure 14.5, *Off* is the start state.

A change of state, called a *transition*, is represented by an arc connecting the states. Most changes of state are conditional; the condition is described in a label on the arc. If some work is to be performed along with the change of state, the work is described in the label, below a horizontal line separating it from the condition (even if there is no condition, the horizontal line is always shown). Any action shown in the label is performed, followed by any work of the state. If a change is to occur by default (i.e., after completing any work of the state if no condition for another change is met), no condition is described. In our notation, an object remains in a state until some condition for change is met (including a default transition). If, for a particular state and condition, the result of the condition's occurring will be a return to the same state, OOSD represents this explicitly by drawing a "transition" that returns to the state it came from.

In many cases, behavior ends in a state from which there can be no change, called a *termination state*. We chose to show a possible cycle from *Off* to *On*, instead of showing a termination state, pending clarification of the requirements for turning the system on and off.

Figure 14.5 shows that the system will change from *Off* to *On* when a toggle power request is received from some other object, and when the request arrives, the system will initialize its components. We have placed question marks on the two transitions because the problem description did not specify how the system is to be turned on or off, nor any requirements related to the often critical issues of initialization and cleanup.

We consider that a *condition* for a change of state will be some event, or the result of some internal test, or both. We consider that an *event* is:

- The receipt of either a request from another object that the object perform one of its operations or a message from another orthogonal part
- A time-out

An *internal test* (shown in a label by brackets) may:

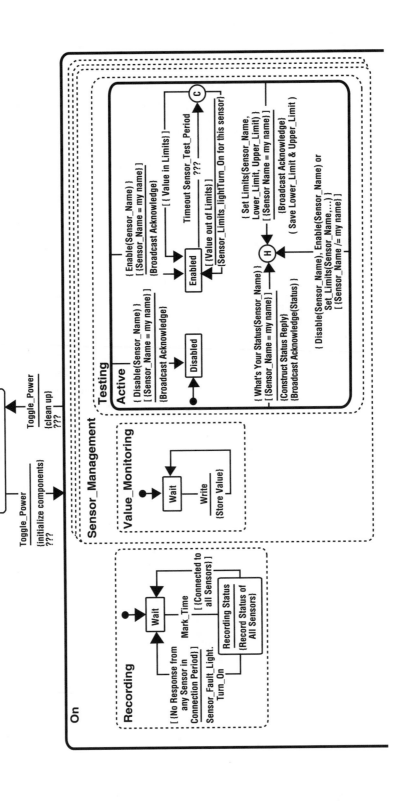

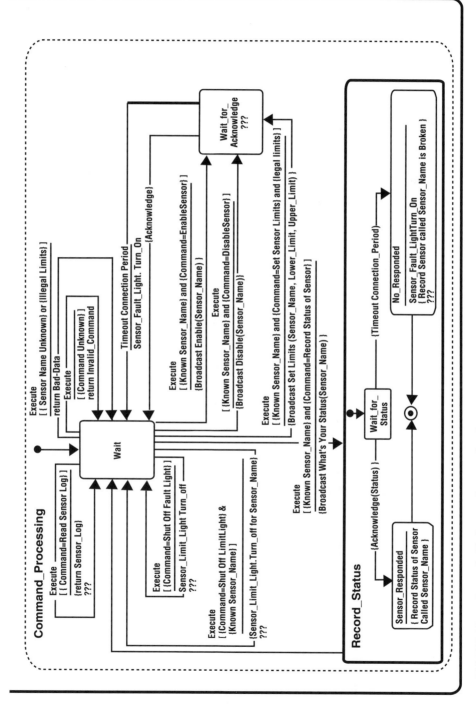

FIGURE 14.6. Expanded behavior diagram for the *Temperature_Monitor_System* (external view).

- Test what state another orthogonal part is in
- Test the value (state) of a parameter of an operation
- Test an attribute of the object whose behavior we are representing

In Figure 14.6, each of the three transitions from *Command_Processing.Wait* to *Command_Processing.Wait_for_Acknowledge* shows a change conditional on both an event and a test result. For example, the system will change when *Execute* is requested, and *Command = Enable Sensor,* and the *Sensor_Name* is known.

When a change leads to a state that has substates or orthogonal parts, we must show clearly which substate is the current state. We specify this in three ways:

- The transition can be directly attached to a specific substate.
- A *default (start) state* can be specified.
- A *state entrance* indicator can be specified.

In Figure 14.5, transitions are drawn from start markers in each orthogonal component, which shows that when changing to the on state, the *Recording*, *Command_Processing*, and *Sensor_Management.Value_Monitoring* orthogonal components each start in their respective wait substates, while *Sensor_Management.Testing* starts in its active substate.

When a change leads out of a state that has substates or orthogonal parts, there is a change out of all substates. In Figure 14.6, the transition from *Sensor_Management.-Value_Monitoring.Active* to *Sensor_Management.Value_Monitoring.Active.Disable* indicates that the system will change to the disable state from the current substate of the active state when a *Disable(Sensor_Name)* message with the appropriate *Sensor_Name* is received.

We consider that work consists of one or more *actions*,[6] and that if more than one action is specified, they are to be performed in the sequence stated. We consider an *action* to be:

- A request that another object perform one of its operations
- A message broadcast from the orthogonal component we are looking at to others
- An "informal description"; that is, a relative abstraction that may later (possibly not until design) need further refinement

Bearing in mind that we want to be "amenable to detailed computerized simulation," it is still often convenient to include conditions and actions at a stage when we are aware of them, but not yet prepared to describe them formally. OOSD encloses these informal descriptions in braces (e.g., *{Initialize.Components}* in Figure 14.6). Although we spoke of broadcast messages and informal descriptions separately in describing actions just now,

---

[6]OOSD does not preserve Harel's distinction between work in states, which he calls *activity*, and work on transitions, which he calls *action*.

broadcast messages are by their nature informal descriptions, and are thus enclosed in braces.

In Table 14.1, the action *Sensor_Fault_Light.Turn_On* in the behavior *Recording* is a request for an operation. The action *{Broadcast Enable (Sensor_Name)}* on the transition from *On.Command_Processing.Wait* to *On.Command_Processing.Wait_for_Acknowledge* is a broadcast message (in this instance received by *Sensor_Management.Testing*). The action *{Recording Status of All Sensors}* in the *On.Recording.Recording_Status* state is an informal description.

When a description of work is associated with a state that may later be expanded, the description summarizes the work refined later in the orthogonal components or substates. For example, the state *On.Recording.Recording_Status* could be expanded to show the detailed behavior represented by the description *{Recording Status of All Sensors}*.[7]

We may wish to abstract away whatever time some particular work may require. We represent such work on a transition. In Figure 14.5 we have placed *{Initialize Components}* on the transition between the *off* and *on* states; relative to the time we expect the system to be *on*, we consider that initializing components takes zero time. When we consider work as taking non-zero time, we associate the work with a state. With these two notations for representing work, which show the abstraction of time in our behavior description explicitly, the object we are examining is always in a defined state at any instant in time, not "in transition."

Note that, more specifically, we have treated initializing components in Figure 14.6 as taking zero time for purposes of the current abstraction. If we later want to expand the transition between *Off* and *On* to show an intermediate state where the work of initializing components is performed, we can treat initializing components as taking substantial time for purposes of that level of abstraction.

OOSD uses the specialized operation state and operation request state to show the precise timing of synchronous communications (including timed and balking). In an operation state, represented by a hexagon, an object is performing the work immediately associated with one of its operations. The operation state is given the name of the operation (with the operation's formal parameter list, if appropriate). The actions (or substates) of an operation state describe the work to performed when the operation is requested. The operation state is shorthand for the frequently occurring pattern *state_name /{perform operation}* which is then expanded to *state_name / {do action_1}, {do action_2},...* where *action_1, action_2*, describes *perform operation* in detail. While the performing object is in the operation state, the requesting object waits (assuming a synchronous communication). Once the performing object leaves the operation state, the requesting object is released.

In an operation request state, represented by an oval and named with the operation requested (i.e. *object_name.operation_name* with actual parameters, if appropriate), an

---

[7]In Harel's nomenclature, work associated with the parent is "concurrent with" the work associated with the substates, but OOSD omits this because his orthogonal components already show concurrency.

object requests that another object perform one of its operations. The operation request state is shorthand for the frequently occurring pattern *state_name /object_name.operation_name (parameters...)*. The object in this state waits for the named object to accept and perform the specified operation. There should be a default transition from the operation request state, describing what state the requesting object will change to when released by the performing object. If the operation request is timed, there should be a transition with a *time-out* to define how long the requesting object will wait for the performing object to accept the request, and what state the requesting object will change to if the time limit expires.

Timing issues are not critical to our present problem, so these states are only noted for completeness.

In many instances, OOSD will allow two or more legal representations of behavior. The user should consider whether a particular representation is more suitable for the purpose at hand. Some representations will be equivalent.

Behavior of the System Object

OOSD describes the behavior of the system object as well as the behavior of system components. This promotes uniformity and guards against uninspected assumptions about the design. In requirements analysis, we describe the behavior of the system object expected (required) by the customer, independent of the components that will be used to build it. For example, Figures 14.5 and 14.6 describe the behavior of the *Temperature_Monitor_System*.

We study the described system behavior, in whatever oral or written statements we are given, for the interactions between the system object and external objects (how the system should respond to requests for each of its operations, when and under what conditions it issues requests to external objects), and what other work the system is expected to do. We want a complete and consistent description of the way the system object is expected to behave (see "Validation of the Requirements" later in this chapter).

As a general rule, I recommend starting the behavior description either with *On* and *Off* states, as in Figure 14.5, or with an "alive state," which is the start state, and a termination state (i.e., "dead"), and then elaborating the "on" or "alive" behavior. Starting the behavior description at the on/off (alive/dead) level protects the developer from overlooking the requirements for start-up and shut-down. How is the system created[8] or activated? What initialization must be performed? How is the system destroyed or deactivated, and what clean-up must be done? Once the system is created, can it be reactivated after it is deactivated?

Our problem statement did not describe the start-up or shut-down behavior of the *Temperature_Monitor_System*, so for completeness we proposed (Figure 14.5) that the *Temperature_Monitor_System* is required to accept a *Toggle_Power* operation request to

---

[8]OOSD allows a distinction between creation or destruction on the one hand, which strictly speaking are performed by an external object, and activation or deactivation on the other hand, which are performed by the system object.

switch from *Off* to *On* and vice versa, that the *Temperature_Monitor_System* will initialize components when going *on*, and that some clean-up will be part of the transition to *Off*. We documented our questions on these points in the dictionary.

Once we have established the expected start-up and shut-down, we next want to describe the system object when it is *on*. If it is to perform multiple simultaneous behavior, we need to represent the *On* state in corresponding orthogonal parts and describe each.

As described in our problem statement, the *Temperature_Monitor_System* must "continually monitor temperatures," and post an alarm if "any of the enabled sensors register an out-of-limits value." It must record the status of the sensors every 15 minutes (set by a timer hardware interrupt). The system must also process user commands. In Figure 14.6, we represented this simultaneous behavior by expanding the *On* state into the three orthogonal parts *Sensor_Management*, *Recording*, and *Command_Processing*, respectively. Since the problem description states that there are ten sensors, we have shown multiple occurrences of the *Sensor_Management* behavior. We have further shown *Value_Monitoring* and *Testing* as orthogonal parts of *Sensor_Management*.

In Figure 14.6, the orthogonal part *Recording* indicates that the *Temperature_Monitor_System* must periodically record the status of all sensors. *Recording* shows that the system starts in a *wait* state, and stays there until receiving a request for the *Mark_Time* operation. Upon receiving that request, the system changes to the state *Recording_Status*, and performs the action *{Record Status of All Sensors}*. Upon completing this action, the system will return to *wait*. If the system *failed to connect* to *any sensor*, it issues the request *Turn_On* to the *Sensor_Fault_Light*. We defer until later the details of how the *Temperature_Monitor_System* performs *{Record Status of All Sensors}*, which is thus shown in brackets. For now, we may treat this as a design decision.

The behavior diagram and object-interaction diagram belong to an integrated description of the system. The behavior diagram is not a separate model, but part of the model of the system object. Every interaction shown in the object-interaction diagram is reflected in the behavior diagram, and vice versa. If the object-interaction diagram shows the system object accepting a request to perform an operation, then the behavior diagram must show at least one condition for state change, with the acceptance of the requested operation, and what the system does in response. If the object-interaction diagram shows the system object issuing a request to an external object, then the behavior diagram must show at least one action where the request is issued. Note that if the object (or its class) has been reused from another system, the behavior diagram may show the acceptance of a request that is not shown as a request in the object-interaction diagram.

Comparing Figure 14.6 with its context object-interaction diagram (Figure 14.1), we can see that there is at least one condition for state change for each request of the *Temperature_Monitor_System* shown. We can also see that for each request issued by *Temperature_Monitor_System* as shown in its context object-interaction diagram, there is at least one action where the request is issued. The behavior diagram shows that the *Temperature_Monitor_System* must accept a request for its *Toggle_Power* operation in order to change between its *On* and *Off* states — which we just noticed the need for, and added. There is still no entry in the context-level object-interaction diagram for the *Temperature_Monitor_System* showing the operation requested, so we must be sure to add this operation here too, with its question marks.

Property Specification

The object-interaction diagrams and the statecharts show which objects *interact* and *under what conditions*, but not how well. For example, Figures 14.1, 14.5, and 14.6 do not show how frequently the *Temperature_Monitor_System* can (or is required to) accept the request for its *Write* operation, nor do they show how easy the system is to use. These "how well" issues belong to property specification.

The property-specification activity defines the quality of an object in terms of *operational characteristics* (properties). During requirements analysis, we specify the required quality goals and resource constraints for the system object.[9]

PROPERTY FORMS AND TABLES

Two textual representations are used: the property specification form and the property summary table (Gilb 1988). The property specification form (Table 14.1) states the unit of measurement ("scale") for each property of an object (including the system object), how the property will be tested ("test"), the minimum ("worst acceptable") and desired ("plan") measures to be met, best-known ("record") and past-performance ("past") measures, current (now) measure, notes, references, and questions. The *test* field should include any separate tests for different phases of the development life cycle, or for different conditions that may affect the object (e.g., wet roads affecting a car's braking distance). Likewise, *worst acceptable, plan, record, past*, and *now* should include any special measures that depend on particular conditions. If in filling out this form or revising it in the process of development, we find a worst acceptable that is greater than the record or plan, we thus discover a risk that a property will fail its minimal or desired achievement. Likewise, as we proceed we can watch the achievement of a property by verifying from time to time that the *now* value is in the range defined by *worst acceptable* and *plan*.

The property summary table (Table 14.2), which summarizes all properties of an object (including the system object), helps analyze trade-offs between properties, risks of failing to achieve desirable or necessary combinations, and alternate designs (see "Validation of the Requirements," later in this chapter).

DEFINING THE SYSTEM OBJECT'S PROPERTIES

Formally defining the properties of an object (including its operations and interactions) is a characteristic feature of OOSD that is absent in most methods. In requirements analy-

---

[9]In the past, these have been called the *non-functional requirements*, perhaps an unfortunate name.

TABLE 14.1. Property specification form for **Write** frequency.

Name	Write Frequency
Applies to	*Temperature_Monitor_System.Write*
Description	How often the *Temperature_Monitor_System.Write* operation can be processed by the *Temperature_Monitor_System* without loss of data
Scale	Cycles/Second
Test	The operation will be initiated repeatedly for 1-hour period at a fixed number of cycles/second, starting at the plan level, decreasing by 1 cycle/second, until each interaction during the hour succeeds. The interval at which all interactions succeed defines the value for this operation.
Worst Acceptable	50 cycles/second
Plan	70 cycles/second
Record	
Past	
Now	
Note	Sample Numbers. The plan level of average interaction is designed as a 40% safety margin (e.g., hardware change).
References	
Questions	

sis, we define the properties required of the system object. We look for quality goals such as those related to reliability, performance, useability, availability, safety, adaptability, security, and for constraints on resources such as equipment, time, people, and money. For each property identified, we fill out a property specification form (Table 14.1).

Often, properties are incompletely described in the documentation we are given. If only a value is specified, we must verify whether the customer meant it as a minimum (worst acceptable) or a desired value. It is also vital to define, and get our customer's agreement to, a test for the property that will be used to determine whether we have achieved an acceptable level. By making sure of this now, we guard against delivering a product that is acceptable according to our tests, but a failure according to the customer's. We may have to research past projects, including literature, to determine past and record values. (Note that we did not attempt to research these for the properties defined in Tables 14.1 and 14.2).

TABLE 14.2   Property summary table for ***Temperature Monitor System***.

Name	Applies to	Scale	Worst Acceptable	Plan	Record	Past	Now
Write Frequency	*Temperature_ Monitor_ System.Write*	cycles/ second	50	70	?	?	
Ease of Use, Time to Learn	*Temperature_ Monitor_ System*	weeks	2 (qualified)	1 (qualified)	?	?	
Ease of Use, Productivity	*Temperature_ Monitor_ System*	operations/ hour	30	60	?	?	
Ease of Use, Error Rate	*Temperature_ Monitor_ System*	errors/ hour	3	1	?	?	

We noted above that problem statements often prove to contain design decisions expressed as requirements. We may likewise expect to find some properties stated to us in terms of expected solutions that the customer hopes will achieve a desired but unspecified result. For example, by way of describing ease of use, a property, the customer may specify the currently popular human interface, a solution (e.g., "I need a mouse-windowing environment."). However, specifying a solution does not ensure that the desired result will be achieved (Gilb 1988). It is part of our task to recognize when a statement has in fact specified a solution. This usually indicates that the intended property was difficult to define. We attack a hard-to-define property by identifying and defining the factors (sub-properties) that compose it. For example, productivity, error rate, and time-to-learn are factors in ease of use (Table 14.2).

To get a complete inventory of the properties a system needs, we must often review similar systems to identify properties omitted from the documentation we are given. While some argue that if it's not described in the documentation, it's not required, we would be remiss in our duties as hired experts and as engineers if we did not pursue our own technical examination of what was needed, and take up any apparent omissions or discrepancies with the customer. Furthermore, if we fail to do so, we run the risk of developing a system that the customer cannot use and will not want to pay for (or if far enough from his needs, may be unable to pay for).

We may be overwhelmed if we try to develop a complete list of properties all at once. One strategy for managing this risk is assigning priorities to each of the properties and using an evolutionary process to develop the system (instead of the waterfall process, which this chapter follows for convenience). In the first build of the system, we focus on the most critical 10 or 20 properties, and in later builds, work on the rest (Gilb 1988). Such procedures also help to evaluate alternate designs.

Object-Class Specification

The object-interaction diagrams, statecharts, and property forms and tables show which objects interact, under what conditions and how well, but not what classes are used to define the objects or the flows, nor the relations between classes, nor structure of the classes. For example, Figures 14.1, 14.5, and 14.6, and Tables 14.1 and 14.2 do not show the class of the *Value* data flow that passes from *Physical_Sensor* to the *Temperature_Monitor_System* with the *write* request. Defining classes is the province of object-class specification.

The object-class specification activity identifies and defines the class (including its attributes and structure) of each object, and the relations between the classes using object-class diagrams and the dictionary. In requirements analysis, object-class specification defines the classes, attributes, and relations required to describe the system object and its interactions with external objects.

Object-Class Diagram Notation

Object-class diagrams (Figure 14.7) describe the class of each object and information flow in the object-interaction diagrams of a system and describe which classes are related to other classes in the system. In identifying the class of an object, the structural and behavioral modularity and properties of the object are established for the class.

An object-class diagram uses the same notation as an object-interaction diagram to describe objects (see Figure 14.1). Active objects are shown by round-cornered rectangles (e.g., *Temperature_Monitor_System*), passive objects are shown by square-cornered rectangles (e.g., *state*), and external objects are shown by trapezoids (e.g., *Sensor_Fault_Light*). Shadowing (e.g., *Sensor_Limit_Light*) indicates multiple objects of the same class, which are distinguished by some form of mapping (e.g., an address). Operations are represented by hexagons (e.g., *write*) and are shown attached to the symbol for the class that defines the operation. Interface operations (i.e., operations proved by or requested by externals) are shown by lines with a dash-dot-dot pattern. The object-class diagram notation for classes is the same as for objects, except that dashed lines are used (e.g., the external *Hardware_Light_Class*). The names of classes should be nouns with the suffix *_Class*.[10]

An object-class diagram represents nine fundamental relations. Three, *has part* (and its converse *is part of*), *collection of* (and *is member of*), *contains* (and *is contained in*),

---

[10]Since the names of both objects and classes will be nouns, OOSD uniformly includes the suffix *_Class* in the names of classes.

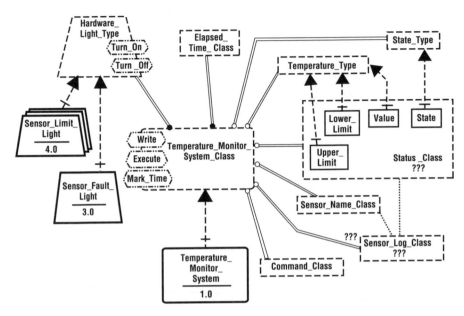

FIGURE 14.7. Object-class diagram for the *Temperature_Monitor_System*.

are represented by graphical enclosure (e.g., **Status_Class** has the parts *Value, Lower_Limit, Upper_Limit,* and *State*; for *collection of* see sensor in Figure 14.9; *contains* is not used in this chapter). The representations for the other six (Figure 14.8) are adapted from Booch's class diagrams (Booch 1991). For example, Figure 14.7 shows that *Temperature_Monitor_System* and *Sensor_Fault_Light* are the *Temperature_Monitor_System_Class* and the *Hardware_Light_Class*, respectively, and that *Temperature_Monitor_System_Class* uses the *Hardware_Light_Class* and the *Elapsed_Time_Class* in its implementation only, and the other classes in its interface.

An attribute is described with its name, its class, and (if appropriate and known) its

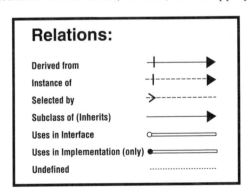

FIGURE 14.8. Object-class diagram relations.

value. To avoid cluttering the object-class diagram, the attributes of objects and classes and the parameters of operations are described in the dictionary. For atomic classes and objects (i.e., ones that cannot be further decomposed, or that the current problem will not require us to decompose further) such as *Temperature_Class* (shown in Table 14.3), OOSD supplies predefined attributes, whose values the developer then specifies. The attributes of non-atomic classes and objects (e.g., *Temperature_ Monitor_System* and *Temperature_ Monitor_System_Class*) are determined by inspecting the behavior description.

Parameters are described with their name, direction of flow, and class name. Table 14.4 shows the parameter descriptions for the operations *Write* and *Execute* of the *Temperature_Monitor_System_Class*.

IDENTIFYING AND DEFINING CLASSES

Unlike most object-oriented methods that identify classes by searching for all possible classes and then eliminating or consolidating classes based on method-specific rules, OOSD identifies specific classes by generalizing from the objects in the model, including their attributes and their operation parameters (except when a class is reused). During requirements analysis, only classes and relations are described which are actually required to define the external view of the system object. For example, each class in Figure 14.7 is needed to define the *Temperature_Monitor_System*, its operations, its interactions with other objects, and its attributes as described in Figures 14.1, 14.5, and 14.6.

We start the object-class specification activity in requirements analysis by identifying the classes of the system object (e.g., *Temperature_ Monitor_System*), and all external objects from which the system object requests operations (e.g., *Sensor_Limit_Light* and *Sensor_Fault_Light*).[11] We add a description of each class to the object-class diagram and dictionary if the class is not yet defined; if we are reusing a class defined earlier in the development, we refine the existing entries as needed; if we are reusing a class from a previous project, we incorporate the definition. We draw an arc for "use in implementation" from the class of the system to each external class.

We add, in the appropriate class, a definition for each operation requested in the object-interaction diagram (e.g., *Write* and *Turn_On*) and not already in the object-class diagram and the dictionary, including definitions for parameters of the objects and information (e.g., *Value*) exchanged during the interaction, improving or creating subclasses of reused definitions as appropriate. We identify the class of each parameter, and confirm that an appropriate description is in the object-class diagram and dictionary. We add or refine attribute descriptions, for the system class, of information (e.g., *Connect_Period*) that the system must know, as shown in the system's behavior description. If a new class is used to define an attribute or an operation parameter, we draw a "use in interface" arc

---

[11]We need not represent the classes of external objects from which our system object requests no operations because our system does not need to know about them — they need to know about our system. For the convenience of reviewers, the object-interaction diagram includes objects that know about our system, but are not known by our system, by providing a complete picture of the interactions between our system object and all externals.

TABLE 14.3. Sample attribute description of classes and objects.

Class/Object	Attributes	
Temperature_Class	Values	−273.15 .. 6,049.0°C (?)
	Precision	.5
	Physical Representation:	16-bit integer multiple of precision
Temperature_Monitor_System_Class	*Connection_Period*	*Elapsed_Time*
	Sensor_Test_Period (?)	*Elapsed_Time*
Temperature_Monitor_System	*Connection_Period*	*Elapsed_Time* = 5 secs
	Sensor_Test_Period (?)	*Elapsed_Time* = ?

from our system class to the new class; otherwise, we draw a "use in implementation" arc.

We create a separate object-class diagram for each new class identified, showing its structure, operations, and relations — easily reused in other systems. (In Figure 14.7 we included the detailed view of **Status_Class** to illustrate some of the points in this paragraph.) For each class added to the object-class diagram, we define its required attributes and operations. We study the behavior diagram of the system object to identify the required operations that each class must provide. For example, the **Temperature_Class** needs to provide comparison operations that our system will use. If the class is atomic, we fill in the values for the predefined attributes (see **Temperature_Class** in Table 14.3). If it is non-atomic, we need to determine what information is known about the class by reviewing the behavior diagram and problem description. For example, our problem description tells us to record the status of a sensor, but omits to specify status; from the expected behavior of the system, we concluded that the **Status_Class** should have four attributes, **Value**, **State**, **Lower_Limit**, and **Upper_Limit**, and we documented our questions. We need

TABLE 14.4. Sample descriptions of operation parameters.

Operation	Parameters		
Temperature_Monitor_System_Class.Write	Value	in	*Temperature_Class*
Temperature_Monitor_System_Class.Execute	*Command*	in	*Command_Class*
	Lower_Limit	in	*Temperature_Class*
	Upper_Limit	in	*Temperature_Class*
	Sensor_Name	in	*Sensor_Name_Class*
	Sensor_Log (?)	out	*Sensor_Log_Class*

our system can integrate with its external objects. For example, in Table 14.3, we define to define the physical representation of any class that is used in an interface to make sure the physical representation of *Temperature_Class* as "16-bit integer multiple of the precision," and in Figure 14.7, we show that the four attributes of *Status_Class* are implemented as component objects (in the dictionary entry, we would specify bit alignment, etc.). We complete the description of each class by adding appropriate relations between the class and other classes.

Validation of the Requirements

We want to verify that our model will meet the customer's needs. We need to eliminate any misinterpretations of the requirements as specified by the customer, and differences between what the customer says and what the customer may actually want. This is validation. Although the topic has, for convenience, been deferred to the end of this chapter, if one defers the activity of validation to the end of development, one risks substantial inefficiency. OOSD facilitates incorporating validation in the process of development. The following steps are done from time to time as the activities described above go on:

1. Verify that the various diagrams, forms, and dictionary that describe the model are consistent. For example, each operation requested of the system object, as shown in the object-interaction diagram, must appear in the statechart as a condition for some change of state, with the possible responses. Each request issued by the system, as shown in the object-interaction diagram, must appear in the statechart as some action, with the conditions that lead to the request. These consistency checks are necessary, but not sufficient to establish that the model is complete and correct.

2. Demonstrate that the behavior of the system object is correct. Since the model is a visual prototype of the system, we can demonstrate that the behavior of the system is correct by studying the interactions described in the object-interaction diagram, devising test scenarios, and "executing" the model against the scenarios. This can be automated by support tools as may be available. If the behavior is not what the customer needs, we revise the model and retest.

3. Verify that the properties as described meet the customer's needs. We review with the customer any properties that pose high risk (i.e., a "worst acceptable" that exceeds the "record" or "plan"), confirm that the customer is aware of the risk, and either establish that the risk will be accepted or explore alternatives. We also need to analyze trade-offs of properties, to discover and see if we can avoid risks of failing to achieve desirable or necessary combinations. We need to identify any properties that conflict (e.g., achieving high efficiency may lower reuseability). We need to include an evaluation of whether we can achieve acceptable levels for all properties combined, including development cost, schedule, and resources.

4. Verify that we can expect the described behavior on schedule. In our problem, the

Temperature_Monitor_System must finish recording the status of sensors before the next *Mark_Time* request arrives.[12] Or, to consider a hypothetical different problem, a bank might have to process all transactions in time to report daily balances to government supervisory agencies. To analyze whether the system will meet its schedule, I recommend the Rate Monotonic Analysis developed by the Software Engineering Institute of Carnegie-Mellon University (Sha 1988; Software Engineering Institute 1990), which predicts mathematically based on the CPU utilization of periodic and aperiodic activities.

Product of Requirements Analysis

By definition, requirements analysis ends when the required context, behavior, and properties of a problem have been clearly identified and validated ("what"). The next step enters preliminary design ("how"). However, managers or customers often extend requirements analysis to include the top-level decomposition of the system so they can review the documentation of this level before authorizing the rest of the design. This request can easily be accommodated by supplying the internal view of the system object, developed at the start of preliminary design, along with the results of OOSD requirements analysis.

OVERVIEW OF OBJECT-ORIENTED DESIGN

The OOSD approach to design refines the model produced during requirements analysis into a software architecture (preliminary design) and creates a representation of that architecture coupled to the implementation language (detailed design). The result of preliminary design is a description independent of language and technology (e.g., what kind of network will be used). Detailed design yields a description specific enough to produce code.

Preliminary Design

In preliminary design, the model of the application that was developed during requirements analysis is now made the top level of the architecture. This architecture is then refined, through considering how the model will be implemented (e.g., the elaboration of Figure 14.1 shown in Table 14.3).[13]

The activities of requirements analysis now take new meaning as they are reused to elaborate the architecture. In this way, the problem model is refined into a solution model.

---

[12]The *Temperature_Monitor_System*, which is watching only an office building, has no close timing constraints. However, it could as easily be watching temperatures in a jet engine or a nuclear reactor.

[13]Note that some of the points mentioned above as properly deferred to design, such as the user interface, will not be taken up in this chapter, which only sketches OOSD design activities.

The products of this activity appear as elaborated versions of the now familiar object-interaction diagrams, object-class diagrams, statecharts, and property specification forms and tables. In addition, we create an object-hierarchy diagram, which illustrates the "has-part" relations of all objects in the system.[14]

In object-interaction specification, we revise the context object-interaction diagram of our system object, incorporating any changes resulting from our discussions with the customer in the course of validating our model. We then create an object-interaction diagram which describes the internal structure of our system (Figure 14.9), called an *internal* or *exploded* view. An internal-view diagram illustrates which objects are part of a higher-level (parent) object by showing them as inside the higher-level object. Object-interaction specification at this stage also shows how a parent interacts with its components, and how the components interact.

Localization and information-hiding are fundamental notions of object-oriented software engineering. The abstraction of an object puts components inside, "hiding" them, while offering a visible set of operations that may be requested. Work in the present system, and any changes, are thus localized and easier to follow. The object-interaction diagram enforces both localization and hiding.

Boldface lines in Figure 14.9 indicate an object that has an internal view in another diagram. Off-page connectors represent objects that the parent object interacts with.

The internal view of an object, and diagrams that represent external views of the object, must consistently show all the interactions between the object (or its components) and objects outside. An operation, which during requirements analysis we viewed as being requested by a parent object may now, at this stage, prove to be only conceptual, and actually implemented as a request by one or more component objects. An interface operation requested of the parent may likewise prove to be only conceptual and implemented as a request on a component.

OOSD develops component objects by applying a set of guidelines, and referring to the system object's properties and to software-engineering goals, to allocate what each parent object is required to know and do (e.g., a component may be created to manage each external object). We want components that have well-defined responsibilities and cooperate to implement the parent object. Components may be reused (e.g., building a new system that incorporates an existing system) or may be instances of reused classes from other systems or other parts of the present system.

With each component object, we repeat the procedure of behavior specification, property specification, and class specification, which we performed for the system object in requirements analysis. If we reuse a component (or a class), we can reuse its behavior diagrams, property tables and forms, and class diagram. If we reuse a component developed outside OOSD, we create diagrams, tables, and forms as needed.

We verify the design of an object (its internal view) against its external view. The design

---

[14]Strictly speaking, object-hierarchy diagram is redundant since its information is already in the object-interaction diagram, but I have found that it helps some people visualize the construction of the system.

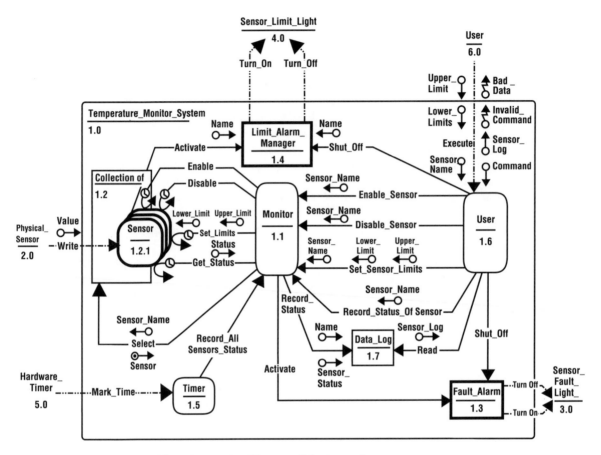

FIGURE 14.9. Object-Interaction Diagram of the internal structure.

of a non-atomic object is best verified before decomposing any non-atomic components. A good design will correctly implement the parent object's external behavior and interactions, and will achieve the parent object's required minimum for every property. The best design will optimize property requirements.

OOSD allows the unusually complete further verification of comparing the results of "executing" the model represented by the internal object-interaction diagram and state-chart of an object, and the external statechart of its components, with the results of executing the model represented by the object's external object-interaction diagram and statechart. We thus obtain a recursive proof, although not a full proof, that the system is correctly implemented and achieves the required properties. We also reapply rate monotonic analysis to verify that the design will perform the described behavior on schedule.

OOSD generally begins with the overall object-interaction diagram and then works down (except where reusing), in a breadth-first instead of "depth-first" strategy. "Breadth first" generally reveals most errors in the external view of an object before we have designed its internal structure. With "depth first", once we found errors in an external-view object, we might have to revise all the lower-level objects used to build it.

Preliminary design formally ends when all non-atomic objects have been represented with internal views (created or reused). A project may, if desired, safely choose to begin detailed design for some or all components without completing preliminary design. For example, we could start detailed design for the *Temperature_Monitor_System* without designing the internal structure of the components *Data_Log, Monitor,* or *User.* If we do carry preliminary design to a formal conclusion, we may get better reuseability, including ease of reimplementation with different technology. This is the usual trade-off of development cost now for potential benefit later.

Detailed Design

We now complete the parallelism of the OOSD process by revisiting the same activities once again, this final time yielding a description detailed enough to generate code. At this stage, our four activities (plus verification) are

1. Language-specific software architecture specification[15]
2. Object-class specification
3. Behavior specification
4. Property specification

These activities modify the graphic and textual representations of the model already produced, and produce new representations. As before, after a first draft of software architecture specification, the activities can be performed in almost any order; since the performance of each generally suggests refinements in the others, an iterative approach is recommended.

For each object and class defined in object-interaction diagrams and object-class diagrams, decisions are now made on how to represent these objects and classes in the implementation language.

Ada and C++ are typical of languages currently used in software development. For Ada, OOSD uses a modified form of Ray Buhr's notation (Buhr 1984, Buhr 1990) in graphic representation, and Ada Program Design Language (PDL) in textual representation. For C++, OOSD uses a notation developed by Mark V Systems Ltd. for graphic representation and a C++ PDL (or pseudocode) for textual representation. There is a straightforward map-

---

[15]Some users like to split software architecture specification in two. Their first activity refines the object-interaction diagrams developed during preliminary design to show specific technology (e.g., a particular type of network or bus) that will be used, independent of language issues. The second creates the language-specific representation.

ping from the objects and class defined in preliminary design to the Ada or C++ software components. Generally, the graphic representation is produced first, then the text.

While partial automation is available for representing the objects as software components, some knowledge of the language is needed for good choices between alternate representations (see Figures 14.10–14.13). Generation of Ada and C++ PDL from the respective graphics and vice versa has been automated.

Object-class specification refines the diagrams produced in preliminary design, capturing any language-specific classes and relations. This is mainly documentation maintenance.

Behavior specification now represents the dynamic behavior of the language-specific architecture and demonstrates that the behavior of the architecture implements the behavior specified for the model. The language-specific structure diagrams and PDL are elaborated to represent the behavior of the software components. Behavior specification:

1. Represents the external view of the behavior of the corresponding object or class in the PDL as a comment, written from the perspective of the user of the component, attached to the declaration of the component
2. Represents the internal view of the behavior of the corresponding object or class

    a. Updates the structure diagram for each component to capture as much detail as possible in the notation
    b. Creates a body for each component and describes the implementation of the component in terms of the internal behavior of the object
    c. For each operation of the object or class, creates a body for the language-specific representation (i.e., a subprogram or entry in Ada or a member function in C++), and describes language-specific logic for the behavior associated with the operation
3. Adds descriptions of any language-specific components needed to complete the representation

Property specification identifies the properties of each software component, and demonstrates that they meet the required properties of the corresponding objects. The property specification forms and tables are used to associate the corresponding properties of objects and components, to govern the choices of mapping to components from preliminary design, and similarly in choosing language-specific implementation.

We verify the language-specific design against the language-independent design. To establish that the correct dynamic behavior has been described for the software architecture, OOSD demonstrates that the dynamic behavior described for each software component is correct, which in turn is done by analyzing or executing the software component to verify that it behaves according to the description of the behavior of the corresponding object. This process could be automated (for example, executing the PDL). Components must be analyzed or executed to verify that they achieve the required properties. We also reapply rate monotonic analysis.

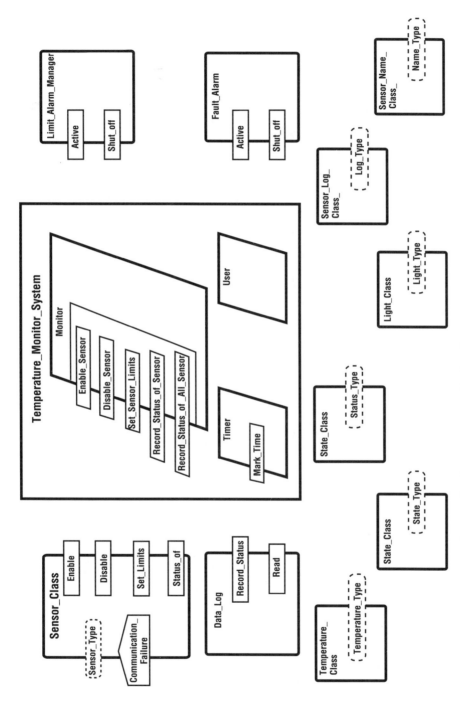

FIGURE 14.10.   Ada structure diagram for the *Temperature_Monitor_System*.

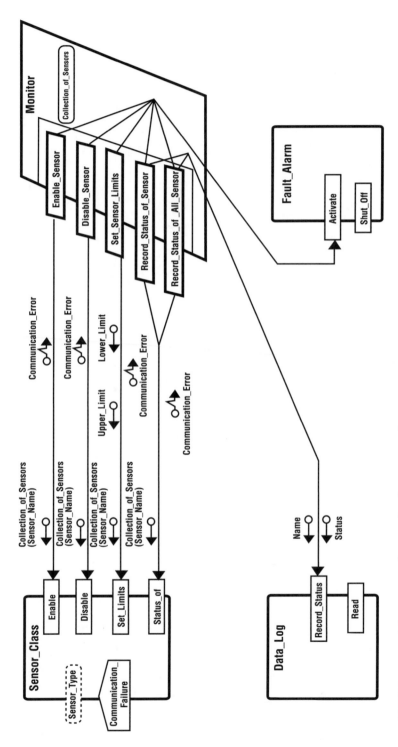

FIGURE 14.11. Ada structure diagram for the monitor object.

Finally, the dictionary is refined to reflect all work to date as a summary and for cross-reference.

CONCLUSION

OOSD develops a single consistent abstract model of the elements of a problem. During requirements analysis, OOSD builds this model from the required objects, classes, functions, behavior, and properties of the problem. During design, the model is refined into an

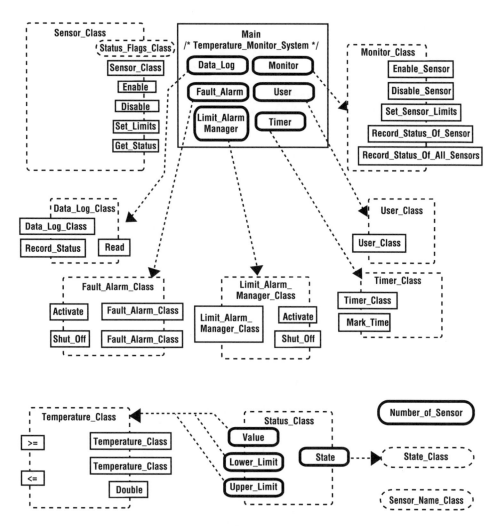

FIGURE 14.12. C++ structure diagram for the *Temperature_Monitor_System.*

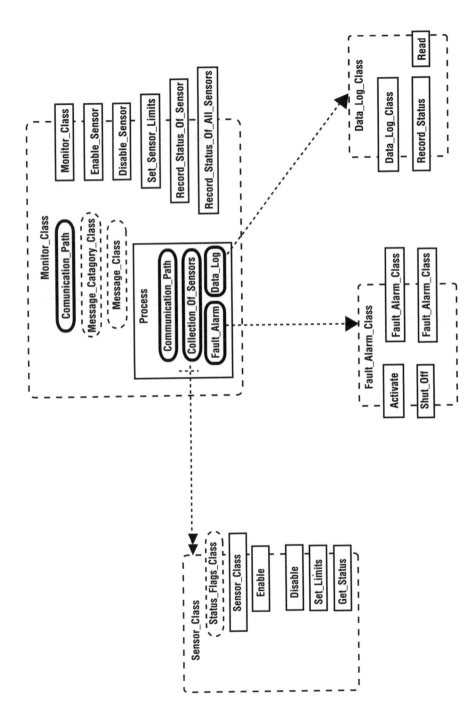

FIGURE 14.13. C++ structure diagram for the monitor class.

architecture for software components, with a smooth transition to code. The constant refinement facilitates the tracing of requirements throughout the process. Careful study of object interactions and behavior makes this method sensitive to real-time issues.

OOSD allows particularly rigorous behavior analysis. This detects errors early. However, the price is more front-end work load, since time and effort must be invested in detailed behavior descriptions (unless descriptions from previous projects can be reused), and a delay in the production of code (even though code production will be more efficient when it occurs). When there is no human-safety or other substantial reliability concern, a less formal use of the method may be adequate.

OOSD's uniform support for localization and information-hiding leads to well-defined objects. Each object is individually testable and provides sufficient information to develop tests. The model developed in requirements analysis provides sufficient information to begin designing integration or acceptance tests for the system, which are then refined as the model is refined. The effects of change can be predicted with assurance, both in the diagrams, forms, and tables of the model, and in the final system.

Formally defining the complete structure, interactions, behavior, and properties of all objects in the system, including the system object, allows validation and verification that the system is correctly implemented. Generating classes from objects in the system yields reliable, reusable components. Carrying out the same essential activities during requirements analysis, preliminary design, and detailed design results in unity of the model. The product is easy to understand and maintain, and closely follows the real world.

REFERENCES

Boehm, B.W. (1981) *Software Engineering Economics*, Prentice-Hall, Englewood Cliffs, NJ.

Boehm, B.W. (1988) A spiral model of software development and enhancement. *Computer*, 21(5): 61.

Booch, G. (1986) *Software Engineering with Ada*, Benjamin/Cummings, Menlo Park, CA.

Booch, G. (1991) *Object-Oriented Design with Applications*, Benjamin/Cummings, Menlo Park, CA.

Buhr, R. (1984) *System Design with Ada*, Prentice-Hall, Englewood Cliffs, NJ.

Buhr, R. (1990) *Practical Visual Techniques in System Design: With Applications to Ada*, Prentice-Hall, Englewood Cliffs, NJ.

Coad, P., and E. Yourdon (1991) *Object-Oriented Analysis*, Prentice-Hall, Englewood Cliffs, NJ.

Gilb, T. (1988) *Principles of Software Engineering Management*. Addison Wesley, Reading, MA.

Goldberg, A., and D. Robson (1989) *SmallTalk-80, the Language*, ed. M.A. Harrison. Addison-Wesley, Reading, MA

Harel, D. (1987) Statecharts: a visual formalism for complex systems. *Science of Computer Programming*, 8: 231.

Harel, D. (1988) On visual formalisms, *Communications of the ACM*, 31: 514.

Orr, K. (1981) *Structured Requirements Definition*, Ken Orr and Associates, Inc., Topeka, KS.

Royce, D.W.W. (1970) *Managing the Development of Large Software Systems*. IEEE WESCON, Institute of Electrical and Electronics Engineers, New York, NY.

Rumbaugh, J.M. et al. (1991) *Object-Oriented Modeling and Design*, Prentice-Hall, Englewood Cliffs, NJ.

Sha, L. (1988) *An Overview of Real-Time Scheduling Algorithms*. Software Engineering Institute, Department of Computer Science, Carnegie-Mellon University, Pittsburgh, PA.

Shlaer, S., and S.J. Mellor (1992) *Object Lifecycles, Modeling the World in States*, Prentice-Hall, Englewood Cliffs, NJ.

Sodhi, J. (1991) *Software Engineering: Methods, Management, and CASE Tools*. TAB Professional and Reference Books. Blue Ridge Summit, PA.

Software Engineering Institute (1990) *Rate Monotonic Scheduling Theory: Practical Applications*. Carnegie-Mellon University, Pittsburgh, PA.

Summerville, I. (1992) *Software Engineering*. Addison-Wesley, Reading, MA.

Wegner, P. (1990) "Concepts and Paradigms of Object-Oriented Programming," *OOPS Nessinger*, 1:8.

chapter **15**

The OOSE Method: A Use-Case–Driven Approach

Ivar Jacobson, Magnus Christerson   *Objective Systems SF AB*

Larry L. Constantine   *Constantine & Lockwood, Ltd.*

Object-oriented software engineering (OOSE) is a disciplined method for the industrial development of software. It is based on use-case–driven design, an approach to object-oriented analysis and design that centers on understanding how a system is actually used. By organizing the analysis and design models around sequences of user interaction and actual usage scenarios, the methodology produces systems that are more useable and more robust, adapting more smoothly to changing usage. Based on more than 20 years of experience, the methods have been applied to numerous application areas and have been embodied in the Objectory computer-aided software engineering case tools.

The approach recognizes three distinct kinds of objects that separate the control and coordination of usage scenarios from interface behavior and from entities embodying the application concepts. By keeping external behavior, internal structure, and dynamics apart, each may be altered or extended independently of the other. Like other methods, OOSE incorporates the concepts of application and enterprise entities, but unlike most

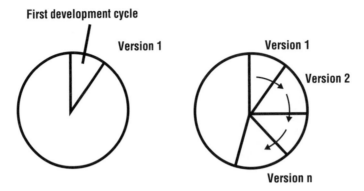

FIGURE 15.1. The first version of a system represents a minor portion of resource consumption during the life cycle of the system.

other approaches, it does not force the entire design into a rigid mold based on this one variety of object. The result is a more robust model of an application: software that is fundamentally more accommodating to extensions and alterations, along with collections of component parts that are, by design, more reusable.

The method divides development into processes or activities that, unlike traditional development phases, can iterate and overlap. These activities produce a series of closely connected models that facilitate seamless development through consistent modeling and high degrees of requirements tracing. Using this approach, it is possible to construct very large and complex designs through a series of stages based on largely independent analyses of distinct use cases. The power of this method thus increases as the size of the system being developed increases.

DEVELOPMENT LIFE CYCLE

All systems change during their life cycles. This must be borne in mind in the development of systems that are expected to last longer than the first version, which means practically all of them. Most development methods today focus on new development (see Figure 15.1), treating revision work only briefly, even though it is known that changes constitute the greatest part of the total life-cycle costs of most systems. A truly industrial process should therefore focus on system changes. A system normally develops through changes in a number of versions, as shown in the figure. New development is, from this point of view, only a special case of the first version. New development is nonetheless an important activity. It establishes an architectural philosophy and constitutes the base of the system, which must last throughout all subsequent development. A faulty base will have serious consequences for the life cycle of the system.

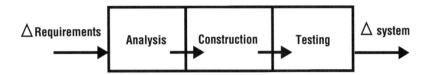

FIGURE 15.2. Processes interact to develop new versions of the system.

In use-case–driven design, we focus on changes in the specific product. The approach thus describes how one version should be changed in the next version. A unique feature of this life-cycle model is that we do not have any specific maintenance phase. All activities throughout the life cycle are actually changes to specific models.

Instead of focusing on how a specific project should be driven, the focus is on how a certain product (deliverable application) should be developed and maintained during its entire life cycle. This means that instead of a conventional waterfall description, we divide the development work for a specific product into processes, in which each process describes one activity in the management of a product. The processes work in a highly interactive manner. Each process handles a specific phase or activity of the system development work. For instance, most types of projects will involve some construction activities. In this manner, the product will be managed by a number of processes. The development work then extends over all these processes, and they exist during the whole system-development life cycle. All development work is thus managed by these processes, and each process can, in its turn, consist of a number of communicating subprocesses.

A system-development project is thus carried out through a number of activities, each of which constitutes a more detailed and concrete development of earlier steps. Thus, system development is a gradual transformation of different models of the system to be developed. The first model describes the customer's requirements, and the last one is the fully tested program. Between these two end points are a number of other models.

Our development life cycle is thus built of different processes that cooperate to take a product from one version to the next by changing the various models. The main processes are analysis, construction, and testing. These describe the activities that are undergone in the development of a product, and which are "alive" during the entire life of the product. When a new version of the product is required, these processes are activated by the development staff (see Figure 15.2).

In the analysis process, we create a conceptual picture of the system we want to build. Here, different models are developed to understand the system and to communicate its essential aspects back to the client as well as to the construction process. In the construction process, we develop the system from the models created during analysis. This includes both design and implementation, resulting in a complete system. The testing process integrates the system, verifying it and deciding whether it should be passed on for delivery. Linked mainly to the construction process is a component process, which develops and maintains reusable components — fully implemented construction parts that can be used in several different applications, mainly during construction. The component process is not tied to a specific product, but is a multi-product-process. We will not discuss the component process further here.

It is the rule, rather than an exception, that the requirements for information systems, as well as for technical systems, are not fully known at the outset of a project. Knowledge of the system grows successively as work progresses. When the first version of the system is in operation, new requirements appear and old ones change. Thus, the system cannot be completely developed on the assumption that the requirement specification will remain constant during development, which may take several years for large systems.

In most cases, it is better to develop the system step by step, beginning with a few of its core functions. As an appropriate path becomes clear, and a better understanding of how the system functionality evolves, new functions can be added. In this way, the system is incrementally enlarged until the finished product is available, normally at a product release. Such an incremental strategy also provides faster feedback during the development process. In practice, incremental system development means that we can divide the system into parts corresponding to customer-requested services. Each new stage extends the system with new functionality up to the finished product comprising the whole of the desired system. All subsequent releases of the system are also developed in a series of incremental stages. For the sequencing of development to be successful, it is essential that later stages do not necessitate changes to the results of earlier stages. Thus, it is important to capture the requirements that form the base of the entire system as early as possible. Each stage is developed in a cycle and is tested before the stage is completed. This means that the processes are run through several times for a specific version of the system.

Analysis

The aim of the analysis process is to analyze, specify, and define the system that is to be built. The models developed will describe what the system is to do. The basis of this modeling is the customer or end-user requirements, expressed in some form, for the system. It is then important to carry on a dialogue with the clients and prospective users to insure that the system to be built is really what is wanted. In the analysis phase, we build models that will make it easier for us to understand the system.

The models developed during analysis are oriented fully to the application and not to the implementation environment They are "essential" models that are independent of things such as the operating system, programming language, DBMS, processor distribution, and hardware configuration. This will be our definition of analysis: modeling the system with no regard to the actual implementation environment. The purpose is to formulate the problem and to build models that can solve the problem under ideal conditions. As the models are entirely problem oriented, and no attention is paid to the real implementation environment, they are fairly straightforward to develop from the standpoint of functionality. We can thus focus entirely on the problem as such and neglect the technical details initially. The models, based on application-oriented concepts, can be discussed with users without using implementation terms.

Eventually, the system will have to be adapted to the implementation environment; this is done in construction. The fact that little attention is devoted to the implementation environment during analysis guarantees that the resulting system architecture will be based on the problem itself and not on conditions prevailing during implementation. It is, of course, impossible to develop the models entirely without consideration of the realization, since the models and their architecture must be realizable. Another great advantage of this procedure is that analysis models can remain intact and usable if and when the implementation conditions change.

Two different models are developed in analysis: the requirements model and the analysis model. These are based on requirement specifications and discussions with the prospective users. The first, the requirements model, should make it possible to delimit the system and to define what functionality should take place within it. For this purpose, we develop a conceptual picture of the system using problem domain objects and also specific interface descriptions of the system if it is meaningful for this system.

We also describe the system as a number of "use cases" that are performed by a number of "actors." The actors constitute the usage environment of the system, and the use cases are what take place within the system. The use case is one of the unique concepts of our methodology.

The analysis model is an architectural model used for analysis of robustness. It gives a conceptual configuration of the system, consisting of various object classes: active controllers, domain entities, and interface objects. The purpose of this model is to find a robust and extensible structure for the system as a base for construction. Each object type has its own special purpose for this robustness: together, the types will offer the total functionality that was specified in the requirements model. To manage the development, the analysis model may group objects into subsystems.

The analysis model comprises a total, functional specification of the system we wish to develop, without any attention to the implementation environment. The design model, developed in the construction process, incorporates such adaptations to the implementation language, the database management system, and the like. The design model and the analysis model both model of the system, but each has a distinct purpose. Traceability is enhanced because objects in one model can be directly related to objects in the other.

Construction

We build our system through construction based on the analysis model and the requirements model created by the analysis process. The construction process lasts until the coding is completed and the included units have been tested.

The testing process follows the construction process; here all use cases and the entire system are tested and verified. This does not mean that we must wait until all parts have been constructed before starting the certification of the system. Instead we try to do as much as possible in parallel. We even try to start the construction before the analysis phase has been completed.

What then is the purpose of the construction process? Could we not write the source code directly from the analysis model, which already describes the objects in the system and how they are related? There are three main reasons for a construction process.

1. The analysis model is not sufficiently formal. To seamlessly change to the source code, we must refine the objects — which operations should be offered, exactly what should the communication between the different objects look like, which stimuli are sent, etc.
2. Adaptation must be made to the actual implementation environment. In the analysis phase we assumed an ideal world for our system. We must now transform the analysis model from the analysis space to the design space, considering, for example: performance requirements, real-time requirements and concurrency, system software, the properties of the programming language, the database management system to be used, etc.
3. We want to do internal validation of the analysis results. As our system is growing and is increasingly formalized, we will see how well the analysis models describe the system. During the construction, we can see at an early stage whether the result of the analysis will be appropriate. If we discover unclear points in the analysis or the requirements models we must clarify them, perhaps by returning to the analysis process.

Construction is divided into two phases, design and implementation, each of which develops a model. The design model is a further refinement and formalization of the analysis model in which consequences of the implementation environment have been taken into account. The implementation model is the actual implementation (code) of the system.

Testing

Testing verifies that a correct system is being built. Testing is traditionally expensive, primarily because many faults are not detected until late in development. A disciplined and well-organized approach to system development is necessary to increase the quality of the system and to decrease testing costs. To do effective testing, the goal must be that every test should detect a fault, and therefore several different testing types and techniques are used. We will summarize some key issues of the testing activities.

Unit testing is performed on a specific unit, which can be of varying size from a class up to an entire subsystem. The unit is initially tested structurally (i.e., "white box testing"). This means that we use our knowledge of the inside of the unit to test it. We have various coverage criteria for the test, the minimum being to cover all statements. However, coverage criteria can be hard to define since, due to polymorphism, many branches are made implicitly in an object-oriented system. The use of inheritance also complicates testing, since we may need to retest operations at different levels in the inheritance hierarchy.

However, polymorphism also enhances the independence of the objects, making them easier to test as stand-alone units. Furthermore, since we typically have less code, there is less to test.

Specification testing of a unit is done primarily from the object protocol (so-called black box testing). Here, we use equivalence partitioning to find appropriate test cases.

In our methodology, testing activities are performed throughout development. Even integration testing may start quite early in development. Instances of different classes may be integrated continuously throughout the process. The use-case concept is crucial for actual integration, with one use case at a time being integrated. Test planning must be done early, along with the identification and specification of tests.

MODELS

Here we will discuss the different models produced during systems development in our methodology.

The Requirements Model

The requirements model consists of: a use-case model, user interface descriptions, and a problem-domain object model.

The use-case model is based on actors and use cases (Figure 15.3). These concepts are aids to defining what exists outside the system (actors) and what the system should be able to perform (use cases).

Actors represent whatever interacts with the system, that is, everything that needs to exchange information with it. An actor is not a user, but a role a user can play in relation to the system. A user is a person (or sometimes a device) that uses the system. Unlike many other objects, actors are nondeterministic in their actions.

We regard actors as a class and users as instances of this class. These instances exist only when the user does something to the system. The same person can thus appear as instances of several different actors. For example, a system may have both pilot and passengers as actors. Jim Smith is a user who sometimes acts the role of pilot and sometimes of passenger, performing different use cases depending on the role he plays.

Every actor can perform a number of different actions with the system and thus participates in the operation of the system. An actor using a system performs a behaviorally related sequence of transactions in a dialogue with the system. Such a special sequence is what is meant by a *use case*. Each use case is a specific way to use the system, a case of usage. A collection of use cases contains the complete functionality of the system to be built. Each use case has a description, and the system should be able to perform everything described in the use case model.

An example of a use case could be to "acknowledge a flight to be performed by some pilot." Just as with actors, we view the use case as a class. When a use case is performed,

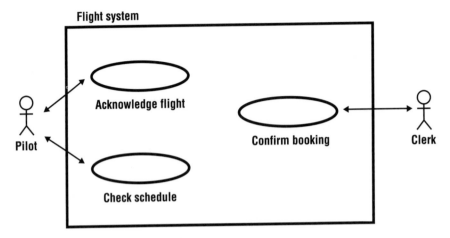

FIGURE 15.3. A sketch of a use-case model.

we view this as instantiating the class. The instance exists as long as the use case is operating. The use case model is structured by various relations among use cases.

Designed in this way, the system model is use-case–driven. When we wish to change system behavior, we remodel the appropriate actor and use case. In this way, the whole system architecture will be controlled by what the users want to do with the system. As we have traceability through all models, we will be able to modify the system from new requirements. We simply ask users what they want to change (which use case) and see directly where these changes should be made in other models.

The requirements model also facilitates discussion of requirements and preferences with system users to insure that we are defining the correct system. The model is easy to understand and is formulated from the user perspective. Since it is the first model to be developed, we can evaluate whether users are pleased with what we are about to design before we start to build the actual system. To support the use-case model, it is often appropriate to develop interface models for the use cases. Interface prototypes can simulate use cases for users by showing them what will be seen when executing the use case in the system to be built.

In addition, to communicate with the potential users and also to get a stable ground for the descriptions of the use cases, a logical and surveyable domain object model of the system is often appropriate. Such a model consists of objects representing entities or constructs from the problem domain and serves as a support for the development of the requirements model.

The requirements model formulates the functional requirement specification based on the needs of the system users. In reality, a requirements model serves effectively as a part of the requirement specification, and could be used for proposals or bidding on system development.

FIGURE 15.4. The object types used to structure the system in the analysis model.

The use-case model is central, controlling the formation of all other models. It is developed in cooperation with the domain object model and may be expressed in terms of objects in this model. The functionality specified by the use cases are then structured into the logical, implementation-independent analysis model, which is robust and stable against changes. This model is then adapted to the actual environment and is further refined in the design model, utilizing use cases to describe how communications flow between design objects. Use cases are then implemented in source code. Finally, use cases become a tool for testing the system, primarily during integration testing.

The Analysis Model

Once the requirements model, which defines the limits of the system and specifies its internal behavior, is developed and has been approved by system users or clients, the actual system development commences with the analysis model. This model defines the logical structure of the system independent of the implementation environment.

Although it is possible to use a domain-object model developed in defining the requirements model as a base for implementing the system, this does not result in the most robust structure. The analysis model represents, from our experience, a more stable and maintainable system structure that will be robust for the entire system life cycle. Since many future changes will come from changes in the implementation environment, they will not affect the logical structuring. We shall see when discussing how to adapt to the actual implementation environment that we want as few changes as possible to this ideal, logical, and stable structure.

Many object-oriented analysis methods recognize only one basic type of object. By employing three distinct kinds of objects, a structure that will be more adaptable to changes results. The object types used in the analysis model are entity, interface, and control objects (Figure 15.4).

Each type of object has a different purpose. An entity object models information in the system that should be held for some period of time, typically surviving after a use case has completed. All behavior naturally and closely coupled to this information is placed within the entity object. An example of an entity is a person with his or her associated data and behavior. The interface object models behavior and information that is dependent on the interface of the system. Thus, everything about any interface to the system is placed in interface objects. An example of an interface object is the user interface functionality for requesting information about a person. A control object models functionality (often mainly behavior) that is not naturally tied to any other object — typically behavior that consists of operating on several different entities, doing some computations and then returning the result to an interface object. An example of a controller is calculating taxes using several different factors. This behavior could be placed on any of the other types of objects (since they can also model behavior), but the actual behavior does not really belong to any specific object.

Since all systems change, system stability is a matter of keeping changes localized so they affect only one object. Distributing functionality in an orderly manner over these three types of objects helps to isolate changes. Changes in any actual system interface should typically affect only interface objects.

Changes in functionality may occur in various ways. In an object-oriented system, functionality may be distributed over all object types. However, if a change involves functionality coupled to information held by the system (e.g., how to calculate a person's age) such changes will typically affect only the entity object representing that information. Changes in the functionality of an interface (e.g., how to receive and collect information on a person) should affect only the corresponding interface object. Changes of functionality involving multiple objects (e.g., how to calculate taxes from several different criteria) will, in the appropriate design, be local to a control object, since such functionality that is unique to one or a few use cases is placed in controllers. Thus, through three distinct types of objects, we encapsulate the areas that are likely to change.

It is clear then that the most stable systems cannot be built using only objects that correspond to "real-world" or problem domain entities. The entity objects in our analysis model will often be very similar to models developed through methods based solely on such real-world objects. Entity objects often represent a problem-domain object, although this is not always necessary. In other methods, however, behavior that more properly belongs in control objects will typically be found distributed over several other objects (entities) or will involve more complex inter-object communication, making it harder to introduce changes in this behavior.

More than 20 years of experience in object-oriented development of telecommunications systems has led to these conclusions. Examining changes to these systems has shown that frequently too much functionality was assigned to typical problem-domain objects. As changes are introduced, the behaviors as allocated are found to be too specialized to facilitate reuse in new operations. With time, an increasing number of limited or specialized operations may be added to such an object. (In one system, a *TrunkLine* object had 23 added operations that were unique to a single use case.) Separating out more specific functionality into control objects results in more generalized behaviors in entity objects. The entity objects thus hold functionality that is more reusable across multiple or new use cases, and the control objects encapsulate interrelated functionality that might otherwise be scattered.

The Design Model

In the construction process, we build the system using both the analysis and the requirements models. Initially, we create a design model, which is actually a refinement and formalization of the analysis model. The main work in developing the design model is to adapt to the actual implementation environment. Our goal is to refine it sufficiently so that it is straightforward to write the source code from it (which is done in the implementation model). Since the analysis model has all the properties we want for the system, this structure should form the base for the design model. However, there will be changes to the model when introducing, for instance, a relational database management system, a distributed environment, performance requirements, a specific programming language, or concurrent processes.

When does analysis end and design begin? On the one hand, we want to do as much work in the analysis model as possible where we can focus on the essentials. On the other hand, we do not want to do so much that we need to change when adapting the analysis to the implementation environment. What we really want is a continuum of refinements in the models, with the switch of models occurring when we see the first consequences of the implementation environment. Hence, the transition from analysis to design must be decided from application to application. If there will be no adaption problems with the database management system, distributed environment, real-time requirements, concurrent processes, hardware adaptations, etc., it is fine to be quite formal in the analysis model. However, if these circumstances will strongly affect the system structure, the transition to design should be made very early. The goal is not to redo any work at a later phase.

This also leads to the question of when changes in the analysis model should be made while working with the design model. A change in the design model that comes from a logical change in the system (e.g., determining that two objects should be logically related), should also be included in the analysis model. However, if the change is a consequence of the implementation environment (e.g., determining that two objects should not communicate directly due to the processor structure chosen), then it should not be incorporated into the analysis model.

The structures we work with are basically the same as in the analysis model, but the view has changed since this is a step toward implementation. We use the concept of a block when talking about design objects, to give an abstraction of how the code works. One block normally implements one analysis object. As in analysis, different types of blocks may be used. However, blocks are not necessarily the same objects as the analysis objects. Changes will be introduced in the design model. For example, one block may be split in two to handle loosely coupled process communication. Such a split should not affect the analysis model; thus, we do not require the two models to be illustrations of the same model.

Another difference between the analysis and design models is that the analysis model should be viewed as a conceptual and logical model of the system, whereas the design model should take us closer to the actual source code. We can view it as a drawing of the code to be developed. This means that we change the view of the design model to an abstraction of the source code to be written later. Hence, the design model should be a drawing of how the source code should be structured, managed, and written. Since we want a strong and easy-to-maintain traceability from the analysis model over the design model to the implementation model (source code), we will try to map the design objects in a straightforward way to the modules used in the targeted programming language.

Blocks are abstractions of the actual implementation of the system, and will thus group the source code. To know how to implement the blocks, we need to refine the design model further by describing how blocks will communicate during execution. To describe the communication between the blocks, we use stimuli. A stimulus is sent from one block to another to trigger an activity in that object. This execution may send new stimuli to other blocks.

Blocks are directly traceable to modules in the target language. For instance, in C++, a typical block will be mapped to one file (actually two, .h and .c files) including one or several classes. In Ada, it is natural to map a block to one package. The target module is referred to as the *object module*. For example, in C++ an object module is the class, in Ada, it is a package. The interfaces of the blocks will thus be mapped onto the object module of the particular language and serve as the interfaces of these modules (the .h file in C++ and the specification-part of the Ada-package). A block may thus be implemented by one or several object modules.

During the construction process complexity increases enormously. It is essential to be able to manage this complexity. We group objects into subsystems, which may be used in both the analysis and the design models. They may also include other subsystems recursively. In this way we have a hierarchical structuring of the system to manage its complexity. The highest level is the system level, which is the actual application and also defines the borders of the application.

INTERACTION DIAGRAMS

Interaction diagrams are used in the design model to describe how each use case is handled by the interaction of communicating objects. Interaction takes place as blocks send and receive stimuli from each other. In an interaction diagram, each block participating in a particular use case is represented by a column drawn as a vertical line (Figure 15.5). Usually, the external environment of the system, the system border, is also represented by the left-most column. It represents the interface to everything outside the blocks in the diagram (e.g., external actors) and can consequently correspond to different external interfaces of the system. To the left of the system border we describe the sequences in the interaction. This description is textual, usually structured text or pseudocode. For pseudocode, constructs in the intended programming language are used to ease migration to the actual implementation later. The text describes what is happening in a particular part of the use case, called an *operation*. The column (hence, the block) to which the operation

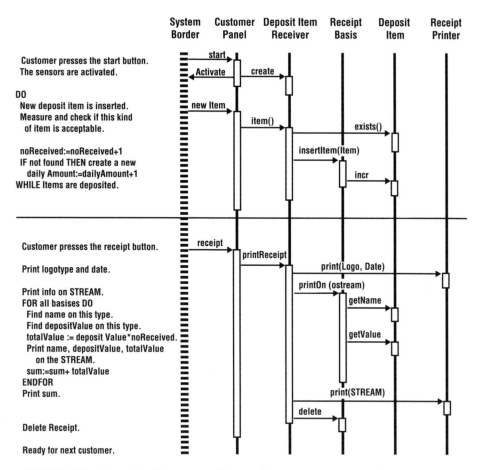

FIGURE 15.5. Example of interaction diagram for a use case in a recycling system.

belongs is marked with a rectangle representing the operation.

Interaction diagrams are controlled by events. A new event gives rise to a new operation. These events are stimuli that are sent from one object to another and initiate an operation. Figure 15.5 gives an example of an interaction diagram.

In the diagram, the use case begins when the customer presses the start button. The block customer panel then activates the sensors that are external to the system. Now the customer can start feeding in the return bottles, empty cans, and crates. This is solved by a DO...WHILE statement that ends when the customer requests a receipt. Items are checked in this loop; if acceptable, we increment the number of things of this type fed in by the customer and the total for today. Note that incrementing the daily total is delegated to the block Receipt Basis.

The Implementation Model

The implementation model consists of the source code with accompanying comments. Note that we do not require an object-oriented programming language; the technique may be used with any programming language to obtain an object-oriented structure of the system. However, an object-oriented programming language is desirable since all fundamental concepts can easily be mapped into language constructs.

The basis for implementation is the design model, which specifies the interface of each block and describes the behavior expected behind this interface. Although it is very desirable to have a close match between blocks and actual object modules, it is not always possible in more complex environments. In one project one entity block ended up using 17 classes in C++ for the implementation. However, it was a very complex implementation due to the use of a relational database management system, requiring things like type conversion, keying, error handling, versioning, etc. This is not a normal case, however. Typically, one block will map to between one and five object modules.

A very powerful implementation tool is the ability to use components. These are fully implemented parts that enable us to build a system with more powerful concepts (higher abstractions) than the programming language can offer us. Components can be regarded as completed building elements that can be used directly in our system.

METHODOLOGY

A method, or methodology, is a planned procedure by which a specified goal is approached step by step. Most methods describe, often abstractly, how one should think and reason in developing a software system. Most also indicate the sequence of steps and substeps to be followed, all describing how the work is to be carried out, assuming a certain underlying basic architecture. This means that the description of the method is formulated in terms of the concepts of the architecture to be realized.

Analysis

REQUIREMENT ANALYSIS

Two different models are developed in analysis based on the requirement specification and discussions with prospective users: the requirements model and the analysis model. The requirements model delimits the system and defines what functionality the system should offer. It is the developer's view of what the customer wants and serves as a contract between the developer and the client. It is essential that this model be readable by those unfamiliar with object orientation and OOSE. The requirements model normally consists of three parts; the use-case model, the problem-domain object model, and user-interface descriptions. The use-case model specifies the functionality the system is to offer from a user's perspective and defines what should take place inside the system. It uses actors to represent roles users can play and use cases to represent what users should be able to do with the system. Each use case is a complete course of events in the system from a user perspective. If appropriate, user-interface descriptions may also be developed. These will specify in detail what the user interface will look like when use cases are performed. To give a conceptual picture and a better understanding of the system, we use objects that represent occurrences in the problem domain. This model will serve as a common base for all people involved in the requirements analysis, developers as well as customers.

To be able to identify what use cases are to be performed, we identify, by means of actors, the behavior of users of the system. Actors model the prospective users. The actor is a user type or category; when a user does something, he acts as an occurrence of this type. One person can instantiate (play the roles of) several different actors. Actors thus define roles that users can play. Actors model anything that needs information exchange with the system, either human users or other systems that communicate with the system. Actors constitute anything external to the system being developed, hence the boundary defining the limits of the system must be specified.

The actors who will use the system directly and most regularly (perhaps in their daily work) are called *primary actors*. Each actor will perform one or more of the main tasks of the system. Besides these primary participants are others overseeing and maintaining the system, called *secondary actors*. Secondary actors exist so that the primary actors can use the system. It is often simpler to find actors that model people than those that are machines or other systems.

Once we have defined what is outside the system, the functionality inside it can be defined through specifying use cases. A use case is a specific way of using some part of the functionality. Each use case constitutes a complete sequence of related transactions performed by some actor and the system in a dialogue. The collected use cases specify all the ways of using the system.

Actors are the major tool for finding use cases. Each actor is involved in a number of use cases. By defining everything that every actor will be able to do in interaction with the system, the complete functionality of the system is defined. To identify use cases, we can read the requirement specification from an actor's perspective and carry on discussions with those users who will function as actors, asking a number of questions, such as:

- What are the main tasks of each actor?
- Will the actor have to read/write/change any of the system information?
- Will the actor have to inform the system about outside changes?
- Does the actor wish to be informed about unexpected changes?

It is not always obvious what functionality should be placed with a separate use case and what is only a variant of another use case. If differences are small, they can best be described as variants of one use case. If the differences are large, they should be described as separate use cases. For instance, in the use case of a telephone call, if the called party does not answer, is that a separate use case? Although it involves different behavior, it is closely related logically and is probably a variation of an answered call.

The identification of use cases is often iterative. Once the picture stabilizes, each use case is described in more detail. First, the basic course, the most important sequence giving the best understanding of the use case, is described. Variants of the basic course and errors that can occur are described in alternatives. These descriptions are not developed earlier, since the requirements model typically undergoes several changes.

When analyzing and describing use cases in detail, it is not unusual to uncover unclear points in the requirement specification. Vague requirements thus become obvious at an early stage. Since use cases often focus on a certain functional area of application, it is possible to develop use cases for different areas separately, joining them later to form the complete requirements model. We can thus focus on one problem at a time, later bringing the results together without having to consider the entire problem at once.

A powerful concept used to structure and relate use-case descriptions is the "built-on" association. *Built on* relates how one use-case description may be inserted into, and thus expand, another description. In this way, extensions of use cases can be described in a compact way allowing easy changes and additions to functionality. The use case another is "built on" must comprise a complete course in itself, entirely independent of the inserted sequence. The original description makes no references to any courses that can be inserted, avoiding compounding the complexity and dependencies. By describing basic use cases independent of any extended functionality, we can add new extensions without changing the original descriptions.

When describing use cases and communicating them to potential users, it is often appropriate to describe user interfaces in more detail. Typically, we can utilize sketches of what the user will see on the screen when performing the use case or more sophisticated simulations using user interface prototyping software. In this way, use cases can be simulated as they will appear to users before even thinking about how to realize them. Such techniques reduce the possibilities for misunderstanding. User interface descriptions are an essential part of the use-case descriptions and should accompany them.

When designing interfaces, future users should be involved early in the process so that the new interfaces reflect their logical view of the system. One of the most fundamental principles of human interface design is to maintain consistency between the user's conceptual picture of the system and the system's actual behavior. By using a problem domain model as a conceptual base to define the constructs and semantics of the system and user interfaces, the user interface will be consistent with the user's logical perspective of the system.

Especially when requirements are vague, it can be difficult to define and delimit the task of a system. It is helpful to develop a logical view of the task using problem domain objects, that is, objects that have a direct counterpart in the environment and about which the system must handle information. A problem-domain model also supports specifying use cases, defining the concepts with which the system should be working. A glossary used to formulate the functionality of use cases is especially valuable when several people are involved in the specifications of use cases. The major benefit of such a model is its usefulness as a tool for communication. Since clients and users will recognize all the concepts, the model can be used when defining what the system will do. By asking customers to draw pictures of their view of the system and reasoning with them, an extensive problem-domain model can evolve. A common terminology for use cases reduces misunderstandings between developers and potential users.

The requirements model as described thus far is sufficient to define the functionality of the system. However, this model can be elaborated to enhance reuse and prepare for transition to the analysis model. This refinement mainly involves identifying and extracting similar parts of use cases, called *abstract use cases*. Abstract use cases are not instantiated by themselves, but serve to describe what is common among other use cases. Common parts need only be described once instead of in every use case showing similar behavior. Changes to this common portion will thus automatically affect all use cases that share this part. Use cases that are actually to be performed are called *concrete use cases*. Abstract use cases are identified through abstract actors. An abstract actor typically describes a role played in relation to the system. Different actors able to play similar roles can inherit from a common abstract actor. The advantage of modeling abstract actors is to express similarities in use cases. If some use case or part of a use case is performed by several different actors, the use case needs to be specified only with respect to one actor instead of to several.

Use cases are the core running through all activities developing subsequent models, helping to maintain a strong focus on the problem. By controlling the work through use cases, a disciplined approach becomes natural. Knowing the number and complexity of use cases also facilitates estimating the work involved in subsequent models and predicting the time required to handle each use case.

ROBUSTNESS ANALYSIS

Once the requirements model has been developed and is approved by the clients, we can start focusing on structuring the system, first by developing the analysis model. In the analysis model, the system is described using three different types of objects: interface, entity, and control objects. Each of these has its own purpose and will model one specific aspect of the system. Objects are also grouped into manageable units called *subsystems*. The analysis model aims at creating a good platform for the system design and will form the basis of the design.

Developing the analysis model really entails distributing the behavior specified in the use-case descriptions among objects in the model. An object can be common to several different use cases, and we must specify which object is responsible for offering which behavior in each use case. Although it is possible, behavior need not be broken down into operations at this stage. Instead, a more natural way is to use a verbal description of the responsibilities or the roles played by each object.

All functionality that is directly dependent on the system environment is placed in interface objects. It is through these objects that the actors communicate with the system. The task of an interface object is to translate the actor's actions with the system into events in the system and to translate those events in the system in which the actor is interested into something presented to the actor. Interface objects, in other words, describe bi-directional communication between the system and its users. Interface objects may involve either interfaces to other systems or to human users. Interface objects are quite simple to identify since either they are clearly identified from the user interface descriptions accompanying the requirements model or, starting from the actors or use-case descriptions, the functionality that is interface specific can be extracted. Having identified and separated interface objects, it will be easy to change an interface in the system. By having everything that concerns an interface in one object, every change to that interface will be local to the object.

What behavior in a use case should be assigned to a particular interface object is generally decided on the basis of potential changes. Any change of functionality directly related to the interface should be local to the interface object. Other changes should not affect interface objects. To identify which part of the sequence of events in a use case should be allocated to interface objects, we focus on the interactions between actors and the use case. This means that we should look for units with the following characteristics:

- Presents information to the actor or requests information from him
- Behavior is changed if the actor's behavior is changed
- Course depends on a particular interface type

To model information the system will handle over a longer time, we use entity objects. Typically, such information survives use cases, that is, the information should be kept even if a use case has been completed. Along with the information itself, we also allocate the behavior that naturally belongs to this information to the entity object. Entity objects are identified from use cases, just as are interface objects. Most entity objects are found early and are obvious from the problem-domain object model. Others may be harder to find. Entity objects usually correspond to something in the real world, outside the system, although this is not always the case. It is all too easy to model too many entity objects in the belief that more information is necessary than is really called for. The hard thing is to model only the entity objects that are actually needed. It is therefore essential to work in a disciplined and structured way. Use cases should be the guide; only entity objects that can be justified by use-case descriptions are included. Every place in a use case where we need to store information is a potential entity object.

To store information, entity objects use attributes. Each attribute has a type, which can be of a primitive data type, such as integer or string, or a composite data type, which is more complex and is specially defined. The attributes of an entity object develop as use cases are analyzed. To decide if a piece of information should be modeled as an entity object or as an attribute, we see how the information will be used. Information that is handled separately should be modeled as entity objects, whereas information that is strongly related to some other information and never used by itself should be an attribute. How the use cases handle the information is decisive. Certain information may become an entity object in one system, while it may very well become an attribute in another system. If it is used from two different places and for different reasons, it should form a separate entity object.

The behavior of the use cases is first allocated to interface objects and entity objects. Sometimes only these two types will be necessary to allocate everything. In more complex cases, certain behavior may not be able to be naturally placed in either interface objects or the identified entity objects. In these cases, objects are used, typically for transaction-related behavior or control sequences specific to one or a few use cases or functionality to isolate entity objects from interface objects. Control objects thus unite courses of events and carry on communication with other objects. If such behavior were distributed over objects already identified, changability would be reduced. Since changes would affect several objects and be more difficult to incorporate. Control objects typically serve as glue or cushions to unite other objects to form a single use case. They are typically the most short-lived of all the object types and usually survive only during the performance of one use case.

It is not easy to strike a balance between what is placed in entity objects and interface objects and what is assigned to control objects. Control objects are normally found directly from the use cases. As a preliminary model, a control object may be created for each concrete and each abstract use case. Each use case normally involves interface objects and entity objects. Behavior that remains unallocated after partitioning the interface and entity objects is placed in the control objects, but departures from this initial approach may be made for several reasons. Where no behavior is left to be modeled from the use case, no control object is needed. If, on the contrary, behavior of a very complicated nature remains unassigned, it may be divided among more than one control object, each with more limited tasks that are simpler to understand and to describe. A control object coupled to several different actors might imply that behavior is different for each actor and should be split up among several control objects. The aim is to tie one actor to each control object, as changes are often precipitated by actors. If each control object is dependent on only one actor, changes in the system can be isolated.

Normally, the analysis model is developed from one use case at a time; related interface objects, entity objects, and control objects are identified before continuing with the next use case. However, since analysis objects are orthogonal to use cases, in the sense that one object may participate in several use cases, this process is iterative. Once a set of objects is identified, these may be modified to fit new use cases. The goal is to form as stable a structure as possible reusing as many objects as possible.

Finding the necessary objects is usually easy; it is much more difficult to identify what operations and attributes these objects are to offer. Since the only way to manipulate an object is via its operations, the identified operations must be sufficient for all users of the object. Detailed descriptions of use cases are extremely valuable for identifying the necessary operations. A structured technique usually used in construction can also be utilzed in analysis to identify operations; but since these operations are likely to change in the design, they are not usually identified in the analysis model.

Once all analysis objects have been identified, the system may contain a large number of objects: between 30 and 100 for a medium-sized project. Getting a clear view and understanding of such a large model is seldom possible, so objects need to be grouped in one or more levels, depending on the size of the system. Groups of objects are called *subsystems*, and subsystems may contain subsystems. At the bottom of the subsystem hierarchy are the analysis objects. Subsystems package objects to reduce complexity and structure the system for further development and maintenance. Subsystems also serve as convenient units in the organization (e.g., for development, marketing, sales, and delivery). Although some subsystems are obligatory in the system, many are optional.

The lowest-level subsystems, called *service packages*, are viewed as change units. These are regarded as indivisible or atomic: the customer either gets all of one or nothing. A minor change should concern no more than one such subsystem. The most important criterion for partitioning into subsystems is predicted system changes. One subsystem should therefore be related to only one actor, since changes are usually instigated by an actor. The division into subsystems should also be based on the functionality of the system so that all objects that have a strong mutual, functional relationship are placed in the same subsystem. To identify objects with a strong mutual coupling, we start from one object and study its environment. Another criterion for division into subsystems is to reduce communication between the subsystems.

Construction

DESIGN

In construction, the system is built on the basis of the analysis model and the requirements model. The construction activity is necessary for three main reasons.

1. The analysis model is not sufficiently formal. For a seamless transition to source code, we must refine the objects in terms of specific operations to be offered, the precise form of communication between objects, stimuli to be sent, etc.
2. Analysis assumed an ideal world for the system, but in reality adaptations must be made to the actual implementation environment (e.g., performance requirements, real-time requirements and concurrency, system software, the properties of the program language, the data-base management system to be used, etc.)
3. The analysis results need to be validated. As the system grows and becomes more formalized, we see how well the analysis model and the requirements model describe it. If we discover unclear points in the analysis model or the requirements model, we must clarify them, perhaps by returning to the analysis process. The construction activity produces two models, the design and implementation models. The design model is a further refinement and formalization of the analy-

sis model, where consequences of the implementation environment have been taken into account. The Implementation Model is the actual implementation (code) of the system.

The design model explicitly defines the interfaces of the objects and the semantics of operations. This model also reflects decisions on how databases, programming language features, distribution, and the like will be handled. The design model is composed of blocks, which are the design objects. These make up the actual structure of the design model and show how the system is designed. Blocks will later be implemented in source code and thus abstract the actual implementation. A block may be implemented by a single object module in the source code or by several. An object module is the actual unit written in the target programming language. In an object-oriented programming language, the object modules are the actual classes definable in the language. In any given language, there is a direct correspondence to some language concept, for example, a class in Eiffel or a package in Ada.

Initially, each analysis object is simply transformed into a corresponding block. If each analysis object can be traced to a block, changes introduced into the analysis model will be localized in the design model and thus also in the source code. Traceability is bidirectional: a class (or other object module) in the source code can also be traced back to the analysis model to see what gave rise to it. This simple system architecture is preferred initially, but may be changed to accommodate the implementation environment. For example, blocks may have to be broken up or divided to distribute them on a computer system, or completely new blocks may be needed to build interfaces to an existing database management system.

Having identified the system architecture, we must describe how blocks are to communicate. For each concrete use case, an interaction diagram is drawn describing how the use case is realized through the interaction of communicating blocks that receive and send stimuli. These stimuli, including the parameters sent, must be defined. The block protocols are defined through use-case design. Based on which analysis objects offer the use case in the analysis model, corresponding blocks are included in the interaction diagram. New blocks, introduced during construction, may also participate in a use case. When all use cases, or at least all use cases for a specific block, have been designed, the block(s) can be designed based on the external requirements determined from the analysis model.

Actual implementation of the blocks in source code can begin when the block interfaces stabilize. Through use-case design, we have implicitly specified the protocol of each block. By taking all interaction diagrams where a block participates and extracting all the operations defined for that block, we have a complete picture of the requirements of a block. Typically, these requirements have appeared through separate design of use cases by several people and have not been collected into a single document. Nevertheless, they exist explicitly and are connected to the appropriate block. It is simple to extract these requirements — this can even be done by means of a CASE tool. From the interaction diagram, the block interfaces can be developed and expressed in a programming language, for example, in C++, but header files of public classes of a block. At this stage it is possible to freeze the interfaces of the blocks, allowing block design activities to be carried out in parallel.

In many cases a block will correspond to exactly one class and its instances, making it easy to map the interface of an object in the design model to a specific class interface in the source code. In other instances, many classes must be used to implement one block, often to handle the implementation environment, but also for the implementation of attributes, use of components, separation of common functionality into abstract classes, etc.

State-transition diagrams can be used as an intermediate-level tool for the internals of an object before looking at the actual implementation. These diagrams form a simplified description to increase understanding of a block without being too dependent on the selected programming language. These diagrams describe which stimuli can be received and what happens when a stimulus is received.

THE IMPLEMENTATION MODEL

Once structuring of the blocks is complete, we define the classes in the system. The goal is to design classes that are robust and highly reusable. Wherever possible, two classes should not offer similar functionality unless they are related through inheritance. Classes should also be highly cohesive and offer functionality that is internally strongly interrelated. For instance, if half of a class's operation accesses half of the instance variables, and the other operations operate on the other variables, we should consider splitting it in to two classes. Other heuristics for good class design include an assessment of the potential reusability of the class. Will a change make the class more reusable to others? Of course, it takes time to design a good class, and it is not always efficient to develop every class in the system to be as general as possible.

Note that traceability has been maintained from the analysis model all the way down to the source code. When we read the source code, we can also directly trace what gave rise to it in the analysis model. This property is invaluable throughout the system life cycle, especially for the engineers who will work on the maintenance and continued development of the system.

The adaptation of the design to the programming language occurs in this late phase, but during the entire design process we will be forced to consider how to solve problems that appear due to the implementation environment. Specialization to the programming language describes how we translate the terms used in the design into the terms and properties of the implementation language. Although the methods described here are general and largely independent of the actual language, all languages will have some special issues and problems during implementation.

The overall picture we have given here may give the impression that the process of construction is a straightforward and easy road to follow. However, real development is an incremental process, and often many iterations must be made.

Glossary

This section summarizes the modeling concepts used in this document.

Associations

The following associations can be used in all models:

Class Associations

Class associations are drawn with a dashed arrow.

- **Inheritance:** the descendant has all the properties of the ancestor. The arrow is drawn from the descendant and points to the ancestor since the descendant knows of its ancestor, but the ancestor does not know of its descendants.
- **Built on:** one object extends another object. The arrow points from the object defined by extension to the object that will be extended through insertion.

Instance Associations

Instance associations are drawn with a solid arrow.

- **Acquaintance:** an object holds a reference to another object. The association has a name and a cardinality that tells how many objects may be associated. The association is named in terms of which responsibilities the object has or which roles it plays to the object that associates to it.
- **Consists of:** an object aggregates a set of other objects. This is a special kind of acquaintance association.
- **Communication:** an object may send stimuli to another object. The arrow points to the receiver of the stimuli. The association may be bidirectional.

The Use-Case Model

- **Actor:** models one or more roles that a user or system interacting with the system can play.
- **Use case:** a specific sequence of transactions in a dialogue between a user and the system representing a particular way to use the system. A use case may have one basic course (or sequence) and several alternative courses.

Domain-Object Model

- **Object:** models a phenomenon in the real world that the system needs to be aware of. Aims at understanding the concepts of the problem domain.

Analysis Model

- **Interface object:** models objects that are directly dependent on the interface of the system. Should separate the functionality of the application from its presentation to actors.
- **Entity object:** models information and the behavior associated with this information of the system. Usually a long-lived (persistent) object that survives a use case.
- **Control object:** models objects of the system that are specific to one or a few use cases. Usually ties together the objects that participate in a use case.
- **Attribute:** models an information element of an object. An attribute has a name, a cardinality, and a type. Attributes are used for encapsulated information elements of an object.
- **Subsystem:** groups objects and subsystems into managing units. Lowest level is called *service package* and is an atomic or elementary unit of management. Subsystems may exist in the analysis model as well as in the design model.

Design Model

- **Block:** models a part of the implemented system. Normally, one analysis object is implemented as one block. A block could be public or private to a subsystem.
- **Object module:** module in the programming language. In an object-oriented programming language, it corresponds to a class. Could be public or private to a block.

CONCLUSION

The use case driven approach of Object-Oriented Software Engineering (OOSE) provides comprehensive coverage of the development life cycle including analysis, construction, and testing. Both the modeling techniques and the definition of the processes involved are addressed, making it a powerful and well-defined methodology applicable to all classes of projects — particularly to large and complex systems that require the application of a repeatable and optimizing process.

REFERENCE

Jacobson I., M. Christenson, P. Jonson, and G. Övergaard (1992). Object-Oriented Software Engineering. Wokingham: Addison-Wesley, Reading, MA.

chapter **16**

The MERODE Method: The Practical Realization of Object-Oriented Business Models

GUIDO DEDENE   *KATHOLIEKE UNIVERSITEIT LEUVEN*

This chapter presents an overview of the practical development of consistent object-oriented business models and their implementation technology. The approach is mapped on the Zachman framework for information architecture to position appropriately the abstraction level of the techniques that are involved. An elaborated course administration example illustrates the building process of business models and their practical use. The results improve the acceptability of object-orientation for information systems to business administrators.

INTRODUCTION

The information systems industry has problems today. The major reason for these problems is the failure to consistently deliver information systems with even the minimal required quality. Each development project seems to be a risky adventure with little or no guarantee for success. Sometimes, as if by accident, a project is successful; it then dominates the covers of information magazines. This depressing picture leads information systems people to desperation. A major increase in development productivity is required.

The industrial world has also been confronted with this type of problem in the past. Experiences with computer-integrated manufacturing demonstrate that an emphasis on productivity improvement is not sufficient. Only an integral quality approach can result in significant productivity improvement. Quality of information systems is based on consistent, well-structured specifications. Hence, system-development methodologists must seek to embed structures and consistency in the specifications themselves. In other words, validation must be encapsulated in the specification process.

Most methodologies lack the power of formal consistency. Moreover, methodologies balance between being process oriented or data driven. The research of the information systems group at the faculty of economics and applied economics of the Katholieke Universiteit Leuven has concentrated for a long time on the search for formal but practical methodologies. Blending the research on the JSD method (Jackson 1983) and entity-relationship modeling (Put 1988) resulted in an object-oriented approach to systems development called MERODE (model-driven entity-relationship object-oriented development). This approach combines the JSD and entity-relationship models in a way that gives formal consistency checks along the modeling process. The main difference between MERODE and other object-oriented modeling techniques that combine entity-relationship models with dynamic specifications such as state diagrams, lies in the fact that in MERODE the behavior of each object is compared with the behavior of the other related objects. This also leads to a natural classification of objects in MERODE. As pioneered in JSD, it becomes clear how an object-oriented business model is the basis for a rich and powerful information functionality. Business models as well as design models can be translated easily and in a straight forward way into implementations. The implementation models can use advanced technology (OOPS, rule-based systems, etc.) as well as conventional technology (regular programming languages in combination with databases and transaction monitors). This feature facilitates the acceptance of the MERODE approach.

This chapter will present an overview of the business modeling process with an extended course and membership administration model. Although the model is not very large, it illustrates all the features of MERODE business models, including relationship objects and generalization/specialization. Some implementation and design considerations are added to motivate the use of business models. The next sections discuss some of the basic features of model-driven development and object orientation.

MODEL-DRIVEN DEVELOPMENT: BEYOND TRADITIONAL ANALYSIS AND DESIGN

Traditional systems development is based on the waterfall view of the life cycle. In this view, systems development starts with the information requirements of the end users. These requirements are translated into a systems analysis, which in turn is further refined into a systems design. From the systems design, an implementation is realized. This implementation is maintained, whereas systems enhancements go through the cycle of analysis and design again.

As conventional systems analysis starts from the information requirements of the user, business functionality is mixed up with information functionality in the analysis models. Michel Jackson pointed out as early as the early eighties (Jackson 1983) how this may lead to systems with artificial complexity. This viewpoint has been reemphasized in the Zachman framework for information architecture, which stresses the need to consider models of business functionality and models of information functionality as being positioned at different layers of abstraction in information modeling (Zachman 1987, Dedene 1991). Figure 16.1 diagram summarizes the layers of abstraction in information models, according to the Zachman framework.

A model of the business functionality is called a *business model*. This is not an intangible construction: It is a concrete, well-structured specification of the functioning of the business, or, in other words, the business reality. Business functionality does not address aspects of information functionality such as input, output, queries, etc. This kind of functionality is addressed in design models, which show how information requests can be responded to by information functions. Information functions also address the notion of transactions, screens, reports, and presentation of information, all in the most user-oriented way. Different design techniques can be applied to model information functions, varying from traditional procedural design, such as JSP (Jackson 1983) to nonprocedural specifications such as those used in fourth-generation languages.

Some techniques don't have a sufficient degree of abstraction to be useful at the business modeling layer. Traditional data flow diagrams, for example, mostly contain hidden implementation choices, as a data flow is nothing but the representation of a pipe or a call between processes. In the same way, the concept of messages between objects suffers from the same drawback. At the business layer of abstraction, only the triggers can be identified that might later give rise to messages across design objects or implementation objects. All of this illustrates that a business model is not another term for what was once called a

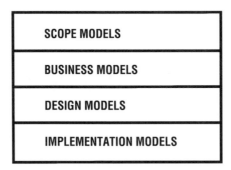

FIGURE 16.1. Layers of abstraction in information models.

systems analysis. In the same way, a design model involves much more than a traditional systems design. The real problem with many actual methods is the fact that they mix business functionality with information functionality, sometimes from the very first specifications for the system.

Another challenge for business modeling formalism is that they should be sufficiently easy to be practiced by business professionals. If business models describe business reality, they are nothing less than a new attempt to provide a formalism for administrational organization. This is an ambitious goal, though not a new one, remembering that COBOL stands for common business-oriented language. Nevertheless, powerful techniques exist that indeed have a sufficient degree of abstraction, (e.g., the notion of relations).

An implementation model is a specification of the implementation choices for the business and design models. Implementation choices include scheduling options, choice of operating system, execution environment, distribution of the systems functionality, etc. In today's technology trends, implementation of business models usually reside on server technology, given the degree of throughput and consistency that is required. Information functions can reside on client technology, using remote procedure calls to establish the communication between the business model and the information functions. The evolving transparency of information technology will ultimately result in transparency of implementations, which is already exemplified by some object-oriented environments today.

The Zachman framework is not a neo-waterfall view of systems development, as if the systems' scope will be modeled, and a business model constructed, around which a design model is developed and then implemented. The Zachman framework stresses the presence of layers of abstraction in information models only, not the order of their production. Considering layers of abstraction as layers of detail results in a step-wise refinement life cycle waterfall model. Nothing dictates a predefined sequence of activities across these layers of abstraction. A business model can be implemented first, for example, to enable information functionality. In the same way, the use of reference models will enable the combination of scope and business modeling.

THE CHARACTERISTICS OF OBJECT ORIENTATION

Object orientation is a fascinating development in information systems. Because this terminology is proliferated throughout the literature, the main characteristics of object orientation are briefly outlined in this section. These characteristics apply to every item in information systems that is using the label *object oriented*: programming languages, design tools, databases, etc.

First of all, object orientation is characterized by encapsulation. This feature refers to the fact that objects hide their implementations from the external world and communicate only through acceptance or rejection of triggers sent to them. This means that objects encapsulate the processes that they invoke to respond to these triggers into their specifi-

```
┌─────────────────────────────────────────────────────┐
│  BOOK-COPY OBJECT CLASS                              │
├─────────────────────────────────────────────────────┤
│  STATE VECTOR : Book-copy-title-id,                 │
│                 Book-copy-state,                     │
│                 Book-copy-#-loans,                   │
│                 Book-copy-#-renews,                  │
│                 ...                                  │
├─────────────────────────────────────────────────────┤
│  METHODS :                                           │
│                                                      │
│  BOOK-COPY-ACQUIRE {                                │
│            Book-copy-title-id  :=                    │
│            Acquire-Book-copy-title-id-input;         │
│            Book-copy-state  := "I";                  │
│            Book-copy-#-loans  := 0;                  │
│            Book-copy-#-renews  := 0;                 │
│                 }                                    │
│  ...                                                 │
│                                                      │
│  BOOK-COPY-RENEW {                                  │
│            Book-copy-#-renews  :=                    │
│            Book-copy-#-renews  +  1;                 │
│                 }                                    │
│  ...                                                 │
└─────────────────────────────────────────────────────┘
```

FIGURE 16.2.   *Book-Copy* **object class.**

cations. The most common specification technique in use today is the abstract data type (Meyer 1988), which consists of an object-state vector (i.e., the collection of all the object attributes) and the methods or services that apply to this state vector. An example of part of an abstract data type for a copy object in a library model follows.

The abstract data type describes how objects of the class **Book-Copy** react to the triggers **Acquire** and **Renew**. Intuitively, the methods describe the elementary transactions against state-vector records. Abstract data types are used in many object-oriented languages and database systems today with triggers that are implemented through messages. Triggers in general, however, should not be confused with messages, which are just one way to implement triggers.

The essence of encapsulation goes further than abstract data types. Encapsulation expresses the fact that information is the duality of data and process, not just a loose com-

```
┌─────────────────────────────────────────────────┐
│                                                 │
│   BOOK-TITLE OBJECT CLASS                       │
│                                                 │
├─────────────────────────────────────────────────┤
│                                                 │
│   STATE VECTOR : Book-title-id,                 │
│                  Book-title-state,              │
│                  ...                            │
│                  Book-title-#-copies,           │
│                  ...                            │
├─────────────────────────────────────────────────┤
│   METHODS :                                     │
│                                                 │
│   ...                                           │
│                                                 │
│   BOOK-TITLE-ACQUIRE {                          │
│                  Book-title-#-copies :=         │
│                  Book-title-#-copies + 1;       │
│                         }                       │
│   ...                                           │
└─────────────────────────────────────────────────┘
```

FIGURE 16.3. Acquisition of an additional *Book-Copy*.

bination of data and process. Duality is a well-understood formal concept and provides the basis for consistency checking in object-oriented methods and techniques.[1] Another consequence of the strong implementation of encapsulation would be the fact that distinguishing databases from programming languages becomes obsolete. As a final remark, note that static rules, such as object invariants (Meyer 1988) can be added to abstract data types to document properties that are independent of the triggering mechanism.

A second characteristic of object-orientation is polymorphism. Encapsulation expresses the fact that objects hide the way they react to triggers. Polymorphism expresses the fact that different objects can react differently to the same trigger. Moreover, sometimes objects can react jointly but differently to the same trigger. The different reactions result in different methods in the abstract data types for each of the reacting objects. In the preceding example, the reaction of the object **Book-Title** to the acquisition of an additional

---

[1]Duality is the property in mathematics whereby some, at first sight, very distinct elements and properties turn out to exist in a self-controlling kind of parallelism. A simple example from geometry can perhaps help. Looking at the fact that two lines intersect in exactly one point, while two points can be connected by exactly one line, shows that points and lines are dual. The dual properties are "connected by" and "intersect in". Many algebraic concepts in mathematics have their dual counterparts, which helps in reducing the size of basic theory that is required. Quantum physics emerged from the full exploitation of duality in physics. In fact, the Einstein equation $E=mc^2$, which can be rewritten as $E/C^2=m$ reads "Energy= mass" or "Dynamics=statics". Encapsulation is an example of duality in information systems.

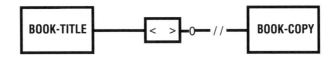

FIGURE 16.4. Entity-relationship representation.

Book-Copy would be documented as shown in figure 16.3 in the abstract data type for the *Book-Title* object.

The last fundamental characteristic of object orientation is the presence of a classification scheme for the objects. One way of classifying objects is by means of inheritance, which classifies objects in supertypes and subtypes, in combination with rules for polymorphism. There is some danger in applying strict single inheritance, as it may induce on developers the same strict hierarchical classification. An alternative classification scheme is multiple inheritance, in which the combination rules with polymorphism are far from trivial. A recent development path, pioneered by OMT (Rumbaugh 1991) is the use of relationships to classify objects. This approach opens some interesting perspectives, as more harmonic rules for polymorphism can be imposed. Imagine, for example, that objects are classified according to the sets of triggers they can accept. In this classification a *Book-Copy* object will be "smaller than" the *Book-Title* object of which it is a concrete copy. This causes an existence-dependency relationship between the objects *Book-Copy* and *Book-Title*, which is represented graphically in Figure 16.4

Using the entity-relationship representation conventions, Figure 16.4 expresses that a *Book-Title* can have zero, one, or more *Book-Copy* existences dependent on it. Classification is based on what is called a *lattice structure* in mathematics, so that an alternative notation is:

Book-Copy < *Book-Title*

Of course, every classification scheme must be in harmony not only with polymorphism, but also with encapsulation. Finding such classification schemes is a challenge, but one that results in further consistency checks in object-oriented specifications.

Classification is a prerequisite for enabling reusability of object-oriented specifications. The inheritance scheme can enable strong reusability by subtyping from object class libraries. Increasingly today it is found that even relationship-based schemes show reusable or generic modeling patterns, which result in meta-models.

To have a genuine object-oriented method, technique, or tool, the presence of encapsulation, polymorphism, and classification must be demonstrated. Moreover, the mutual harmony between these characteristics has to be clarified. Many so-called object-oriented techniques have only partial answers as they fill in only some of the characteristics or have no proven way of harmonization across the attributes. These techniques use the name *object oriented* only because of its commercial attraction today and might disappear rapidly in the future due to their lack of consistency.

THE SPECIFICATION OF OBJECT-ORIENTED BUSINESS MODELS

The specification of object-oriented business models in MERODE involves three major activity sets: object/event analysis, object/structure analysis, and abstract-data-type analysis. There is no predetermined sequence for these activity sets. For example, object/structure analysis may correct some of the object/event analysis results. However, clearly the specifications must be consistent across the activity sets. As an example, a business model for a course administration in a computer association will be constructed, starting from the following description of the computer association (adapted from (Verhelst 1992)):

EVENT	OBJECT					
	MEMBER	STUDENT	PERSON	COURSE-TOPIC	COURSE-SESSION	REGISTRATION
CREATE-MEMBER	C		C			
CHANGE-PERSON-DETAILS			X			
PAY-MEMBERSHIP-FEE	X		X			
STOP-MEMBERSHIP	X		X			
CREATE-STUDENT		C	C			
REGISTER-FOR-COURSE-SESSION		X	X	X	X	C
SHOW-UP-FOR-COURSE-SESSION		X	X	X	X	X
PAY-COURSE-FEE		X	X	X	X	X
CANCEL-COURSE-REGISTRATION		X	X	X	X	X
REFUND-COURSE-FEE		X	X	X	X	X
ANNULATE-COURSE-SESSION				X	X	
START-COURSE-SESSION				X	X	
CREATE-COURSE-SESSION				X	C	
CREATE-COURSE-TOPIC				C		

FIGURE 16.5. Object/event table.

BCA, the Belgian Computer Association, is an association of computer users and computer specialists. Members have to pay each year their membership fee. Members can attend courses at reduced course fees. Nonmembers can also attend courses, but have to pay the full course fee.

From time to time courses are announced. If not enough participants register, the course may have to be cancelled. Sometimes, people who have registered cancel their registration or do not attend the course. BCA is an extremely friendly organization, and in these cases, the course fee is refunded almost completely.

In MERODE, a business object is, in a first instance, the set of all the business events in which it participates. A business event happens in the real business world, has no duration and cannot be deconstructed further into sub-events. This also implies that business events are thought of as happening at one point in time. Even if they might take some time outside our universe of discourse, they are recognized at one point in time. The participation of business objects to business events can be represented in an object/event table. Figure 16.5 shows an example of such a table for the BCA model.

A C-sign indicates the fact that the business event creates the participating object. Observe how each object must have at least one creating event. Moreover, in MERODE, business objects belong only to the universe of discourse when they are created in the relevant business reality. This explains why the BCA association itself is not a business object: it is not created within the relevant reality for this system; it is just there. For the same reason, "date" can never be a business object within MERODE — how could time be created?

Business events are the triggers of business objects. A business model is a set of objects participating in business events. No internal communication between business objects is defined. The business model as a whole is confronted with triggers from the business reality-business events, which may later on be implemented as messages to the business model. The model accepts or rejects the triggers, according to business rules to be determined later in the business modeling process. Figure 16.5 shows how these simple constructs are already fully object oriented.

- Encapsulation is clear from the fact that objects exist only by means of the events to which they participate. A business event without participating objects is invalid. The same applies for an object without relevant business objects to which it participates.
- Polymorphism is based on the fact that different business objects can participate jointly in some business events.
- Classification will in the first instance be based on the subset classification, which classifies objects according to the events they respond to.

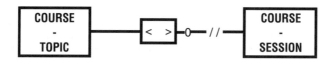

FIGURE 16.6. Existence dependency relationship.

The object/event table documents the participation of objects in business events and enumerates the objects as sets of events. For example,

REGISTRATION = {REGISTER-FOR-COURSE-SESSION,
*   SHOW-UP-FOR-COURSE-SESSION,*
*   CANCEL-COURSE-REGISTRATION,*
*   PAY-COURSE-FEE,*
*   REFUND-COURSE-FEE}*

It is easy to see how some objects (regarded as sets of events) are subsets of other objects. The **Course-Session** object is a subset of the **Course** object. This means that every **Course-Session** is the session of some **Course**. It also indicates how all triggers for **Course-Session** are also triggers for the **Course** of which it is a session. As explained in the previous session, this results in an existence dependency relationship between these two objects (Figure 16.6).

Some objects are subsets of several other objects, such as the **Registration** object, which is a subset of both **Course-Session** and **Student**. In MERODE this can be represented by a relationship object. A graphical representation is given as in Figure 16.7.

Relationship objects can be defined only if there exists a nontrivial set of common events between the objects that are related by the relationship object. In this particular case, this can be observed easily from the object/event table.

The equivalent representation by existence dependencies demonstrates what is known as the instantiation equivalence in entity-relationship modeling.

From this it becomes clear how existence dependency is the mother of all relationships, and becomes the principle mechanism for classifying objects in MERODE business models. A remarkable object is **Person**, which is a generalization of the **Member** and **Student** object. Members are persons who pay membership fees, without necessarily attending any course sessions. Students participate to **course-sessions** by means of registrations.

FIGURE 16.7. Relationship object.

EVENT	OBJECT	MEMBER	STUDENT	PERSON	COURSE-TOPIC	COURSE-SESSION	REGISTRATION
CREATE-MEMBER		C		C			
CHANGE-PERSON-DETAILS				X			
PAY-MEMBERSHIP-FEE		X		X			
STOP-MEMBERSHIP		X		X			
CREATE-STUDENT			C	C			
REGISTER-FOR-COURSE-SESSION			X	X	X	X	C
SHOW-UP-FOR-COURSE-SESSION			X	X	X	X	X
PAY-COURSE-FEE			X	X	X	X	X
CANCEL-COURSE-REGISTRATION			X	X	X	X	X
REFUND-COURSE-FEE			X	X	X	X	X
ANNULATE-COURSE-SESSION					X	X	
START-COURSE-SESSION					X	X	
CREATE-COURSE-SESSION					X	C	
CREATE-COURSE-TOPIC					C		

FIGURE 16.8. Common events between objects.

Member students pay different course fees to nonmember students. Specialization is modeled by one-to-one existence–dependency relationships. In other words, *Member* and *Student* are two different roles of a person object. The full object-relationship diagram for the BCA organization is given in Figure 16.10.

This diagrams shows *COURSE-SESSION*, being existence dependent on *COURSE-TOPIC* by means of a one-to-many existence dependency. *REGISTRATION* is a relation-

FIGURE 16.9. Instantiation equivalence.

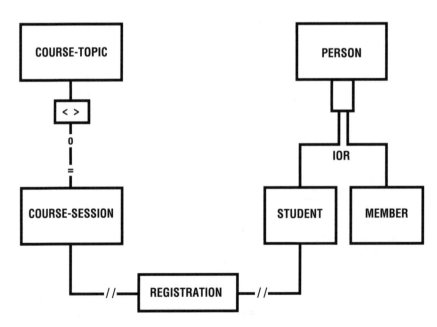

FIGURE 16.10. The BCA organization.

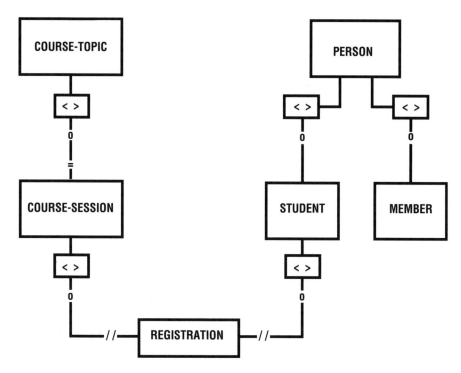

FIGURE 16.11. Entity-relationship diagram showing existence dependencies.

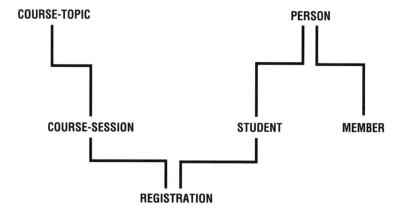

FIGURE 16.12. Classification lattice.

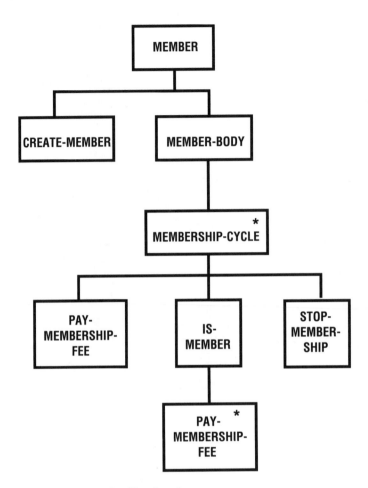

FIGURE 16.13. JSD diagram for *Member* object.

ship object, relating **COURSE-SESSION** and **STUDENT** in a many-to-many fashion. **STUDENT** and **MEMBER** are specializations of **PERSON**, related in an inclusive selective way (IOR). Instantiation of all the objects leads to the diagram in Figure 16.10, which shows all the objects with their respective existence dependencies.

Observe how the instantiated existence dependency relationships are at most one-to-many relationships. The existence dependencies give a way to classify, or order, objects with respect to each other. This allows us to arrange MERODE business objects in a lattice fashion.

By a happy accident — or maybe by design — the bottom objects in this structure are the revenue-generating objects of the BCA organization. They are also the starting point for the next activity set in MERODE business modeling: the object-structure analysis.

Object-structure analysis attaches a regular expression to every object, putting the business events in which it participates together in a well-structured way. Regular expressions can be developed in different ways. The easiest method is to use Jackson structure diagrams, as pioneered in JSD (Jackson 1983). The structure for a MEMBER object for example is given in Figure 16.13.

A much more compact way to describe these object structures involves the use of process algebra (Kuich 1986), using "." for sequence, "+" for selection and "*" for iteration, resulting in the following formula, or regular expression, for the MEMBER object.

MEMBER = CREATE-MEMBER .
[PAY-MEMBERSHIP-FEE] *. [STOP-MEMBERSHIP]

Another bottom object in the object classification is **REGISTRATION**. Remembering the very flexible behavior of the BCA association with respect to course participation and refunding of course fees, it is interesting to build up the structure of the **REGISTRATION** object in the JSD notations. The result is shown in Figure 16.14.

The corresponding regular expression is again much more compact, but perhaps less transparent.

REGISTRATION =   REGISTER-FOR-COURSE-SESSION .
[CANCEL-COURSE-REGISTRATION +
(SHOW-UP-FOR-COURSE-SESSION .
PAY-COURSE-FEE) +
(PAY-COURSE-FEE .
{ SHOW-UP-FOR-COURSE-SESSION +
(CANCEL-COURSE-REGISTRATION .
REFUND-COURSE-FEE) })]

Some of the formal aspects of MERODE can now be explored. (The properties of the structure primitives in MERODE induce on the set of business events the structure of an idempotent semi-ring (Kuich 1986, Dedene 1992). Business objects are elements of the free semi-ring generated over the set of business events in the universe of discourse. A key feature of idempotent semi-rings is that they allow only one way to order their elements consistently with the semi-ring structure. The formal definition, adapted to MERODE business models, is the following:

P <=' Q if and only if P + Q_(P) = Q_(P)

$Q\backslash\_(P)$ is the **Q** structure in which all events not present in **P** are replaced by the neutral element of the sequence operator ".", the "do-nothing" event. If there is only one way to classify regular expressions for objects consistently, the classification must be consistent with the existence-dependency classification. This introduces an additional consistency

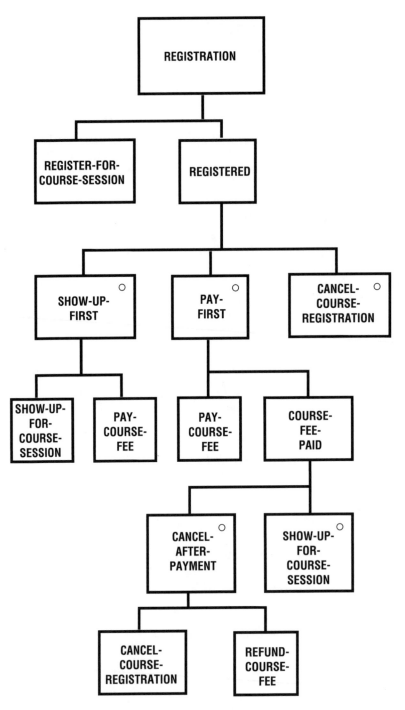

FIGURE 16.14. JSD diagram for registration object.

check on MERODE business model specifications. The regular expressions for the remaining objects of the BCA business model are the following:

```
STUDENT =        CREATE-STUDENT .
                 [REGISTER-FOR-COURSE-SESSION +
                 PAY-COURSE-FEE +
                 CANCEL-COURSE-REGISTRATION +
                 SHOW-UP-FOR-COURSE-SESSION +
                 REFUND-COURSE-FEE ]*

PERSON =  (CREATE-STUDENT + CREATE-MEMBER)
                 [CREATE-STUDENT + CREATE-MEMBER +
                 PAY-MEMBERSHIP-FEE + STOP-MEMBERSHIP +
                 CHANGE-PERSON-DETAILS +
                 REGISTER-FOR-COURSE-SESSION +
                 PAY-COURSE-FEE +
                 CANCEL-COURSE-REGISTRATION +
                 SHOW-UP-FOR-COURSE-SESION +
                 REFUND-COURSE-FEE ]*

COURSE-SESSION = CREATE-COURSE-SESSION .
                 [REGISTER-FOR-COURSE-SESSION +
                 PAY-COURSE-FEE + REFUND-COURSE-FEE +
                 CANCEL-COURSE-REGISTRATION]* +
              {(CANCEL-COURSE-SESSION .
                 [CANCEL-COURSE-REGISTRATION +
                 REFUNND-COURSE-FEE]* ) +
                 (START-COURSE-SESSION .
                 [CANCEL-COURSE-REGISTRATION +
                 PAY-COURSE-FEE + REFUND-COURSE-FEE +
                 CREATE-COURSE-REGISTRATION +
                 SHOW-UP-FOR-COURSE-SESSION]* )}

COURSE-TOPIC = CREATE-COURSE-TOPIC .
                 [CREATE-COURSE-SESSION +
                 STAART-COURSE-SESSION +
                 CANCEL-COURSE-SESSION +
                 REGISTER-FOR-COURSE-SESSION +
                 PAY-COURSE-FEE + REFUND-COURSE-FEE +
                 SHOW-UP-FOR-COURSE-SESSION +
                 CANCEL-COURSE-REGISTRATION]*
```

It is straightforward to verify that existence-dependent objects also satisfy the semi-ring-based classification of regular expressions. As an example

REGISTRATION + STUDENT_(REGISTRATION) =
STUDENT_(REGSTRATION)

STUDENT_WHERE (REGISTRATION) = [REGISTER-FOR-COURSE-SESSION
+   PAY-COURSE-FEE + CANCEL-COURSE-REGISTRATION +
*   SHOW-UP-FOR-COURSE-SESSION + REFUND-COURSE-FEE]**

This strong classification principle for business objects in MERODE introduces an additional consistency check on the behavior of objects in object-relationship models. Because of the object classification, the conditions under which MERODE business models do not contain dead-locking business rules can be shown (Snoeck 1993). Moreover, the classification of the objects provides methodological guidance for building business rules.

Object structures allow us to model the dynamic business rules that describe the behavior of the business objects. These rules depend only on the state of the object. The object state is already a first example of how objects and events can be made visible by means of attributes. This is a starting point for the next stage in MERODE business modeling, the abstract-data-type analysis.

Business events as well as business objects can use attributes to make themselves visible. Attributes of business events allow us to write down unique instances of business events. As an example, a *REGISTER-FOR-COURSE-SESSION* business event can be made visible by attaching to it the following attributes:

REGISTER-FOR-COURSE-SESSION :
COURSE-SESSION-ID-INPUT, STUDENT-ID-INPUT
COURSE-TITLE-ID-INPUT, PERSON-ID-INPUT
REGISTER-FOR-COURSE-TIME-STAMP

Object attributes allow us to denote unique instances of business objects. The set of all the attributes of a business object is called the *object-state vector* (inspired by the fact that each object has at least its state to achieve controllable behavior). Each participating object will react to a business event with its own method. Some examples include:

COURSE-SESSION :
REGISTER-FOR-COURSE-SESSION {
*   COURSE-SESSION-#-PARTICIPANTS =*
*   COURSE-SESSION-#-PARTICIPANTS + 1 ;*
*   ... }*
STUDENT :
REGISTER-FOR-COURSE-SESSION {
*   STUDENT-#-COURSE-SESSIONS-REGISTERED =*

> *STUDENT-#-COURSE-SESSIONS-REGISTERED + 1;*
> *... }*

This feature also makes polymorphism visible in MERODE business model specifications. Each business object becomes visible through its own abstract data type, including the object-state vector and a business method for every business event to which the object participates. An example for the BCA organization is the data type shown in Figure 16.15.

A practical way to imagine business methods is to consider them as sets of operations that must be committed to the object-state vector at single points in time. This is why methods are denoted as sets of operations and not as sequences of operations: The actual sequence doesn't matter as long as the operations have a common checkpoint.

Business objects with abstract data types can be dressed with static business rules (or invariants) specifying extra rules based on attributes of business objects. An example might be a rule stating that nonmembers can register for no more than five course sessions. Flags with the corresponding rule numbers can be attached graphically to the object relationship models to indicate the presence of static business rules.

Figure 16.15 shows all of the features of the specification of a business model in MERODE. To be complete, a specification must contain the following elements:

- A list of the business objects and business events
- A description of each object as a set of events, by means of the object/event table
- A structure diagram (or equivalent regular expressions) for the dynamic business rules
- A list of business event attributes
- An abstract data type for each business object
- A list of static business rules

There are no internal communication mechanisms, such as messages, between the objects. The only connections between objects are caused by joint participation in business events. The mutual consistency of the specification elements leaves little room for errors in the specification process. This should not be interpreted as a limitation to systems developers: They are guided by the structure present in MERODE. A typical example of this is the way the existence dependencies among objects provide a natural way to build up the regular expressions for the business objects.

THE USE OF OBJECT-ORIENTED BUSINESS MODELS

Business models are simply formal simulation models of business behavior. They do not contain any functionality on input or output of information. However, it is easy to enable this functionality once a business model is completed. The most trivial way is to connect it to the real world by means of input functions that send event messages to the business model. Each message contains identification for the event it represents and the participating objects. The business model can accept the message or reject it on the basis of violation of (at least) one of the business rules. The implementation of such a "business engine" is simple and straightforward. The JSP-like pseudocode for such a procedure is summarized in Figure 16.16.

This business engine can be realized in conventional technology. Most CASE tools are

---

MEMBER OBJECT CLASS

STATE VECTOR : Member-id
                            Member-person-id,
                            Member-state,
                            Member-total-membership-payment,
                            Member-stop-time-stamp

METHODS :

CREATE-MEMBER {
                    Member-id := Member-id-input;
                    Member-person-id :=
                     Member-person-id-input;
                    Member-state := "I";
                    Member-total-membership-payment
                       := 0;
                    Member-stop-time-stamp := " ";
                    }

PAY-MEMBERSHIP-FEE {
                    Member-state := "II";
                    Member-total-membership-payment :=
                    Member-total-membership-payment +
                     Membership-fee-input;
                       }

STOP-MEMBERSHIP {
                    Member-state := "I";
                    Member-stop-time-stamp :=
                         Stop-membership-time-stamp-input;
                       }

FIGURE 16.15. An abstract data type.

```
BUSINESS-ENGINE itr (until no more messages)
  KIND-OF-EVENT sel (create event)
    CREATION-EVENT posit
      CREATION-EVENT-OK seq
        Check non-existence of object to be created;
          Quit if object exists;
        Get ADT, and in particular the state vector of the other
        participating objects;
          Quit if some objects not found;
        Check business rules for other participating objects;
          Quit if one business rule is violated;
        Execute business methods for the creation event;
        Store new ADT's for the updated objects;
      CREATION-EVENT-OK end
    CREATION-EVENT admit
      CREATION-EVENT-NOT-OK seq
      Send rejection message with rejection code;
      CREATION-EVENT-NOT-OK end
    CREATION-EVENT end
  KIND-OF-EVENT alt
    NON-CREATION-EVENT posit
      NON-CREATION-EVENT-OK seq
      Get ADT, and in particular the state vectors
      of the participating objects;
          Quit if some objects not found;
      Check business rules for the participation objects;
          Quit if one business rule is violated;
      Execute business methods for the event;
      Store new ADT's for the updated objects;
      NON-CREATION-EVENT-OK end
    NON-CREATION-EVENT admit
      NON-CREATION-EVENT-NOT-OK seq
        Send rejection message with rejection code;
      NON-CREATION-EVENT-NOT-OK end
    NON-CREATION-EVENT end
  KIND-OF-EVENT end
BUSINESS-ENGINE end
```

FIGURE 16.16. Pseudocode for "business engine."

also oriented toward this conventional technology and can be invoked for easier construction of implementation models. However, increasingly, technology helps to facilitate implementation. Examples are object-oriented languages and database managers in which the abstract data types of the objects can be taken over exactly from the business model specifications. The problem of user interfaces can be solved easily using, for example, class libraries and environments for graphical-user interfaces.

Input functionality can be enhanced for the user by means of input transactions. Input transactions are triggered by means of transaction requests. The output of an input transaction is the set of relevant event messages resulting from the transaction. Take for example assistance in searching the object identifications for the participating objects. Suppose some one is paying a course fee. The full event message format is given by the event attributes for the event *PAY-COURSE-FEE*, with the appropriate identifications for the participating objects.

> *PAY-COURSE-FEE :*
> *COURSE-SESSION-ID-INPUT, COURSE-TITLE-ID-INPUT,*
> *REGISTRATION-ID-INPUT, STUDENT-ID-INPUT, PERSON-ID-INPUT,*
> *PAY-COURSE-FEE-TIME-STAMP, PAY-COURSE-FEE-AMOUNT-PAID*

A transaction object *PAY-COURSE-FEE-TRX* can be created that is triggered by a message that contains only the *REGISTRATION-ID* and the *AMOUNT-PAID*. The transaction method will query the object base for the involved objects, collect their identifications, and add the system time as the relevant time-stamp. The result is a full event message.

A second use of input transactions would be where events are combined into single transactions for the user. A *REGISTRATION-TRX* could, for example, automatically generate the *CREATE-STUDENT* and *CREATE-PERSON* event messages for a new student.

Output functionality is used to make objects or events visible, to extract or summarize information from the business models. This feedback type of function will be referred to as *information functions* (by analogy with JSD). Their output is a stream of information to the real world. Some functions also present a feed-forward type of functionality. Their output will suggest some business events as a result of the current state of the business model. These functions interact with the business model as they generate a stream of business event messages. Once the users acknowledge the scheduling of business events — acknowledging in this way that they have been accepted by the real business — they are forwarded to the business model. Two simple examples will illustrate these concepts, although a lot more examples can be found in (Dedene 1993).

A typical information function might produce a list of all persons who are no longer members, but were members last year. This function, triggered by request messages, will use state-vector inspections to query all the *MEMBER* objects and their corresponding *PERSON* objects to produce the list (Figure 16.17).

The abstract data type for *FUNCTION_1* is shown in Figure 16.18, in which the *GetSV* operations declare the queries.

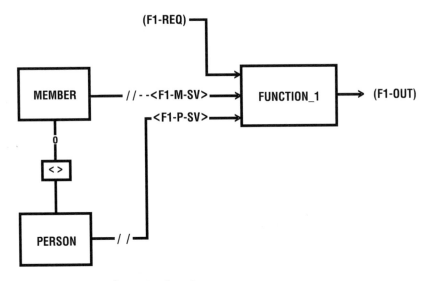

FIGURE 16.17.   An information function.

A typical feed-forward function might suggest the cancelation of a course session if at the last time-stamp for acceptance of registrations the number of registrations is insufficient. This function will query the **COURSE-SESSION** object to find the attached number of registration objects to make a decision.

Observe how business models are not changed as a consequence of the functions: The business model is the nucleus of the system, which is invariant for the information requirements. At most, information requirements may add new attributes and the corresponding operations to the business model. These are inessential changes as they don't add new objects, relationships, or behavior rules.

Business models can be implemented directly before doing any function design whatsoever. In fact, implemented business models can enable the prototyping of information functions by means of fourth-generation languages or query and reporting tools. As such, business models reanimate the old idea of information center functionality, which was explored in the early eighties.

Moreover, a natural coherence exists with client/server technology. Business models will normally be implemented on server technology, given the fact that the business interaction is reflected in a business model. Client technology can be used to implement functions, involving local power at the client workstation to process the functions and present the information results. The messages between the business model and the function objects can be implemented using the remote procedure calls of the client/server technology.

The overall architecture of an implementation model can be represented as a data-flow diagram (Figure 16.19). This extends the idea of the business engine by adding input transaction functionality and functions to the system.

```
┌─────────────────────────────────────────────────────────────────────┐
│ FUNCTION_1 Abstract Data Type                                         │
├─────────────────────────────────────────────────────────────────────┤
│ FUNCTION_1 State Vector : -                                           │
├─────────────────────────────────────────────────────────────────────┤
│ FUNCTION_1 Methods                                                    │
│                                                                       │
│ Function_1 {                                                          │
│                                                                       │
│    C-F1-REQ-P-F1-OUT  seq                                             │
│       *Query members  into Member-cursor-stream                       │
│       GetSV MEMBER  (  Member-person-id  )                            │
│                where (  Member-state  = 'I'   and                      │
│                          Year(  F1-REQ-timestamp-input  ) -           │
│                          Year(  Member-stop-time-stamp  ) <2  )        │
│                on F1-REQ-timestamp-input                               │
│                into Member-cursor-stream;                             │
│       Send  ( 'Membership last year cancellations report'):          │
│       Receive Member-cursor-stream-message;                          │
│       C-F1-REQ-P-F1-OUT-BODY  itr  (until end-of-Member-cursor-stream) │
│          P-F1-OUT-MESSAGE  seq                                        │
│            GetSV PERSON  (  Person-name-address  )                     │
│                 where  (  Person-id = Member-person-id  )             │
│                 on Member-person-id;                                  │
│             Send  ( 'Member',  Person-name-address  , 'Cancelled');   │
│             Receive Member-cursor-stream-message;                    │
│                                                                       │
│          P-F1-OUT-MESSAGE end                                         │
│       C-F1-REQ-P-F1-OUT-BODY end                                      │
│    C-F1-REQ-P-F1-OUT  end         }                                   │
└─────────────────────────────────────────────────────────────────────┘
```

FIGURE 16.18.   Abstract data type for *FUNCTION_1.*

The different processes shown in the figure can be distributed, whereby the message streams are implemented by means of remote procedure calls. Moreover, many of the components of this diagram are reusable in constructing other implementations. This provides another reusability feature, which may contribute to productivity increases in system development.

DISCUSSION AND OUTLOOK

This chapter has emphasized the practical realization of object-oriented business models. It has been shown how these models act as the engines of systems that have to be

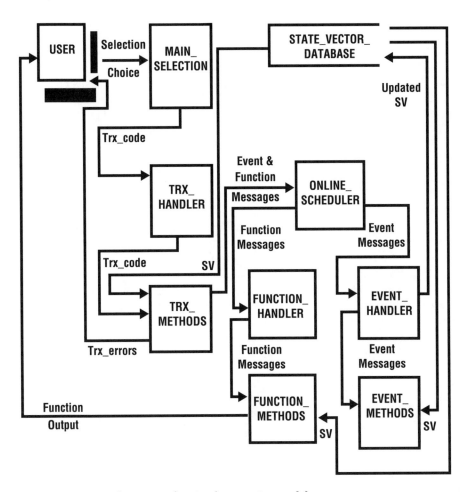

FIGURE 16.19. Architecture of an implementation model.

integrated in a particular business environment. From this it is obvious that the use of such development techniques radically changes the current roles and tasks of systems developers.

In fact, the only people who can really design a business model and evaluate whether it is a true reflection of the business are the actual business experts. In today's industry, with much pressure on middle management, this may open some new perspectives. Formal business models are a new specification language for administrational organization. Its formal nature allows for consistency and optimization. Business areas can be reengineered to reduce the business complexity. MERODE business models enable us to visualize these reductions in complexity. In this way, people not personally involved in information systems may become the business architects in this object-oriented system architecture. Information system development is no longer a spectator sport for business managers. The functioning of the business and its appropriate representation is the driver for appropriate information functionality.

The quality resulting from object orientation and the proper use of structured techniques is encouraging. The current lack of quality of information systems is a real economic threat for the whole information business. The more technology facilitates the realization of consistent models, the more rapidly the information technology business will be able to keep pace with actual business developments.

REFERENCES

Dedene, G. (1991) Productive application development using an object-oriented business modeling approach, *2nd International Conference on Repository and AD/Cycle*, Chicago, October 1991.

Dedene, G. (1992) MERODE: A practical approach to the specification of consistent object-oriented business models, *Proceedings of the 5th International conference on putting methods and techniques for systems design into practice*, University of Nantes.

Dedene, G. (1993) MERODE by examples: A tutorial on object-oriented business modeling, *Proceedings of the Object Technology 93 Conference*, Cambridge, UK.

Jackson, M. (1983) *System Development*, Prentice-Hall, Eaglewoods Cliffs, NJ.

Kuich, W., and A. Salomaa (1986) *Semirings, Automata, Languages*, Springer-Verlag, Berlin.

Meyer, B. (1988) *Object-Oriented Software Construction*, Prentice-Hall, Eaglewood Cliffs, NJ.

Put, F. (1988) *Introducing dynamic and temporal aspects in a conceptual database schema*, Doctoral thesis, Faculty of Economics and Applied Economics, K.U.Leuven.

Rumbaugh, J., M. Blaha, W. Premerlani, F. Eddy, and W. Lorensen (1991) *Object-Oriented Modeling and Design*, Prentice-Hall, Eaglewood Cliffs NJ.

Snoeck, M. (1993) Requirements for Correct Business Models, L.I.R.I.S. K.U.Leuven Research Notes.

Verhelst, M. (1992) *MERODE*, Kluwer Bedrijfswetenschappen.

Zachman, J. A. (1987) A framework for Information Architecture, IBM *Systems Journal*, 26(3).

chapter 17

The SSADM Method:
An Object-Oriented Approach?

MIKE GOODLAND   *KINGSTON UNIVERSITY, UK*

SSADM (structured systems analysis and design method) is well established as the UK's foremost systems development methodology. It is an open standard practiced by many end-user organizations, taught by many training organizations and universities, and consulted upon by many consulting organizations. First developed in 1982 by LBMS for Central Government, its use has spread throughout the UK information technology community and beyond. Surveys indicate that more than half of the organizations using structured methods in the UK are using SSADM. Since its inception in 1982 SSADM has always taken a three-dimensional perspective of information systems: functional, data, and dynamic.

Object orientation has been a topic of much recent interest as evidenced by the many seminars, courses, and books published. This chapter first briefly explains SSADM and then demonstrates how it uses object-oriented concepts. Object-oriented methodologies are compared with SSADM in terms of their structural components and general approach. Finally, some suggestions are made as to how SSADM could move to a fuller object-oriented approach.

SSADM

Although SSADM is well described by the reference manual (CCTA 1990) and by several books (Goodland 1993), a brief description of SSADM Version 4 is given here. SSADM covers the feasibility analysis and design phases of a systems development project; strategic planning, construction, and project management are not explicitly covered by SSADM, but the method provides strong hooks to these important areas. There are five modules in SSADM: feasibility, requirements analysis, requirements specification, logical systems specification, and physical design. Each module breaks down into stages and steps that are prescriptively defined in terms of their tasks, inputs, and outputs. Generally, SSADM is used in large projects and strongly follows the waterfall life cycle with clearly defined end points for each stage and formal quality reviews of end products. The modules are designed to be self-contained so that projects may use components of SSADM for, say, requirements specification and requirements analysis and then use a different approach for systems design.

In this chapter we will concentrate on the analysis aspects of SSADM met in the requirements analysis and requirements specification modules; the design modules of SSADM are oriented toward 3GL or 4GL implementations and contain little in the way of object-oriented components. However, in the requirements specification module, SSADM provides as detailed a picture as some of the so-called, object-oriented design methods. Thus, it is felt that the requirements analysis and specification modules encompass object-oriented analysis and the early stages of object-oriented design.

During requirements specification, three models of the system are built: a logical data model, which is a form of entity-relationship-attribute model; a functional model, which is derived from data flow diagrams and attempts to package the system into functional units to solve specific business problems; and finally, an event-entity model showing the business rules governing the behavior of the system. Figure 17.1 shows these three models: the functional model is represented by a data flow diagram; the data model is represented by a logical data structure which would be supported by entity, attribute, and relationship descriptions; and the part of the event-entity model shown is an entity life history, which uses Jackson notation to represent the sequence, selection, and iteration of events affecting typical entity occurrences. These models are created in separate steps, but are strongly linked (shown schematically by the bold double-headed arrows linking them). In the next section of the chapter we describe how these basic models support the object-oriented concepts.

OBJECT-ORIENTED CONCEPTS IN SSADM

Object-oriented concepts and ideas come from a wide variety of sources: initially from object-oriented programming, but also from knowledge-based systems and semantic data modeling. Through much of the published work on object-oriented ideas, there is considerable consensus on what the underlying concepts are, some consensus on the

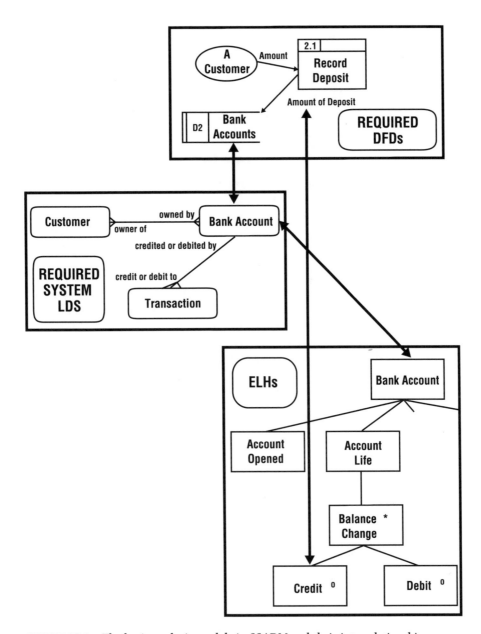

FIGURE 17.1. The basic analysis models in SSADM and their interrelationships.

terminology used, and little consensus on the notations used to represent these concepts in diagrammatic form. Many of these ideas and concepts are familiar to practitioners of information systems development methodologies, particularly those of the data-orienta-

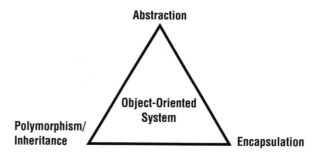

FIGURE 17.2.   The Henderson-Sellers object-oriented triangle.

tion school such as Information Engineering, Oracle CASE method, and SSADM. However, these structured practitioners will find the object-oriented terminology and notation unfamiliar.

A neat way of understanding an object-oriented system is given by Henderson-Sellers (1991). He regards an object-oriented system as requiring three major components — abstraction, encapsulation, and polymorphism — represented as a triangle in Figure 17.2. One of the important object-oriented ideas is that the same or very similar models are preserved through analysis, design, and construction; therefore, an object-oriented analysis and design method must also demonstrate these three components. Each of the concepts of abstraction, polymorphism/inheritance, and encapsulation is described using examples from SSADM to demonstrate how each concept is supported.

ABSTRACTION

The real world, which we are attempting to model in computer software, consists of individual objects: particular people, machines, invoices, etc. We classify groups of individual objects (each identified by a name or by other properties) by giving the group a name. For example, the name *cat* can refer to a set of objects called Rupert, Flossie, etc. This concept of abstraction is an important component of the object-oriented world and of the SSADM world. The term **class**[1] is used in object orientation, meaning a description of a group of **objects** with the same properties, common behavior, common relationships, and common semantics. In the SSADM world, this maps to an *entity type*. The term **instance** refers to an individual **object** that belongs to a **class**. Thus, the **instance** or **object**, "Rupert," would belong to the **class** "cat" (instance perhaps implies a system-world implementation of a real-world object, but the terms are often used interchangeably in the object-orientation literature). In SSADM, we have *entity occurrences* showing the occurrences of a particular type.

---

[1]Terms set in **bold** come from the object-oriented world. Terms set in *italics* come from the SSADM/structured systems world.

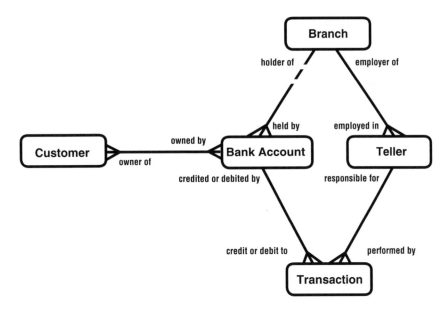

FIGURE 17.3.   Logical data structure in SSADM.

Within the idea of abstraction, we will deal with the idea that different **classes** can interact with each other. Three major kinds of interaction are described in the object-orientation literature: **association**, **aggregation**, and **inheritance** (dealt with under **Polymorphism/inheritance**).

Association

This indicates a relationship among instances of two or more classes describing a group of links with common structure and common semantics. Two particular kinds of relationship are specified by **aggregation** and **inheritance**. These will be described later and their SSADM equivalents given. The idea of **association** (as distinct from aggregation or inheritance) is not popular among all object-orientation experts, but is acknowledged by many of the more pragmatic object-orientated analysis methods (e.g., Rumbaugh (1991) and Coad/Yourdon (1991)). In SSADM, associations are shown by binary *relationships* between entity types. Figure 17.3 shows a typical SSADM *logical data structure* representing diagrammatically these relationships.

The definition given above for **association** is interpreted differently by different object-oriented approaches. Some adopt the binary model, like SSADM, and do not allow associations to contain attributes and functional properties. Other models are closer to the Chen entity-relationship model, which allows multiple participants in a relationship and allows attributes to be attached to the relationship. In SSADM a multiple relationship or a relationship with attributes would be treated as an entity type. In the object-oriented world

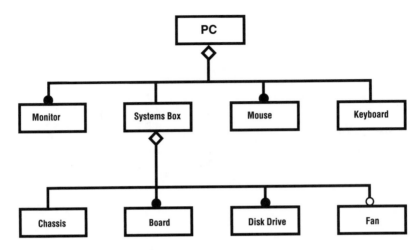

FIGURE 17.4. Rumbaugh notation for aggregation/composition.

class diagrams are used that show multiple associations or show binary associations, as well as the aggregation and inheritance relationships between classes.

Aggregation

This is sometimes known as *composition* and refers to a relationship between **classes**, where a whole is composed of various parts. Typical names for this sort of relationship would be "consists-of," "has-a," "part-of," etc. An example (adapted from Rumbaugh in Figure 17.4) would be where a personal computer consists of a monitor, system box, mouse, and keyboard, and the system box, in turn, is composed of a chassis, board(s), disk drive(s), and fan. The diamond shape below PC and below systems box shows the aggregation relationship. The circles at the other end show the number of occurrences; a solid blob indicates many, an open blob indicates that there may be zero.

These types of relationship are not treated as a separate concept in SSADM, but are dealt with in a variety of ways. These include: creating a relationship that a generic type (e.g., Part) has with itself (sometimes called a *recursive relationship*), or by creating separate types and using normal relationships or by using "bill-of-material" type structures. However, each of these seems rather unnatural and more difficult to explain than the separate aggregation construct. The construct is not available in many object-oriented programming languages or even in some so-called object-oriented databases.

POLYMORPHISM/INHERITANCE

Henderson-Sellers treats these two ideas together as another vertex of the object-oriented triangle. Polymorphism broadly relates to the idea that a message can be serviced

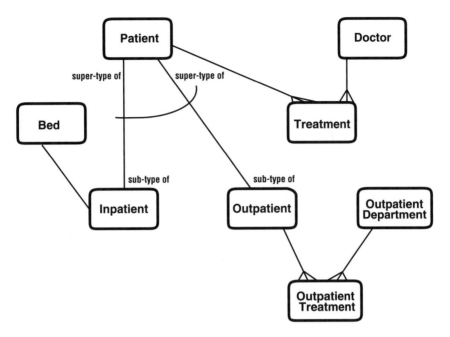

FIGURE 17.5. Formal SSADM representation of inheritance.

differently by different classes — when a message is received by a class/object, the resulting actions will depend upon the receiving class. Objects that are able to respond to a polymorphic message must share certain characteristics, which they will have **inherited** from a base class. There is no direct equivalent to the concept of polymorphism in SSADM, although the concept of inheritance is supported.

Inheritance

Classes can **inherit** the functional properties and attributes of other classes, leading to the concept of **subclasses** and **superclasses**. In a hospital, we could have a superclass of *Patient* and subclasses of *In-Patient* and *Out-Patient*. All patients would share certain attributes such as *Patient Number*, *Home Address*, *Date of Birth*, but only in-patients would have an association with beds, and have the attribute *Dietary Requirements*. Other terms met are **generalization**, that is the creation of superclasses (thus, *Patient* is a generalization of *In-Patient*), and **specialization**, that is the creation of subclasses (thus, *In-Patient* is a specialization of *Patient*). In SSADM, inheritance is handled by *entity sub-typing*. The formal SSADM notation for this is shown in Figure 17.5 although many projects use the notation shown in Figure 17.6 where the supertype encloses the subtypes. These diagrams demonstrate only hierarchical inheritance, but multiple inheritance is also possible where a subclass inherits features from several superclasses. However, this is rarely encountered in SSADM models.

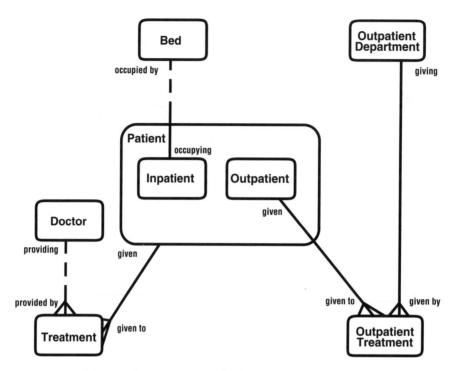

FIGURE 17.6. Often-used representation of inheritance.

ENCAPSULATION

Earlier we discussed one of the components of the object-oriented triangle, **abstraction**, and extended it to cover the types of relationships between different classes. A second important component of the object-oriented world is known as **encapsulation**. This is a modeling and implementation technique that separates the external aspects of an object from the internal implementation details of the object. It is also related to the idea in analysis and design that an object (or class) has both data properties (attributes) and functional properties. It relates to the idea in programming languages of **information hiding** whereby functional and data properties are encapsulated within objects and can be private or hidden from the rest of the system. When a **message** is received by the object, it is dealt with, its results are presented, and further messages are sent.

This concept is foreign to most structured systems analysis methods, but has been an important feature of SSADM, since its inception in 1982. In SSADM, entities have data properties, known as *attributes*, and both high-level (*events* and their *effects*) and low-level functional properties (*operations*) that can be performed upon them. These functional properties are shown through a particular diagram known as an *entity life history*, which

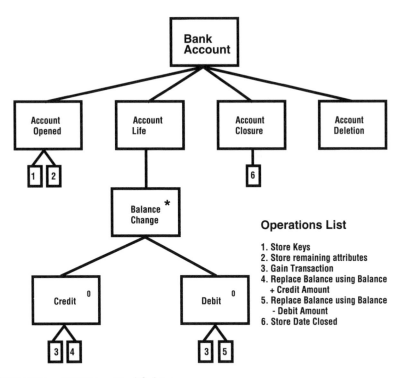

FIGURE 17.7.   SSADM entity life history.

uses Jackson notation to show the sequence, selection, and iteration of events that can effect an entity occurrence. The operations are shown as a separate list to annotate the diagram. Figure 17.7 shows an example of an SSADM *entity life history*.

In the object world the term **method** (although Rumbaugh uses **operation**, and Coad/ Yourdon use **service**) is often used to refer to a functional property of a class. This refers to the implementation of an operation for a specific class and relates to the SSADM *effect* of an *event* on an *entity*. In SSADM, the operations on an entity and the attributes are normally shown in separate diagrams, but some SSADM CASE tools are capable of showing this information on the same screen at the same time in a different window or in the same window. The equivalent diagrammatic notation used by Coad/Yourdon is shown in Figure 17.8.

Objects receive **messages** (some authors use the term **event** or **request**) that trigger methods into action. Thus a message might be received by the *Transaction* class, causing it to instantiate a *Transaction* object and to transmit a message *Credit* to a related *Bank Account* object, there causing an update to the *Balance* attribute. This maps closely to the SSADM term *event*: the event *Credit* affects a *Bank Account* occurrence and a *Transaction* occurrence.

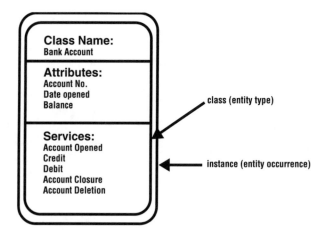

FIGURE 17.8. Coad/Yourdon notation for a class that may have instances.

In SSADM an *event occurrence* may affect different *entity occurrences* in different ways. This is shown formally in SSADM by the use of *effect-correspondence diagrams* and informally by the *event/entity matrix*. In Figure 17.10 the event/entity matrix shows an event **Credit**, which affects occurrences of the **Bank Account** and **Transaction** entities. This interaction of an event with different entity occurrences is further characterized by Figure 17.11, which shows the effect correspondence diagram. These diagrams can go beyond simple message passing to consider control aspects, showing whether a number of occurrences of an entity are affected by the event and showing conditions under which the event affects the occurrence. Control is considered to be a weak feature of many object-oriented analysis and design methods (Monarchi 1992).

COMPARISONS OF NOTATIONS

Having considered the main constructs of object-oriented approaches, it is useful to consider the notations employed to represent those constructs. Figure 17.12 compares the

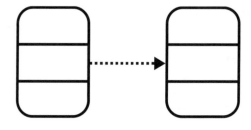

FIGURE 17.9. Coad/Yourdon notation for message passing.

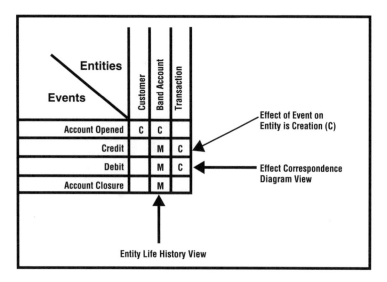

FIGURE 17.10. SSADM event/entity matrix.

notations of Coad and Yourdon, Rumbaugh, and SSADM. This represents but two of the object-oriented approaches, Monarchi and Puhr (1990) list 23 in their paper, and several other approaches and notations have been published since[2]. This illustrates well the confusion and lack of standards throughout the industry.

OBJECT-ORIENTED METHODOLOGIES

For an approach to be considered a methodology, it requires more than just a notation for representing the information about the system. An approach to developing those representations is also needed. SSADM has a very detailed structure that provides considerable guidance on how each of its models is derived, checked, and related to other models. None of the object-oriented approaches can yet claim this level of detail in their approach to the process of systems development.

Object-oriented approaches tend to concentrate more on software than on systems development. By *system* we refer to a set of interrelating components intended to serve some function or to solve certain problems. Object-oriented approaches tend to be conceptual — concentrating on identifying clusters of objects — rather than practical and are intended to deliver solutions to real problems. It is felt that this makes object-oriented approaches in their present form difficult to sell to end users. One of the great strengths of SSADM is that the user is very closely involved in the development—this does not seem

---

[2]The forthcoming Object Management Group report studies over 30 approaches.

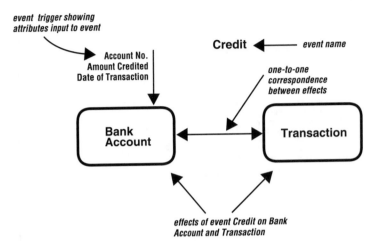

FIGURE 17.11. Effect correspondence diagram for the event Credit showing notation.

to be a strong feature of the emerging object-oriented methodologies in which this is only implied by their use of the evolutionary life cycle.

Object-oriented approaches tend to follow evolutionary life cycles rather than waterfall life cycles. The tendency of SSADM, particularly in its early days, has been the development of large monolithic systems following (or attempting to follow) the waterfall life cycle. However, recent practice with SSADM (prototyping was incorporated into Version 4 of the method) has been smaller subprojects that follow a faster life cycle — nothing about the underlying concepts of object-oriented approaches or of SSADM requires either an evolutionary or a waterfall approach. However, the object-oriented concepts of both approaches make an evolutionary development more viable.

CONCLUSIONS

The concepts met in SSADM are a subset of the full set of object-oriented concepts (this is true of many approaches designated object oriented). The additional features, described by the full object oriented set, deal with problems that have not been encountered on the "normal" SSADM information systems projects. However, as SSADM is increasingly used in more complex projects, these ideas will become more important. The movement toward GUI and client-server systems will lead to extensions to SSADM. These are likely to follow some of the object-oriented approaches.

Although inheritance structures are recognized within SSADM, their strengths in aiding the development of reusable code will lead to a greater emphasis in the future. This

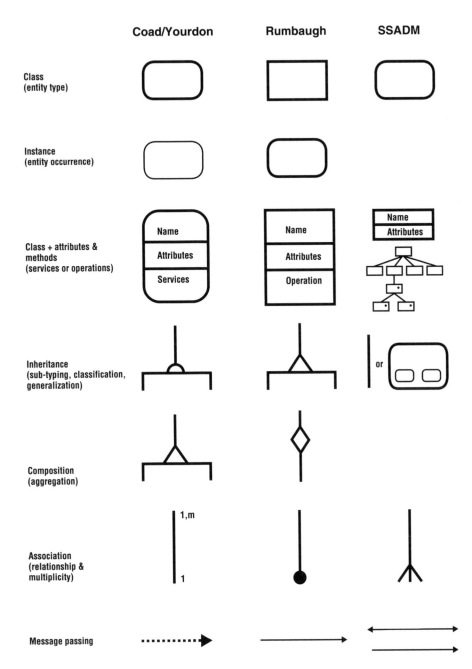

FIGURE 17.12. Comparison of Coad/Yourdon, Rumbaugh, and SSADM notations.

use of inheritance structures needs to be carried through to full support in encapsulation using entity life histories.

It is proposed that object-oriented extensions should be made to SSADM while maintaining existing notations and terminology that are well understood and established within the SSADM community, and are in broad agreement with the concepts expressed by the object-oriented community. Extensions to areas not covered by SSADM concepts should use the best-developed and understood of the object-oriented approaches while attempting to maintain consistency and continuity with the SSADM notations and terminology.

It is also felt that the object-oriented community can learn from SSADM, which has practiced object-oriented ideas for more than ten years on a very large number of successful projects. In particular, it is felt that structural process ideas from SSADM are useful. SSADM's appreciation and identification of the users' problems in requirements analysis and its approach to quality control and user involvement throughout the development are other features from which the object-oriented community can learn.

A well-established methodology like SSADM, which has in the UK more than 4,000 trained, certified practitioners, offers a way of introducing object-oriented techniques and methods without revolutionizing the way that many systems developers work. In short, we are proposing that moving from SSADM to an object-oriented analysis and design methodology should be, and is, evolution — *not* revolution.

ACKNOWLEDGMENT

The author thanks Brian Saxby for his constructive comments on this paper.

REFERENCES

CCTA (1990) *SSADM Version 4 Reference Manual*, NCC Blackwell, Oxford, UK.

Coad, P., and E. Yourdon (1991) *Object-Oriented Analysis*, 2nd Edition, Yourdon Press/Prentice-Hall, Englewood Cliffs, NJ.

Goodland, M. (1993) *SSADM Version 4: A Practical Approach*, McGraw-Hill, Maidenhead, UK.

Henderson-Sellers, B. (1991) *A Book of Object-Oriented Knowledge*,Prentice-Hall, Englewood Cliffs, NJ.

Monarchi, D.E., and G.I. Puhr. A research typology for object-oriented analysis and design, *Communications of the ACM*, September 1992, 35–47.

Rumbaugh, J., M.Blaha, W. Premelani, F. Eddy, and W. Lorensen (1991) *Object-Oriented Modeling and Design*, Prentice-Hall, Englewood Cliffs, NJ.

part **5**

THE EVOLVING DEVELOPMENT ENVIRONMENT

chapter 18

Object-Development Environments

RICHARD DALEY   *RICHARD DALEY ASSOCIATES*

In this chapter, the author expresses his view of the requirements for object-development environments. These include CASE tools and environments for current methods and languages, but also embraces many other requirements of development and management.

INTRODUCTION

It looks as if the world has gone object-oriented. Well, the world always was object-oriented, but now we are expected to make our software systems and applications, which model a part of the real-world, not only to act object-oriented, but to be analyzed, designed, and implemented using object-oriented concepts, methods, and languages.

As is usual within industry, we work inside-out. Initially, we came up with object-oriented programming languages, then we thought about how to design systems using the language, and finally we got around to considering what the problem is and how to represent our thoughts on the problem, so that we can design and implement the system using our object-oriented language.

To this end, we need to provide methods, tools, and environments that allow developers to build systems and support the much-vaunted capabilities of the object-oriented paradigm. Compared to the structured analysis and design ideas of the last two decades the object-orientation paradigm is considered to require no sudden leaps or changes in the underlying concepts. The job of implementing systems can proceed through analysis, design, and implementation by fleshing out the work of the previous phase; in fact many people consider that there are no phases of analysis, design, and implementation — rather, that the system evolves to meet its intended goal.

This difference is most widely seen in systems based upon the Smalltalk language. Indeed calling it a *language* is a misnomer. Smalltalk provides a development environment in which objects are created. A system or application in Smalltalk ends up as an extension to the Smalltalk environment. There is essentially no difference between the development environment and the run-time environment of the application. The Smalltalk paradigm is one of rapid prototyping through establishing classes, defining methods, exploring and adaptation. It starts at the programming-language level and offers little support for thinking about the problem, or reflecting on a design. This do-or-die approach is one that has less likelihood of success with large systems development.

Languages like C++ represent the adaptation of existing third-generation languages to support the object-oriented concepts of object classes, inheritance, etc. While they lend themselves to the development concept of prototyping, they are just not as amenable to it as Smalltalk. This difference reflects the underlying difference between these two types of language — or, rather, a language (C++) and an environment (Smalltalk).

COMMON THEMES

Although there are many different methods for object-oriented analysis and design, the very nature of developing object-oriented systems means that they need to represent certain aspects of the system during analysis and design.

Class Definitions

An expectation of objected orientation is reuse. To achieve this at the analysis and design stages will require each class' definition to be specified.

The appearance of a class in any other representation is an implicit reference to the class definition. The appearance of the class elsewhere will show some of its aspects, although it is only in the class definition that all the information on the class is available.

Static Structures

Static structures is not a common term. It is chosen to avoid the specific terminology of any particular object-oriented method. The static structure establishes the underlying architecture of the system (or application). The diagrams created show the classes of the system and two specific connections between them. First, the static structure shows how a class inherits from other classes, and second, it shows how the methods (also known as *operations, services,* or *functions*) communicate with each other through the sending and receiving of messages.

These diagrams are essentially static; they show nothing going on. They show what is possible in terms of messages and they represent the architectural organization of the system. The presence of a class in a static structure is showing a class being used. Its definition is held as a class definition.

Dynamic Structures

The static structures show what can be, while the dynamic structure is a simple form of animation. Many object-oriented methods provide the means of describing a slice of the action. The diagrams show *instances* (objects) of classes communicating through specific messaging. These diagrams are intended to illustrate that the chosen architecture of the system, as represented by the static structures, can achieve the desired results.

In many senses this is a step towards "testing" the specification if not "executing the specification."

Internal Behavior

Each class represents one or more objects of that class. Over time objects of the class are created, updated, and potentially deleted. For any object of the class what may happen to it between creation and deletion may be complex, with it willing to only accept certain messages at certain times. This leads to the need to be able to model the behavior of the class (sometimes referred to as its life cycle) to show how its instances react according to changes in their data.

A bank account class illustrates this changing of internal behavior. Between the account object being created and deleted, the account may be in credit or overdrawn. While in credit an account object can accept "credit" messages and "debit" messages from other objects. When overdrawn the account object may choose to only accept "credit" messages, unless at an earlier point in time it received an "overdraft" message.

Classes that represent complex objects need to have their internal behavior modeled using existing techniques such as entity life histories or state-transition diagrams.

Packaging

Large systems are never developed as single monolithic systems. Instead, the system is partitioned into smaller subsystems, and these may themselves be further partitioned until the work is apportioned to project teams to develop each subsystem. Large objected-oriented systems are no exception to this rule and it is necessary to package classes together to form coherent groupings that allow the system to be developed in parallel.

To achieve this requires a higher-level concept than a class. In conventional systems development, this is a subsystem. An object-oriented subsystem is a collection of classes, which have a defined interface to other subsystems as defined by the list of all messages that may be received by the classes within the subsystem. Some of the messages received by the classes may only be present to allow communication between classes of the subsystem and need not be *exported* outside the confines of the subsystem.

SUPPORTING COMMON THEMES

Requirements that we can place in our object development environment to support the common themes of objected-oriented analysis and design are outlined in the following sections.

Representation

The following requirements are typical of those for today's CASE tools supporting object-oriented methods.

- It should be possible to represent the different graphical representations and to allow changes to be made dynamically to the diagrams.
- Navigation between the different representations should be possible. An example is the ability to navigate from a class (usage) in a static structure to its class definition.
- The CASE tool should be capable of validating the consistency and correctness of the information entered. For example, the appearance of a method for a class in a static structure should be validated against its underlying class definition.
- The introduction of a class in a static structure or dynamic structure should be based upon information from its class definition, so that the methods required may be chosen from those available.
- The use of the analysis and design tools should allow the richness of the proposed development language to be represented. For example:
  - The notions of single inheritance or multiple inheritance will influence the design of the system.
  - In C++, the language allows for virtual member functions and virtual base classes. It is important to be able to represent this graphically as it has significant effect on the design of the class hierarchy.

Connections

Within the CASE tool used to support object-oriented analysis and design, it is important to be able to show how classes connect to other classes and how objects connect with other objects. The types of connection are many, and are often influenced by the designated programming language. For example:

- The C++ language allows private methods (to which no external access is permitted), protected methods (which are accessible from derived classes only), public methods (which are accessible by all classes), plus the concept of "friend" (classes that share access to the internals of the class). The visibility of a method therefore needs to be represented.
- Some languages have the concepts of templates (or generics), which are instantiated at run-time. Consequently, this use of templates and the act of instantiation needs to be represented.
- In dynamic structures, it is necessary to show messages being sent from class to class (or object to object). These connections are different from those found in the static structure where the connections indicate all possible messages. The ability to overlay these two views is advantageous when trying to assess the legality or feasibility of a particular design.

Queries

The concepts of object orientation include inheritance and polymorphism (resulting in overloading of names), which, while providing much of the power of object orientation, also contribute to the difficulty of understanding a particular analysis or design due to the "hiding" of critical information. It is therefore very important that tools supporting object-oriented analysis and design offer interactive querying features that enable:

- The inheritance tree for a particular class to be browsed or reviewed, especially where multiple inheritance occurs.
- The effect of overloading on a particular class, so that it is possible to see which methods are taking effect, and at which points in the class hierarchy overloading is in force.
- The production of metrics that assist in assessing the "goodness" of a proposed design. These might include the average number of classes in a class hierarchy, number of methods overloaded, number of virtual methods, or number of methods reused.

These queries may offer their results in a textual form, although a graphical representation may be preferable. The queries can also provide navigation facilities so that the developer may traverse the results of a query to see the information being reported.

Reuse

A claimed benefit of object orientation is, of course, that it offers significant opportunities for reuse, although we must not expect too much. Biggerstaff and Richter (1989) warn that less than half of a typical system can be built of reusable objects. It is also essential that we raise the level of what is reused to some higher plane than code.

Organizations are looking for higher levels of reuse so that new systems can be created through the reuse of existing class libraries with some specific new classes added. The new classes offer the functional differences that make the resulting system different from the original system that provided the class library.

Object orientation offers part of its reuse within a system by effectively letting functions be normalized. Functions (or methods) are refined and placed high in the class hierarchy so that they can be inherited by all classes that need them. Only those classes with more specific needs override the function.

Therefore, through the good design of classes and the effective use in hierarchies, it is possible to generalize common functions so that they appear in base classes and are reused by classes that inherit from these base classes. The danger is that this is potentially not very different from the concept of common subroutines at the coding level, although the mechanisms in object-oriented languages make it more likely that it is reusable (at least in the first system).

Support for reuse of designs requires that it is possible to quickly identify and understand existing designs (as represented in class hierarchies or libraries) and existing classes and how to use those classes and extend both class hierarchies and classes. This means that facilities to inquire, comment, navigate, and extract information on class libraries, class hierarchies, and classes are available.

While the concept of reuse libraries is a good start, the issue is predominantly one of understanding. Class libraries may provide a framework to help understanding, but the quality of the class library and the information describing the classes and their methods are just as critical. Just as in the good-old days, developers are likely to go ahead and do their own thing because the existing system is hard to comprehend!

When a class library is poorly constructed and badly documented, the incentive to learn it is reduced, and the time to appreciate it is significantly increased; this is important when a class library has several hundred classes. A developer may also need to understand several class libraries to be able to build a system that has a high reuse content. At the moment good library/class browsers exist at the code level, although little has been achieved at the design level.

Repository

In many respects, the structure and content of the underlying repository of the object development environment could be said to be an implementation issue for its developers. It is, however, an important component of the environment that is critical to its effectiveness and flexibility, particularly if it is intended for use with different methods of object-oriented analysis and design and different object-oriented programming languages.

It is preferable that the repository be object oriented so that the richness of the methods and languages used in development can be supported without losing information or richness — the semantic gap is avoided.

The repository should be accessible to end users and extensible. End users should be able to develop scripts that allow information to be extracted for query or reporting purposes. The scripting language should be object oriented and should operate on objects from the repository using the same terminology as the tools and users who entered the information originally.

A further consideration about the repository relates to many of the object-oriented systems currently being developed. Going back in time we see that many object-oriented systems used objects that were created and updated and that survived the run-time of the system. Persistence was not much of an issue. This is one of the reasons that GUIs led the way in object orientation. Today's systems are applying object-oriented concepts to information that has a longer lifetime than the system (or application). The object is created by one program, modified by others, and finally deleted by another program over the course of several years, although each may run only for seconds at a time. This leads to object-oriented systems having requirements for an object repository to manage persistent objects — something also needed by the object development environments. Therefore, we can expect our environment to need to be able to use (and possibly share) the same repository as the applications and systems developed with it.

Reporting and Documentation

Good reporting facilities that allow the easy production of good quality reports and documents is needed. As indicated in the preceding section, this should be achieved through a scripting language that operates at the same level as the information captured by the object development environments. To facilitate the application of the environment, a number of predefined report scripts should be provided that produce high-quality, well laid-out reports that present relevant information in a concise, easy-to-read style. They should act as the starter kit for end users when developing custom reports.

Reports should duplicate the query features offered so that users may perform inquires on line and produce reports for later consumption or documentation purposes.

OTHER CONSIDERATIONS

The preceding sections concentrated on the core areas of software development concerned with analysis, design, and construction. Software development has a far broader spectrum, encompassing activities that top and tail those already described, as well as activities that occur in parallel.

Examples of these activities include the initial establishment of requirements, the tracing of requirements from initial specification through the life cycle to delivery of the finished system, configuration management, testing, and test management.

Establishing Requirements

Whether establishing requirements is treated as part of analysis or separately, there is an activity where requirements are gathered. The analysis is intended to take in the requirements and develop a model that shows that an understanding of the problem has been gained. The model is used for many purposes, including validation and verification, resolution of contradictory and conflicting requirements, and finally as the input to the design phase where the model is further refined.

Many objected-oriented analysis methods suggest some form of fact-finding where relevant information is collected, reviewed, and categorized. The information collected might include written descriptions, drawings, project proposals, documents, forms, completed forms, and information on existing systems. Using this information, the analysis will make a first pass looking for information that helps identify embryonic objects and classes and potential methods for a class. The different analysis methods may use the information to create an entity model or a first-cut list of candidate classes and objects. Abbott (1983) proposed scanning textual information looking for verbs (methods) and nouns (objects); this has been adopted, to some degree or other, in many object-oriented methods. While simplistic, it does get projects moving and deals with the "blank sheet of paper" syndrome that paralyzes people.

Second, it is suitable for automating in the object development environment through text scanners that create lists automatically and then allow the user to manipulate the information. While, as far as I am aware, this is not a feature of requirements tracing tools like RTM and Life*Link, it certainly allows such tools to be considered for supporting the initial fact-gathering and analysis phase.

Requirements Tracing

If early analysis starts with the identification of information that is used to evolve the analysis, then tools such as RTM and Life*Link can be used to assist the tracing of how a requirement is actually supported. This does mean that the object development environment must provide suitable links within its repository; hence the previously stated need for the repository to be extensible.

Scenario Management

With the creation of a class hierarchy, which is static, it is important to be able to create different dynamic models to assess the acceptability of the proposed class organization. The object development environment should allow these scenarios to be created through manipulation of the static structures. The environment should be able to "play" the scenarios automatically so that it is feasible to develop many varied scenarios.

Similarly, if the static class hierarchy is modified, the object development environment should assist in recreating scenarios and playing them back to ensure that the modifications still meet the expectations for the system. Support of this nature allows for early verification of concept and may also be useful in helping the end users of the proposed system appreciate what is planned, which in some ways brings us back round to prototyping — but in a more controlled manner.

Testing and Test Management

If reuse is to gain a hold on software engineering, then it is essential that what is reused is considerably more than code. We need to reuse more interesting higher-level elements than code by being able to reuse both design and analysis specifications as discussed by Graham (1991).

The object development environment must also allow a packaging of more than the specification by including the associated test specification, test cases, and test results.

FUTURE TRENDS

Although many companies today have a software development environment of some sort, often with a CASE tool to support conventional structured analysis and design, there is often little — if any — support for the process followed. As the object-oriented paradigm takes an ever firmer foothold, it will become essential to change this attitude about process.

The ability to evolve systems more elegantly through object-oriented methods will require that we give much more consideration to the process for that transition from analysis to design to implementation and to facilitate it with the simplicity and elegance required.

At least for the foreseeable future, while many objected-oriented methods rely on scenario management to represent the dynamic behavior of the proposed system, there will be a strong need to consider how best to manage and exploit the need for various levels of animation — at early stages of the development process.

I foresee through the object repository on the tools' side and through the object repository on the application/systems side, a much stronger connection and interaction between the development of applications or systems and their deployment. It is in development that we identify and create artifacts that model parts of the real world, and it is in the use of the application or system that we deploy the artifacts to mimic what is happening in the real world.

REFERENCES

Biggerstaff, T., and C. Richter (1989) Reusability framework assessment and directions, tutorial: software reuse, *Emerging Technology*, IEEE Computer Society, EH0278-2, 3–13.

Abbott, R. J. (1983) Program design by informal english descriptions, *Communications of the ACM* 26(11): 882–894.

Graham, I. (1991) *Object-Oriented Methods*, Addison-Wesley, UK.

chapter **19**

Toward a Common
Object-Oriented Meta-Model
for Object Development

ANDY CARMICHAEL   OBJECT UK LTD.

In this chapter, we consider the information exchange required in an object development environment. To do this we must appreciate how the semantics of object-oriented analysis and design methods can be unified, thus allowing components from any stage in the development life cycle and from different environments and methods to be shared via a common "meta-model." A proposed Common Object-Oriented Meta-Model (COOMM) is discussed, first in terms of the aims and scope of the meta-model and then in terms of the principles and concepts used in its definition. The meta-model is modular to allow the integration of partial models from different sources. The module types in the meta-model are identified and an overview of their definition is presented.

CASE AND OBJECT ORIENTATION

Object-oriented development is not a new idea. Simula, for example, an object-oriented language widely used in simulation environments, is over 25 years old. However it *is* an idea whose time has come. The complexity of systems that we are now attempting to build, coupled with the powerful technology (the virtual machine) on which we may now build, demands that the methods and languages used in building systems match natural models of human thinking and classical techniques for organizing information, rather than requiring immediate transformation into structures that correspond to conventional computer architectures or procedural languages. Object orientation provides methods and languages with these qualities, and the implementation systems now being brought to the marketplace are of sufficient power to transform the resulting structures into efficient and effective systems.

The growth in the application of object-oriented development has only started. Its penetration into major software producers is universal (they all have some object-oriented technology in use), but shallow (they are mostly small projects). This is therefore a major opportunity for further growth. The degree to which CASE systems have and will share in this growth is open to question. Some have suggested (Cook 1992) that CASE is irrelevant, at least in its current manifestations, to the key issues affecting the adoption of object-oriented techniques and technology. Nevertheless, many of the current CASE tools are converting their offerings to greater or lesser degrees to support object technology. Their success may be limited by a number of factors.

First, object orientation requires a change in the life-cycle model from static chronological ordering of phases (eg., analysis, followed by design, followed by implementation) to a flexible and iterative process that incorporates prototyping, the use of class libraries, reuse and reengineering of other application code, and late configuration to changing requirements. This is well represented by the additive life-cycle model, for example, proposed by the Object Management Group (see Figure 19.1 and OMG 1992). While this clearly cries out for support from automated tools, the underlying models within the tools must change.

Second, since most of the code in object-oriented developments should be reused and all of it should be reusable, consistency checking will include modules not developed by the current team. Documentation of the other classes may well have been produced using different methods, notations, and tools. Therefore, open exchange of information between different methods and notations is required.

Third, the object-oriented development environment will include myriad powerful and varied tools; cooperation between tools is the only way in which large and complex systems will be developed and verified. Traditional CASE tools form only a part of this verification matrix, but unfortunately such tools are often structured so that verification can only take place within their own repositories, thus excluding consistency checking of information from other sources.

Nevertheless, object-oriented development supported by ad hoc procedures and coding tools is similarly flawed! CASE tools, based on formal meta-models and the underlying software engineering principles of object orientation, hold the key to efficiency and consistency in the all important activities of analysis and design. To overcome the problems outlined above, CASE support must be fully modular (e.g., able to browse and select

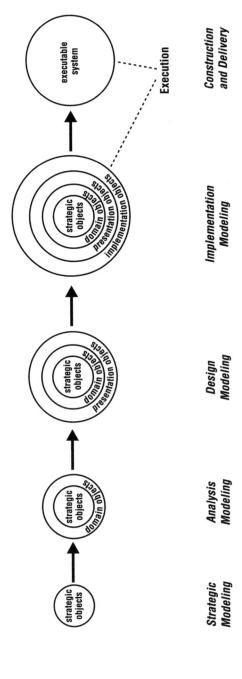

FIGURE 19.1.   The additive life-cycle model. [Source: Object Analysis and Design Reference Model (OMG)]

classes from external libraries), and fully open (i.e., able to integrate and be integrated with methods, tools, and design information from many other sources).

This chapter examines how the problem of semantic data exchange between tools that are using different object-oriented methods can be addressed. It draws on practical work being carried out at VSF, where a meta-CASE development environment is being used to build tools that share information even though they use different diagraming techniques. The problem is addressed by defining a common object-oriented meta-model (COOMM), effectively a data model for multiple object-oriented CASE tools supporting multiple object-oriented methods and notations. The aims and scope of the COOMM are discussed in this chapter, as are its foundation concepts and how, for example, the concepts of attributes, relationships and operations can be unified.

An Introduction to **COOMM**

The common object-oriented meta-model is a definition of the information model for object-oriented methods of analysis, design, and implementation. It was developed to provide a basis for object-oriented CASE, reengineering, and management tools offered by VSF Ltd. and may equally be applied by other development tools and environments.

Aims of COOMM

One of the key aims of COOMM is to unify concepts from multiple objected-oriented methods. In doing this it is necessary to separate issues of presentation from semantics. By *presentation* we mean not just issues of notation (e.g., the shape of boxes, symbols on links to indicate optionality and cardinality, etc.), but recognizing the semantic equivalence between different method concepts. For example, class behavior can be characterized by event-type diagrams as in the Ptech method (Foster 1994; Martin 1992), entity life histories (SSADM), and state transition diagrams (Texel, Rumbaugh, Shlaer/Mellor, etc.). However, it is possible to show the formal equivalence of these notations and then let designers choose which "presentation" of the information they wish to use. COOMM will therefore allow the exchange of design information between methods since the definition of the meta-model also implies an exchange format definition. The format currently used conforms to SYNTAX.1 of the CDIF international standard (CDIF 1991). This, in turn, enables support for:

- Common libraries
- Common code generation / reverse engineering tools
- Common interfaces to other tools

Although COOMM itself is not a standard, it is and will be maintained to be compatible with emerging standards (e.g., CDIF, CORBA, OMG Reference Model, PCTE). It also provides the basis for methods development facilities, particularly Methods Factory, an object-oriented CASE product for developing VSF workbenches.

Scope of COOMM

Given the high ambition for COOMM, it is necessary also to recognize the limitations of its scope and purpose. In particular, the focus of the model is the information content, as opposed to development process. There are many different object-oriented methods — 21 are surveyed in the OMG reference model, which is by no means exhaustive (Hutt 1993) — and the differences among them are significant and important. However, their commonality is more important, and there is some agreement in key areas, particularly concerning the goal of the methods — namely to define the structure and behavior of classes or types. This is the focus of COOMM — a common expression for the definition of classes and types — rather than the process of definition, the notations for presenting the information, or the approach in terms of teaching the method.

There is also an emphasis in COOMM on "what we finally get and keep," as opposed to "what we used to get it." Although particular tools should provide a means of storing and examining the information concerning the development process and the rationale behind design decisions, the meta-model itself does not explicitly address this area.

It is relevant to ask how COOMM is different from other initiatives and standards in similar areas, for example CDIF (CDIF 1991) and the OMG reference model (OMG 1992).

CDIF (CASE Data Interchange Format) is a draft international standard that lays out an approach for defining meta-models (the "meta-meta-model"), a protocol for the exchange of meta-models and models, and standard meta-models in a number of areas of interest, particularly entity-relationship modeling and data-flow diagramming. Unlike COOMM, it is not specific to the objected-oriented paradigm, although in due course it is expected that a standard meta-model will emerge, for which COOMM is in fact a candidate starting point.

COOMM goes further than CDIF in some areas in that it is not just an exchange format. It also includes the definition of an approach to the modular construction of models and systems that allows modules to be reused in multiple models. CDIF is used in the definition of COOMM and is an important standard that COOMM will track, however COOMM's implementation is taking place before CDIF standardization would be feasible (even if it was underway).

The OMG reference model is a framework for comparing objected-oriented methods for business and system modeling. As such, it is an important source for COOMM and provides a context to understand the contribution of specific methods. The reference model does not attempt to unify the semantics of methods, although as with CDIF this is a logical next step and is likely to be undertaken in the future. In this case, COOMM will first be a candidate starting point for this work, and second will be able to track the progress of the work, incorporating agreed-upon features as the consensus grows.

PRINCIPLES OF THE META-MODEL

The COOMM seeks to draw concepts from many of the methods discussed in this book and others. The aim is that differences in the presentation of information will be allowed, either by storing additional information about how information is presented in a particular method or by fixed transformations from a common semantic model. Having said this, certain basic principles must be applied. Our starting point is that object-oriented methods have at least these properties:

- Modularity based on classes or types
- Separation of "inside" and "outside"

The meta-model is therefore component-based and should allow:

- Semantics interchangeable between methods (for either complete or partial models; e.g., a single class or group of classes)
- An additive rather than transformational model of development (which keeps the loss of information between stages to a minimum). See Figure 19.1.

The layering of information represented in the meta-model seeks to recognize (at the deepest semantic level) the equivalence of relationships and attributes, and of attributes (with specified access) and operations. The presentation choices of the designers (and of methods) must be stored, but at a presentation rather than semantic level. This aspect is discussed in more detail later in this chapter.

Classes, Types, and Sets

Classes, types, and sets are all distinguishable and useful concepts in the meta-model (Blair 1991, 1994). Classes provide an object with both an interface (type) and an implementation (class body). Subclasses share parent classes behavior through inheritance.

Types (and subtypes), on the other hand, define the interface of classes and, therefore, their compatibility. It is the type of an object (rather than its class or even the inheritance hierarchy) that defines the possibility of polymorphism. Types may also be defined to show the interface required by other classes. In this case, they would not necessarily have corresponding classes that implement the type directly, provided that there were classes that "conformed" to the required type, that is, classes that were subtypes.

Sets are a more general concept than either types or classes. Sets group together a number of objects independently of their interface or implementation either by naming the objects explicitly (definition by extension) or by specifying a necessary condition for membership of the set (definition by intension). If sets are derived (or "inferred") from a necessary condition, generally defined as a predicate or query, we may say that the "intent" of the set is the query definition, the "extent" of the set is the query result.

Another difference of sets, as opposed to classes or types, is that objects may belong to multiple sets, irrespective of the defined subset relationships. For example, a car may belong to a set of "English objects" and, simultaneously, a set of "green objects," where neither set is an explicit subset of the other. However, an object in COOMM is defined as having only one class and type (even though it may be used — through polymorphism — wherever a supertype is referenced); this explicit class or type does not change during the life of that object. Thus, the interface of the object is statically determined even though the responses to accessing the interface (e.g., "are you green?") will depend on the internal state of the object at any point in time. Note that this definition is not consistent with the use of the word type in a number of methods (e.g., Ptech, Martin 1992) in which the concept of dynamic reclassification is used. This is not to say that these methods are excluded from COOMM (Carmichael 1993), but it does require the resolution of conflicting terminology.

Module Types of the Meta-Model

The fundamental building blocks, or module types, of models conforming to COOMM are classes and types. A class consists of two parts: the outside, which may also be referred to as its *type*, and the inside, the class body or implementation. Larger modules are basically collections of classes and types such as subsystems, packages or products, and they may of course contain additional descriptive or other information. Smaller modules, such as the code for an operation, might be defined, although COOMM does not currently recognize finer granularity than the type or class.

In this outline, therefore, three module types are considered:

- Type
- Class body
- Class category (also known as subject, subsystem, domain, or folder)

The dependency among these module types is explicitly defined, as shown in Figure 19.2. For example a class body is dependent on class bodies it inherits from, its interface (type) and used types, whereas types are dependent only on other types. Note that the analysis of these interdependencies in the meta-model and the direction of dependency is crucial to the usability — and particularly to the reusability — of the resulting model. This principle has been well expressed in the term *connascence* by Page-Jones (1992).

Meta-Model Notation

The notation used in these figures needs to be briefly explained. Boxes represent "meta-entities," or concepts in the method, and may be related to each other by binary relationships (directed arc with a name) or by inheritance (hierarchical structure with no arrowhead on the lines, e.g., Figure 19.3). Bold outlines for meta-entities (the boxes on the diagram) indicate that they are module types and therefore can be shared between differ-

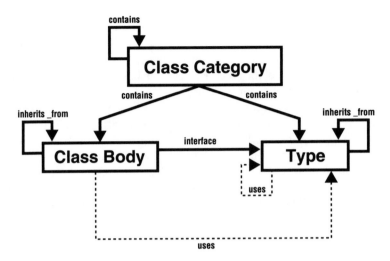

FIGURE 19.2. The module types in COOMM.

ent models (e.g., for the purpose of reuse). Meta-entities with "non-bold" outlines are not themselves module types, but will belong to a module type as defined by the dependency relationships.

Non-bold relationships indicate that the instances of the relationship exist within one module. Bold relationships, on the other hand, indicate that an instance of the relationship would occur between modules and implies the dependency of one module on another. In Figure 19.2, for example, all the relationships are between module types, and therefore the instances of those relationships in a model will be between modules. Inter-module relationships must be handled slightly differently than those within modules to ensure that reuse occurs consistently — for example, when a module is imported that refers to a module that is missing from the new model.

Dashed lines in the meta-model notation show inferred relationships. Such relationships are read-only since they are derived from actual "asserted" relationships that are defined at a lower level of detail than is shown on this diagram (Figure 19.2) For example, the "uses" relationship between a class body and a type may in fact be inferred from calls within the body of an operation of the class or from the declaration of a particular variable within the implementation. By defining the inferred relationship at the higher level, we can use this relationship name to define high-level rules for the meta-model to ensure consistency. Sets may also be shown in a similar way (dotted box) although there are none in this example.

An important contrast between an asserted relationship and an inferred relationship in the meta-model is the "inherits-from" relationship and the "subtype-of" relationship. Inherits-from is asserted by the definer of a type when he wishes, for example, to reuse an existing type definition. However, the subtype-of relationship may be inferred from the

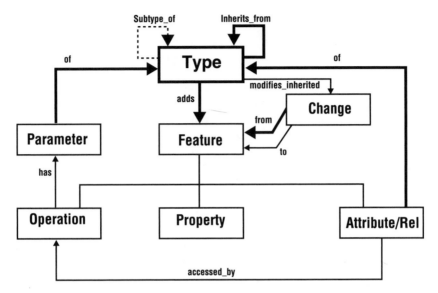

FIGURE 19.3. Part of the meta-model for the "type" module type.

two independently defined types using the rules of subtyping (e.g., see Blair 1991).

The module types shown in Figure 19.2 are now discussed in slightly more detail.

THE "TYPE" MODULE TYPE

The type defines the interface to an object or class. It must therefore contain all the information necessary for a class conforming to this interface to be used or reused. Part of the meta-model is shown in Figure 19.3.

Types have features that may be specialized as operations, attribute/relationships, or properties. Properties include such items as type invariants, timing constraints, and non-functional requirements. They are not discussed further in this chapter. Operations are the accessible interface — the services — that can be invoked on objects of this type. The full operation definition should include the description or formal specification of the semantics of the operation. Attribute/relationships are a part of the type (the interface), only if they are accessible via operations.

Inheritance is used in the definition of types; this is shown as the inherits-from relationship. Note that this implies that subtypes depend on the supertypes they inherit from rather than vice versa. The meta-model does allow a different inheritance hierarchy to exist for types (the interface definition) from that defined for the class bodies, although in most current methods the two structures would be constrained to be identical. It should be noted that type conformance (subtype-of) is the relationship between types required, for example, to achieve polymorphism. Conformance may be inferred from the type definitions independently of the specified inheritance hierarchy, using the rules of subtyping. In fact, the same rules that are used to infer subtyping (e.g., to check the validity of polymorphism), should be used to constrain assertions within the inheritance hierarchy to ensure that only valid redefinitions of the properties of supertypes are made in subtypes.

The subtyping relationships of a type results in an inherited set of attribute/relationships, properties, and operations being specified. The rest of the information held by the type defines extensions to this definition, which may be

- Changes to existing features (operations, invariants, descriptions, or other properties), which must nevertheless preserve the subtype relationship to inherited types,

and/or

- The addition of features, e.g., ones that result from additional access operations on existing attribute/relationships, additional attribute/relationships, or additional operations.

THE "CLASS BODY" MODULE TYPE

The class body defines the implementation of a class. It contains all the information necessary for the class to work. It will include the full definition, and ultimately the implementation of the class, and a full specification of the dependencies of the class on other types as well as any hardware/operating system constraints. A similar structure — "adds", "Feature", "modifies_inherited", "Change", and "inherits_from" — exists in the meta-model for class body as exists for type, as shown in Figure 19.4.

THE "CLASS CATEGORY" MODULE TYPE

A simple model of class categories is currently supported in COOMM. They are used in different contexts for a variety of purposes and thus only a basic structure is defined which is then readily extensible (as with other parts of COOMM) in the context of a specific method or tool. The class category module type contains descriptive information, a list of other components and "other properties". This basic meta-model structure is shown in Figure 19.2.

Equivalence of Concepts

In this section, the semantic equivalence of some commonly distinguished concepts are discussed.

ATTRIBUTES AND RELATIONS

Analysis and design methods generally distinguish between attributes of classes and relationships or associations between classes. Attributes (in deference to the relational

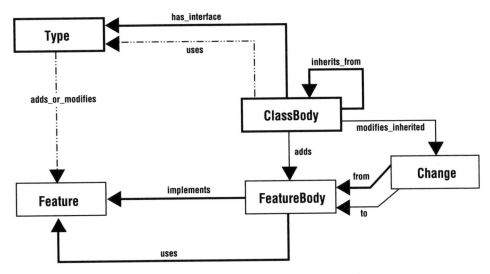

FIGURE 19.4. Part of the meta-model for the "class body" module type.

model) are usually single-valued and of simple types. Relationships between classes, on the other hand, may have a specified cardinality (one-to-many, many-to-many, etc.) and optionality (i.e., whether the relationship is mandatory in valid objects). The direction of the relationship in many methods is either undefined or written purely to aid the reading of the relationship name (e.g., *Person* owns *Vehicle* rather than vice versa). Other methods use the direction to imply important information about the dependency between classes; this is the case with COOMM, which preserves this information when available.

The semantic equivalence of relationships and attributes may be shown if multivalued attributes of complex types are allowed and all types (domains) are classes. For example, a diagram showing a *Vehicle* having an attribute *owner* of type (or class) *Person* means exactly the same as two classes with a directed arc from *Vehicle* to *Person* labeled *owner*.

ATTRIBUTES AND OPERATIONS

Interestingly, at the semantic level we may also unify the attribute/relationships with operations by clarifying the concept of the inside of a class and the outside (its type). Some methods allow only operations on the outside. Others show attributes on the interface as it is implied that they are also accessible to other classes (Rösch 1994). Specifications differing in these ways may be shown to be equivalent if the external access mechanisms on attribute/relationships (e.g., create, read, update, delete) are specified. These access mechanisms are semantically equivalent to operations. The presentation of the information in different diagram notations and different instances of diagrams requires considerable flexibility and choice to be given to the designer.

Some of the presentation choices can be carried between methods in an intermethod transfer, but in most cases the presentation choices (e.g., whether an attribute is shown on the interface of the class or only by showing the operations that access the information will be stored in a separate presentation layer.

Extension/Customization of COOMM

Specific methods and tools have meta-models that are larger than COOMM in that only concepts that are common to multiple methods are included in COOMM. However, the COOMM structure does allow such additional information to be stored in a standard format so that when modules are exchanged and changed in different methods, information is not inadvertently lost through the transfer. Therefore, COOMM provides a sound basis for class libraries that will be used over many years during which time the methods will likely evolve — perhaps almost as rapidly as the analysis and design models they are used to produce and represent.

CONCLUSION

The opportunity represented by the growth in object-oriented methods and languages is significant. However, to support this growth, CASE environments need to be modular in structure and open — open not only to other tools, but to multiple methods and notations that support the object-oriented paradigm as well.

This chapter has reported on work to define a common object-oriented meta-model, capable of representing information from different analysis and design methods. This meta-model and its direct support on workbenches such as Texel-SF (Texel 1993) and VIEWS-SF (Bent 1993) is the foundation of a strategy for supporting object-oriented software development into the future. In conjunction with much other work in standardization of methods, meta-models, exchange formats, and object management systems, it promises to provide, more generally, a foundation for object development.

REFERENCES

Bent, S. (1993) *Realizing a Comprehensive Object-Oriented Application Development Method*, IBM Corporation (forthcoming).

Blair, G.S., J.J. Gallagher, and D. Hutchison (eds) (1991) *Object-Oriented Languages, Systems and Applications*, Pitman Publishing, London.

Blair, G.S. (1994) The four dimensions of object-oriented methods and languages, Chapter 3 in this volume.

Carmichael, A.R. (1993). Mapping OOPAL to an OOPL (dynamic reclassification in COOMM), Internal document. VSF Limited.

CDIF. (1991) CASE Data Interchange Format, Interim Standard EIA/IS-83.

Cook, S. (1992) The future of object-oriented CASE, *Object Magazine* 2(2): 30–35.

Foster, E., A.J. Barnard, S.A. Roberts, et al. (1993) PoeT: Object Engineering in Public Transport. *Object Technology '93 Conference*, British Computer Society, London.

Fowler, M. (1994) A comparison of object-oriented analysis and design methods, Chapter 6 in this volume.

Hutt, A. (1993) Object Management Group: review of object analysis and design methods, *Object Technology '93 Conference*,. British Computer Society, London.

Martin, J., and J.J. Odell (1992) *Object-Oriented Analysis and Design*, Prentice-Hall, Englewood Cliffs, NJ.

OMG Object Analysis and Design Special Interest Group (1992) Object Analysis and Design, Draft 7.0. OMG.

Page-Jones, M. (1992) Comparing Techniques by Means of Encapsulation and Connascence, *Communications of the ACM*, 35(9): 147–151.

Rösch, M. (1994). The Coad/Yourdon method: simplicity, brevity and clarity — keys to successful analysis and design, Chapter 10 in this volume.

Texel, P.P. (1994) The Texel method: a pragmatic and field-proven approach to object-oriented software development, Chapter 13 in this volume.

INDICES

Author Index

Subject Index

Clip this page and mail to:

▼

ROAD
c/o SIGS Publications
71 West 23rd Street, New York, NY 10010

▼

For faster service,
fax to: 212.242.7574 or
send email to: poo976@psilink.com

Success depends on knowledge...stay informed!

Written for both the newcomer and the experienced user, OBJECT MAGAZINE provides information on how you can apply the latest advances in object technology to every stage of your software development project. Published 9 times a year, OBJECT MAGAZINE provides case studies, practical guidelines and proven techniques for real-world object development projects.

Each issue provides you with new information on:

• ODBMS • Methodology • Applications • Education & Training
• Project Mgmt. • Languages & Environments • Standards
• Migration Strategies

Plus—Candid perspectives from such industry notables as:
Philippe Kahn, Bill Gates, Grady Booch, Adele Goldberg, Larry Constantine, Bertrand Meyer & others.

The Manager's Guide to Object Technology

☐ **Please rush me the next issue of OBJECT MAGAZINE to examine without obligation or commitment.**

If I like it, I'll pay the low subscription price of $39 for the full year and receive an additional 8 issues. If I choose not to subscribe, I'll write "cancel" on your invoice and owe nothing. The free issue is mine to keep.

BKS95

Name _____
Address _____
_____
City_____State____Zip _____
Country_____Postal Code _____
Phone_____
Fax _____

Don't miss another issue. Return the offer card today!

JOOP is <u>the</u> technical publication for O-O programmers & developers.

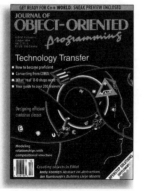

The *Journal of Object–Oriented Programming* is written by and for programmers and developers using object technology. International in scope, editorial features are code–intensive, technical, and practical offering readily usable advice and programming techniques.

Stringent editorial guidelines and peer-reviewed articles ensure that JOOP's subscribers receive the most accurate, leading–edge and objective information available. Learn from leading O–O authorities and language originators including: Andrew Koenig (C++), Bertrand Meyer (Eiffel), John Pugh & Wilf LaLonde (Smalltalk), Mary Loomis (Databases), and noted methodologists Grady Booch, Stephen Mellor & Sally Shlaer, and Jim Rumbaugh.

☐ **Please rush me the next issue of JOOP to examine without obligation or commitment.**

If I like it, I'll pay the low subscription price of $69 for the full year and receive an additional 8 issues. If I choose not to subscribe, I'll write "cancel" on your invoice and owe nothing. The free issue is mine to keep.

BKS95

Name _____
Address _____
_____
City_____State____Zip _____
Country_____Postal Code _____
Phone _____
Fax _____

* Non-U.S. orders must be prepaid. Add $25 for Canadian and Mexican orders. Add $40 for all non-North American orders. Checks must be in U.S. dollars and drawn on a U.S. bank.

Clip this coupon and mail to:
▼

OBJECT MAGAZINE
c/o SIGS Publications
71 West 23rd Street, New York, NY 10010

▼

For faster service,
fax to: 212.242.7574 or
send email to: p00q76@psilink.com

....

....

Clip this coupon and mail to:
▼

JOURNAL OF OBJECT-ORIENTED PROGRAMMING
c/o SIGS Publications
71 West 23rd Street, New York, NY 10010

▼

For faster service,
fax to: 212.242.7574 or
send email to: p00q76@psilink.com